ILLUSTRATED PROJECTS™

Microsoft® Office 2000

Y0-BPX-397

PROFESSIONAL EDITION

Carol M. Cram

Capilano College, North Vancouver, B.C.

COURSE
TECHNOLOGY

Thomson Learning™

ONE MAIN STREET, CAMBRIDGE, MA 02142

Australia • Canada • Denmark • Japan • Mexico • New Zealand • Philippines
Puerto Rico • Singapore • South Africa • Spain • United Kingdom • United States

Microsoft® Office 2000, Professional Edition — Illustrated Projects™

is published by Course Technology.

Sr. Product Manager:	Kathryn Schooling
Production Editor:	Megan Cap-Renzi
Product Manager:	Rebecca VanEsselstine
Associate Product Manager:	Emily Heberlein
Editorial Assistant:	Stacie Parillo
Acquisitions Editor:	Christine Guivernau
Marketing Manager:	Karen Bartlett
Composition House:	GEX, Inc.
Quality Assurance Testers:	John Freitas, Jeff Schwartz, Jon Greacen, Matt Carroll
Text Designer:	Joseph Lee Designs
Cover Designer:	Doug Goodman Designs

Trademarks

Course Technology and the Open Book logo are registered trademarks of Course Technology.
Illustrated Projects and the Illustrated Series are trademarks of Course Technology.

Some of the product names and company names used in this book have been used for identification purposes only and may be trademarks or registered trademarks of their respective manufacturers and sellers.

For more information contact:

Course Technology
One Main Street
Cambridge, MA
02142
Or find us on the World Wide Web at:
www.course.com

Disclaimer

Course Technology reserves the right to revise this publication and make changes from time to time in its content without notice.

ISBN 0-7600-6159-9

Printed in the United States of America

4 5 6 7 8 9 BAW 04 03 02 01 00

A Note from the Author

As instructors, what is our goal? I believe that we can and should teach our students to fly—to become independent learners with the confidence to tackle and solve problems. My greatest satisfaction in the classroom comes when my students learn the information, skills, and techniques necessary to function effectively in the workplace and to accomplish tasks related to their own needs and interests.

Several years ago, I was teaching a second-level word processing course to students who had completed the introductory word processing course. These students knew a series of functions and had proven their ability to pass "fill in the blanks" tests. But when I asked the students to produce an attractively formatted business letter, they were at a loss. That's when I realized that teaching a series of functions wasn't enough. Students needed—and deserved—to learn *what* to do with a software application. They needed to "see the forest" and not just the trees.

I developed a philosophy of teaching software applications that has evolved into the Illustrated Projects series. Each text in this series provides students with step-by-step instructions to create documents or perform tasks appropriate to the software package they are learning. As students complete the projects, they learn how a variety of functions combine together to produce a tangible product.

But the real core of the Illustrated Projects approach to teaching software doesn't stop with the projects. In my classroom, the significant learning occurs when students are then given the opportunity to create their own version of a project document. That's when I feel a kind of magic creeping into my classroom. Students take the structure offered by a project and then, in the Independent Challenges, adapt this structure to explore practical business applications and to express their own interests. Suddenly, my students are willing to take risks, to solve problems, to experiment with new features as they work towards the creation of a document that belongs to them. Pride of ownership inspires learning!

I hope you enjoy working with the projects in this book as much as I have enjoyed creating them. And I hope that you too can experience the magic that occurs in your classroom when your students begin to fly!

Carol M. Cram

Preface

Welcome to *Microsoft Office 2000—Illustrated Projects*. This highly visual book offers a wide array of interesting and challenging projects designed to practically apply the skills learned in any beginning Office 2000 book. The Illustrated Projects Series is for people who want more opportunities to practice important software skills.

Organization and Coverage

This text contains a total of eight units. Four units contain projects chosen for the individual programs: Word, Excel, Access, and PowerPoint. Three other units contain projects that take advantage of the powerful integration capabilities of the suite. The eighth unit contains projects that help students practice gathering and using the information available on the World Wide Web. Each unit contains three projects followed by four Independent Challenges and a Visual Workshop. (A Hot Spots page replaces the Visual Workshop in the World Wide Web unit.)

About this Approach

What makes the Illustrated Projects approach so effective at reinforcing software skills? It's quite simple. Each activity in a project is presented on two facing pages, with the step-by-step instructions on the left page, and large screen illustrations on the right. Students can focus on a single activity without having to turn the page. This unique design makes information extremely accessible and easy to absorb. Students can complete the projects on their own and because of the modular structure of the book, can also cover the units in any order.

Each two-page spread, or "information display," contains the following elements:

Road map–It is always clear which project and activity you are working on.

Introduction–Concise text that introduces the project and explains which activity within the project the student will complete. Procedures are easier to learn when they fit into a meaningful framework.

Hints and Trouble? comments–Hints for using Microsoft Office 2000 more effectively and trouble shooting advice to fix common problems that might occur. Both appear right where students need them, next to the step where they might need help.

Numbered steps–Clear step-by-step directions explain how to complete the specific activity. These steps get less specific as students progress to the third project in a unit.

Time To checklists–Reserved for basic skills that students should do frequently such as previewing, printing, saving, and closing documents.

Word

PROJECT 1

ONE-PAGE RESUME FOR JOYCE ALLAN

activity:

Enhance and Print the Resume

You need to decide whether you like the heading styles you created, make some modifications, apply some formatting to the individual sections of the resume, use the Shrink to Fit option to fit the resume on one page, and print a copy. You first decide to modify the Resume Heading Style by reducing both the font size and the border size. When you modify a style, the changes are instantly applied to all the text in the document currently formatted with that particular style.

steps:

1. Click **Format** on the menu bar, click **Style**, select **Resume Heading Style**, click **Modify**, click **Format**, click **Font**, change the font size to **14**, then click **OK**

2. Click **Format**, click **Border**, change the Border size to **1½ pt**, click **OK**, click **OK** again, then click **Close**
   A little more text now appears on page 1, but still not enough.

3. Change the font size in the **Resume Title Style** to **16 pt**, then remove the Shadow border
   You will need to select None in the Borders and Shading dialog box to remove the Shadow border.

4. Click the **Print Preview button** 🔍 on the Standard toolbar, then click the **Shrink to Fit button** 🔲
   The resume now fits on one page.

5. Click **Close**, select the text from **Computer Skills** to **Internet Communications**, then click the **Bullets button** ☰, as shown in Figure P1-7

6. With the text still selected, double-click the **Format Painter button** 🖌 on the Standard toolbar, drag ⬇I across the list of responsibilities for Best Bookkeeping, drag ⬇I across the list of responsibilities for Camp Haida, then click 🖌 to turn it off

7. Refer to Figure P1-8, then use **Format Painter** to enhance selected text so that it appears as shown
   Joyce's resume is looking great.

8. Select the heading text from **Joyce Allan** to the **e-mail address**, then click the **Center button** ▣ on the Formatting toolbar

9. Click in each table, click **Format** on the menu bar, click **Borders and Shading**, click **None**, then click **OK** to remove the gridlines

10. View the resume once more in Print Preview, then print a copy and save the document

Hint

You click Close, not Apply, when you have finished modifying the style because you do not want to apply the style to the text at your insertion point. Instead, you want only the text already formatted with a style to be modified.

Trouble?

If a button does not appear on the Standard toolbar, click the **More Buttons button** 🔻 on the toolbar to view a list of additional buttons.

Time To
✓ Save

The Projects

The two-page lesson format featured in this book provides students with a powerful learning experience. Additionally, this book contains the following features:

▶ **Meaningful Examples**—This book features projects that students will be excited to create, including a resume, a job search form letter, and a budget to amortize a car loan. By producing relevant documents that will enhance their own lives, students will more readily master skills.

▶ **Different Levels of Guidance**—the three projects in each unit provide varying levels of guidance. In Project 1, the guidance level is high, with detailed instructions keeping the student on track. Project 2 provides less guidance, and Project 3 provides minimal help, encouraging students to work more independently. This approach gets students in the real-world mindset of using their experiences to solve problems.

▶ **Start from Scratch**—To truly test if a student understands the software and can use it to reach specific goals, the student should start from scratch. This adds to the book's flexibility and real-world nature.

▶ **Outstanding Assessment and Reinforcement**—Each unit concludes with four Independent Challenges These Independent Challenges offer less instruction than the projects, allowing students to explore various software features and increase their critical thinking skills. The Visual Workshop follows the Independent Challenges and broadens students' attention to detail. Students see a completed document, worksheet, database, or presentation, and must recreate it on their own.

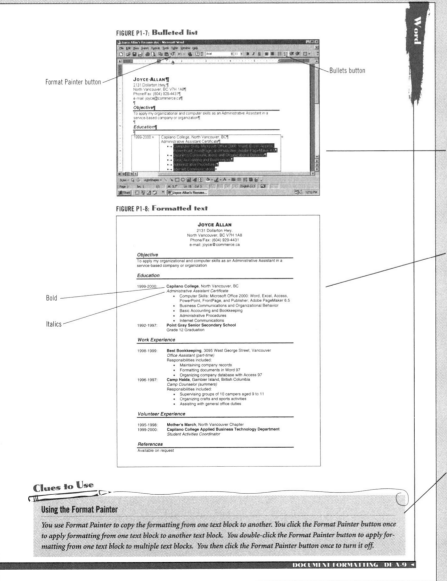

Screen shots—Every activity features large representations of what the screen should look like as students complete the numbered steps.

Completed document—At the end of every project, there is a picture of how the document will look when printed. Students can easily assess how well they've done.

Clues to Use Boxes—Many activities feature these sidebars, providing concise information that either explains a skill or concept that is covered in the steps or describes an independent task or feature that is in some way related to the steps. These often include both text and screen shots.

Instructor's Resource Kit

The Instructor's Resource Kit is Course Technology's way of putting the resources and information needed to teach and learn effectively into your hands. With an integrated array of teaching and learning tools that offer you and your students a broad range of instructional options, we believe this kit represents the highest quality and most cutting edge resources available to instructors today. Visit us on the Web at http://course.com. Briefly, the resources available with this text are:

Course Online Faculty Companion

This World Wide Web site offers Course Technology customers a password-protected site where you can find everything you need to prepare for class. Here you can obtain the Instructor's Manual, Solution files, and any updates and revisions to the text. Contact your Customer Service Representative for the site address and password.

Instructor's Manual

This is quality assurance tested and includes:
- *Solutions to end-of-unit material*
- *Lecture notes which contain teaching tips from the author*
- *Extra Projects*

Solution Files

Solution Files contain every file students are asked to create or modify in the lessons and end-of-unit material. A Help file on the Instructor's Resource Kit includes information for using the Solution Files.

Figure Files

The figures in the text are provided on the Instructor's Resource Kit CD-ROM to help illustrate key topics or steps. Instructors can create traditional overhead transparencies by printing the figure files, or they can create electronic slide shows by using the figures in a presentation program such as PowerPoint.

Contents

Microsoft
► Word
Projects

Document
Formatting

In This Unit You Will Create:

 **One-page Resume**

 **Business Cards**

 **Sales Letter**

You can use Microsoft Word to produce an enormous variety of documents—from simple one-page letters and resumes to multiple-page reports, newsletters, brochures, and even novels. Once you are comfortable with the many features of Microsoft Word, you can concentrate on how to *use* these features to produce just about any document you can think of and even preview how a document will appear when published on the World Wide Web. In this unit, you will apply your Microsoft Word skills to modify styles, use the Format Painter, create WordArt objects, apply borders, create labels, and use the Click and Type feature.

One-page Resume for Joyce Allan

Joyce Allan recently earned an administrative assistant certificate from Capilano College in North Vancouver, British Columbia. She now needs to create an attractive one-page resume that she will include with her job applications. Three activities are required to complete the one-page resume for Joyce Allan:

Project Activities

Enter Text

When you need to create a document such as a resume that will require a great deal of formatting, you will save time by first entering all the text and *then* applying the required formatting. You can also use the Table function to enter data in columns. The text in the Education, Work Experience, and Volunteer Experience sections of Joyce Allan's resume was created in a table form.

Modify Styles

Once you have entered all the text required for the resume, you can select and then modify the styles you wish to apply to the various parts of the resume. In Joyce's resume, the font style and font size in the normal document style were changed to Arial and 12-point, and then an attractive style was created and applied to each of the headings. By using styles to format a document, you save time and attain a consistent look.

Enhance and Print the Resume

At first, Joyce's resume did not fit on one page. The margins were therefore changed so that all the text fits on one page without reducing the font size, which would affect the overall readability of the resume.

When you have completed Project 1, the resume will appear as shown in Figure P1-1.

JOYCE ALLAN

2131 Dollarton Hwy.
North Vancouver, BC V7H 1A8
Phone/Fax: (604) 929-4431
e-mail: joyce@commerce.ca

Objective

To apply my organizational and computer skills as an Administrative Assistant in a service-based company or organization

Education

1999-2000:   **Capilano College**, North Vancouver, BC
Administrative Assistant Certificate
- Computer Skills: Microsoft Office 2000: Word, Excel, Access, PowerPoint, FrontPage, and Publisher; Adobe PageMaker 6.5
- Business Communications and Organizational Behavior
- Basic Accounting and Bookkeeping
- Administrative Procedures
- Internet Communications

1992-1997:   **Point Gray Senior Secondary School**
Grade 12 Graduation

Work Experience

1998-1999:   **Best Bookkeeping**, 3095 West George Street, Vancouver
Office Assistant (part-time)
Responsibilities included:
- Maintaining company records
- Formatting documents in Word 97
- Organizing company database with Access 97

1996-1997:   **Camp Haida**, Gambier Island, British Columbia
Camp Counselor (summers)
Responsibilities included:
- Supervising groups of 10 campers aged 9 to 11
- Organizing crafts and sports activities
- Assisting with general office duties

Volunteer Experience

1995-1998:   **Mother's March**, North Vancouver Chapter
1999-2000:   **Capilano College Applied Business Technology Department**
Student Activities Coordinator

References

Available on request

activity:

Enter Text

You will first enter all the data required for the resume. To save time, you will enter this data without worrying about formatting. You will also use the Tables feature to quickly enter the data required for the Education, Work Experience, and Volunteer Experience sections of the resume.

steps:

Trouble

If a button does not appear on the Standard toolbar, click the **More Buttons button** >> on the toolbar to view a list of additional buttons.

1. Start Word, type just the name and address as shown in Figure P1-2, then press [Enter] twice

2. Type **Objective**, press [Enter], type **To apply my organizational and computer skills as an Administrative Assistant in a service-based company or organization**, press [Enter] twice, then save the resume as **Joyce Allan's Resume** to the disk where you plan to store all the files for this book

3. Type **Education**, press [Enter] twice, click the **Insert Table button** 🔲 on the Standard toolbar, drag the mouse to create a table that is 2 columns by 4 rows, then reduce the width of column 1 to 1 inch
   To reduce the column width, you point the mouse between columns 1 and 2 and drag the ◄║► until the marker on the Ruler Bar appears at 1.

4. Enter the text for the first two table entries, as shown in Figure P1-2
   Joyce Allan does not have any more entries for education.

5. Point the mouse to the left of row 3, click the **left mouse button**, drag the mouse to select rows 3 and 4, **right-click** one of the selected rows, then click **Delete Rows**

6. Press [Enter] once following the table, type **Work Experience**, then press [Enter] twice

7. Click anywhere in the table, move your mouse over the top left corner of the table to show the **Table Select button** ✛, click ✛ to select the entire table, click the **Copy button** 🖹 on the Standard toolbar, click the second paragraph mark below Work Experience, then click the **Paste button** 🖹 on the Standard toolbar
   To replace existing text, click the cell to select it, then start typing the new text.

8. Enter the text for Work Experience in the table, as shown in Figure P1-3, click below the table, press [Enter] once, type **Volunteer Experience**, then press [Enter] twice

9. Copy and paste the Work Experience table, enter the text required for Volunteer Experience, type the remaining text below the table, as shown in Figure P1-3, click the **Spelling and Grammar button** 🔤 on the Formatting toolbar, make changes where required, then save the document

Clues to Use

Restoring Default Toolbars and Menus in Word 2000

Word toolbars and menus modify themselves to your working style. The Standard and Formatting toolbars you see when you first start Word include the most frequently used buttons. To locate a button not visible on a toolbar, click the More Buttons button 🔘 *to see the list of additional toolbar buttons. As you work, Word adds the buttons you use to the visible toolbars and moves the buttons you haven't used in awhile to the More Buttons list. Similarly, Word menus adjust to your work habits, so that the commands you use most often automatically appear on shortened menus. Click the double arrow at the bottom of a menu to view additional menu commands. You can return toolbars and menus to their original settings by clicking Tools on the menu bar, then clicking Customize. On the Options tab, click Reset my usage data. An alert box or the Office Assistant appears asking if you are sure you want to do this. Click Yes, then click Close in the Customize dialog box. Resetting your usage data erases changes made automatically to your menus and toolbars. It does not affect the options you customize.*

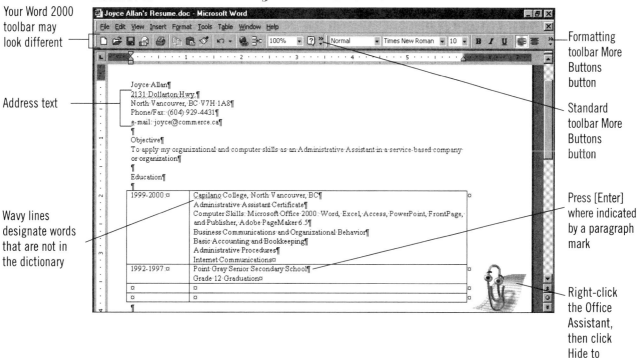

FIGURE P1-2: Resume heading and education text

Your Word 2000 toolbar may look different

Address text

Wavy lines designate words that are not in the dictionary

Formatting toolbar More Buttons button

Standard toolbar More Buttons button

Press [Enter] where indicated by a paragraph mark

Right-click the Office Assistant, then click Hide to remove it

FIGURE P1-3: Remaining text for the resume

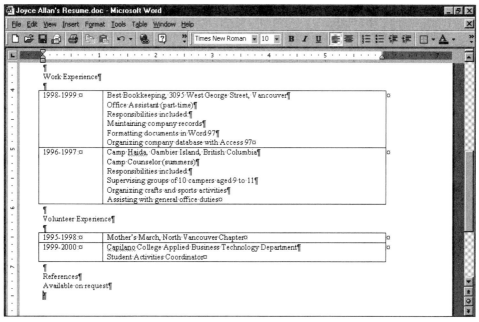

activity:

Modify Styles

You need to modify the normal document style to change the font style to Arial and the font size to 12-point for the entire document. You will then create an attractive heading style and use Format Painter to apply the style to each heading in the resume.

steps:

1. Click **Format** on the menu bar, click **Style**, click **Modify**, then click **Format**

2. Click **Font**, select the **Arial** font and a font size of **12**, click **OK**, click **OK** again, then click **Apply**
   The Normal style for your current document now includes the Arial font and a font size of 12.

3. Click **Format** on the menu bar, click **Style**, then click **New**

4. Type **Resume Heading Style**, click **Format**, click **Font**, select a font size of **16**, click **Bold Italic**, then click **OK**

5. Click **Format**, click **Border,** select a line width of **2¼ pt**, click **Box**, click the **top**, **left**, and **right** borders to remove these lines in the sample Border, as shown in Figure P1-4, click **OK**, click **OK** again, then click **Close**

6. Double-click **Objective** to select it, click the **Style list arrow** on the Formatting toolbar, as shown in Figure P1-5, then click **Resume Heading Style**
   Your heading looks great.

7. Double-click **Education**, click the **Style list arrow**, click **Resume Heading Style**, repeat the procedure to apply the style to **Work Experience**, **Volunteer Experience**, and **References**, then click anywhere in the text to deselect References
   Make sure you select only the text required and not *the previous paragraph marker. If the previous paragraph marker is included in the style, extra space will appear in your document. Don't worry if your resume expands to two pages. You'll fix this problem in a later activity.*

8. Select **Joyce Allan** at the top of the page, click **Format**, then click **Style**

9. Create a new style called **Resume Title Style**, which includes the **Arial Black** font, a font size of **18** and **Small caps**, and a 1½ point **Shadow** border in the Borders and Shading section, click **OK**, click **OK** again, click **Apply**, click anywhere in the resume to deselect the text, then save the document
   Compare your screen to Figure P1-6. Joyce Allan's resume is coming along very nicely.

FIGURE P1-4: Borders and Shading dialog box

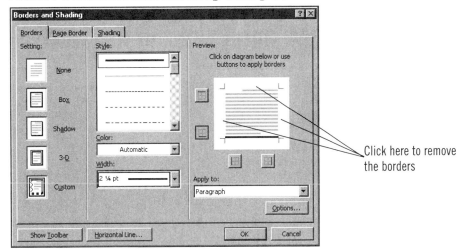

Click here to remove the borders

FIGURE P1-5: Resume Heading Style selected

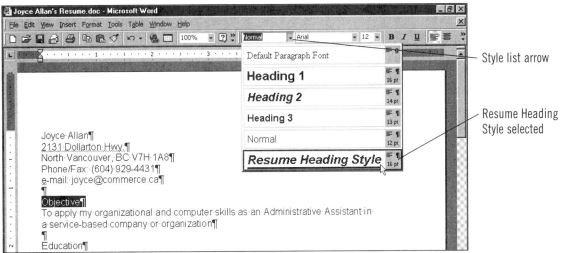

Style list arrow

Resume Heading Style selected

FIGURE P1-6: Resume styles applied

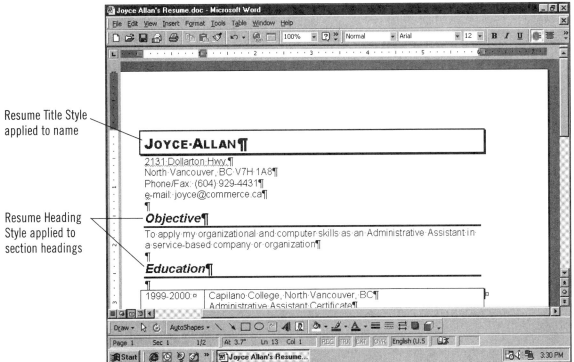

Resume Title Style applied to name

Resume Heading Style applied to section headings

activity:

Enhance and Print the Resume

You need to decide whether you like the heading styles you created, make some modifications, apply some formatting to the individual sections of the resume, use the Shrink to Fit option to fit the resume on one page, and print a copy. You first decide to modify the Resume Heading Style by reducing both the font size and the border size. When you modify a style, the changes are instantly applied to all the text in the document currently formatted with that particular style.

Hint

You click Close, not Apply, when you have finished modifying the style because you do not want to apply the style to the text at your insertion point. Instead, you want only the text already formatted with a style to be modified.

steps:

1. Click **Format** on the menu bar, click **Style**, select **Resume Heading Style**, click **Modify**, click **Format**, click **Font**, change the font size to **14**, then click **OK**

2. Click **Format**, click **Border**, change the Border size to **1½ pt**, click **OK**, click **OK** again, then click **Close**
   A little more text now appears on page 1, but still not enough.

3. Change the font size in the **Resume Title Style** to **16 pt**, then remove the Shadow border
   You will need to select None in the Borders and Shading dialog box to remove the Shadow border.

4. Click the **Print Preview button** 🔍 on the Standard toolbar, then click the **Shrink to Fit button** 📑
   The resume now fits on one page.

5. Click **Close**, select the text from **Computer Skills** to **Internet Communications**, then click the **Bullets button** ☰, as shown in Figure P1-7

6. With the text still selected, double-click the **Format Painter button** 🖌 on the Standard toolbar, drag 🖌 across the list of responsibilities for Best Bookkeeping, drag 🖌 across the list of responsibilities for Camp Haida, then click 🖌 to turn it off

7. Refer to Figure P1-8, then use **Format Painter** to enhance selected text so that it appears as shown
   Joyce's resume is looking great.

8. Select the heading text from **Joyce Allan** to the **e-mail address**, then click the **Center button** ▤ on the Formatting toolbar

9. Click in each table, click **Format** on the menu bar, click **Borders and Shading**, click **None**, then click **OK** to remove the gridlines

10. View the resume once more in Print Preview, then print a copy and save the document

FIGURE P1-7: Bulleted list

Format Painter button

Bullets button

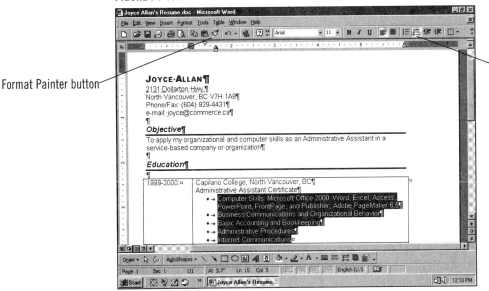

FIGURE P1-8: Formatted text

Bold

Italics

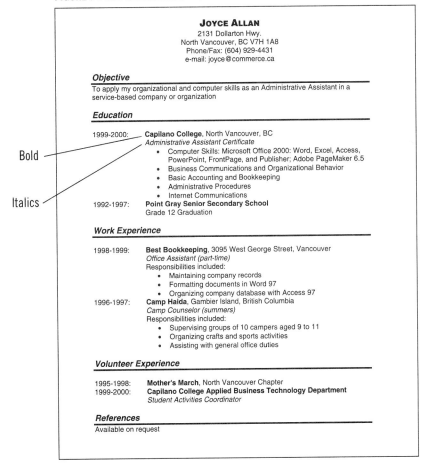

Using the Format Painter

You use Format Painter to copy the formatting from one text block to another. You click the Format Painter button once to apply formatting from one text block to another text block. You double-click the Format Painter button to apply formatting from one text block to multiple text blocks. You then click the Format Painter button once to turn it off.

Business Cards for Günther Schmidt

Günther Schmidt works from his home in Philadelphia as a freelance computer systems analyst. He has just purchased a package of business cards that are produced in pre-punched sheets of 10 business cards to the sheet. Günther wants to use these sheets to create his personal stack of business cards. In the Labels Options dialog box, he finds a form that he can use to create his business cards. To create Günther Schmidt's business cards, you will **Create Labels and Enter Text, Add a WordArt Logo,** and **Format the Label Sheet for Printing.**

activity:

Create Labels and Enter Text

steps:

1. Open a new document, click **Tools** on the menu bar, click **Envelopes and Labels,** then click the **Labels tab**

2. Click **Options,** then scroll the **Product Number list box** until **5371 - Business Card** appears

3. Click **5371 - Business Card** to select it, click **OK,** then click **New Document**
   You click New Document because you want to show the label sheet as a table in which you can include both the text for the business card and a WordArt object.

4. Type **G**

5. Click **Insert** on the menu bar, click **Symbol,** select **(normal text)** as the Font type (if necessary), click the **ü** as shown in Figure P2-1, click **Insert,** click **Close,** then type **nther Schmidt**

6. Save the document on your disk as **Business Cards for Gunther Schmidt**

7. Press **[Enter]** once, then enter the remaining text for the business card as shown in Figure P2-2

8. Select the six lines of text, change the font to **Arial,** click the **Center button** 🖩 on the Formatting toolbar, enhance **Günther Schmidt** with **Bold** and a font size of **12,** and **Computer Systems Analyst** with **Italic,** then deselect the text
   Your business card appears as shown in Figure P2-3.

9. Save the document

Trouble

If a button does not appear on the Standard toolbar, click the **More Buttons button** 🔳 on the toolbar to view a list of additional buttons.

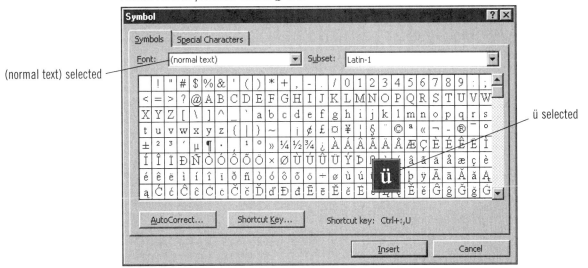

FIGURE P2-1: **Symbol dialog box**

(normal text) selected

ü selected

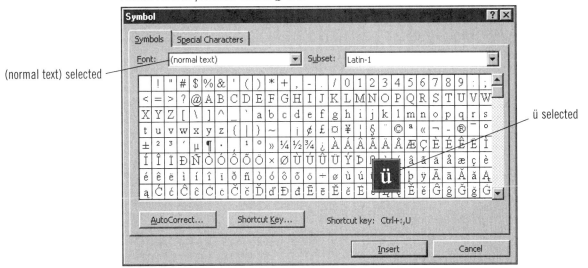

FIGURE P2-2: **Text for business card**

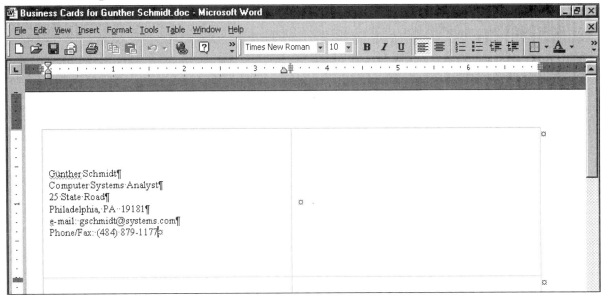

FIGURE P2-3: **Business card text formatted**

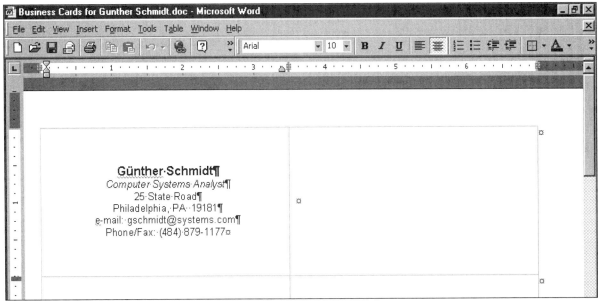

PROJECT 2

Word

activity:

Add a WordArt Logo

You need to modify the paragraph formatting for the business card text, add a WordArt object, then copy the object and text to the remaining nine cards. Your first step is to increase the Before Paragraph Spacing for the first line of the business card to 36 points to make room for the WordArt object.

steps:

1. Click to the left of the **G** in Günther, click **Format**, click **Paragraph**, select the contents of the **Before** box, type **36**, then click **OK**

2. Click the **Insert WordArt button** ▣ on the Drawing toolbar
The WordArt Gallery dialog box appears as shown in Figure P2-4.

3. Select the second option from the left, as shown in Figure P2-4, then click **OK**
The WordArt Gallery dialog box closes.

4. Type **GS**, change the font style to **Forte**, then click **OK**
The WordArt object appears in the document.

5. Click the **WordArt Shape button** ▣ on the WordArt toolbar, then select the **Cascade Up Style** shape, as shown in Figure P2-5

6. Click the **Format WordArt button** ▣ on the WordArt toolbar, click the **Size tab**, select the contents of the **Height box**, type **0.5**, press **[Tab]**, type **0.5**, then click **OK**

7. Click the **Shadow button** ▣ on the Drawing toolbar, then click **Shadow Style 9**

8. Drag the **WordArt object** to the top-left corner of the first business card, as shown in Figure P2-6, then click away from the object to deselect it
The initials appear on the first business card.

9. Save the document

FIGURE P2-4: WordArt Gallery dialog box

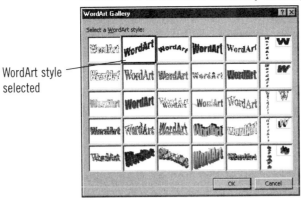

WordArt style selected

FIGURE P2-5: Cascade Up style selected

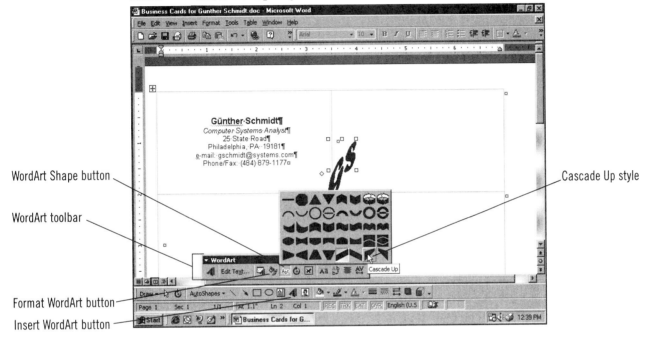

WordArt Shape button

WordArt toolbar

Format WordArt button

Insert WordArt button

Cascade Up style

FIGURE P2-6: Completed business card

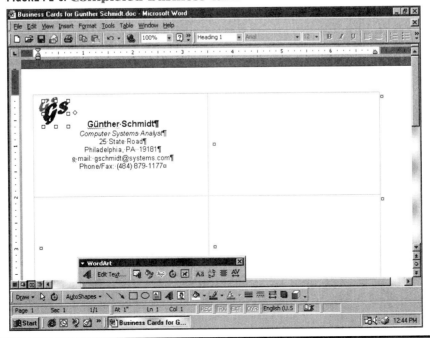

activity:

Format the Label Sheet for Printing

Günther's business card is complete. Now all you need to do is copy it to the remaining nine cards, and print the label sheet.

steps:

1. Click **Table** on the menu bar, click **Select**, then click **Cell**

2. Click the **Copy button** 📋 on the Standard toolbar, click in the top-right card, then click the **Paste button** 📋 on the Standard toolbar

   If the Clipboard toolbar appears at any point, just click its Close button.

3. Click to the left of the first business card to select the entire first row

4. Click 📋, click to the left of row 2, then click 📋

5. Click to the left of the next row, press [F4], press [F4] again, then press [F4] again

6. Click the **Zoom Control List Arrow** on the Standard toolbar, click **Two Pages**, select the blank cards including the entire row on page 2, then click the **Cut button** ✂ on the Standard toolbar

   A complete sheet of business cards appears on one page.

7. Click the **Print button** 🖨 on the Standard toolbar

   Compare your completed sheet of cards to Figure P2-7. If Günther Schmidt were really printing his business cards, he would insert several sheets of the pre-punched cards he purchased into his printer before he clicked the Print button.

Günther Schmidt
Computer Systems Analyst
25 State Road
Philadelphia, PA 19181
e-mail: gschmidt@systems.com
Phone/Fax: (484) 879-1177

Günther Schmidt
Computer Systems Analyst
25 State Road
Philadelphia, PA 19181
e-mail: gschmidt@systems.com
Phone/Fax: (484) 879-1177

Günther Schmidt
Computer Systems Analyst
25 State Road
Philadelphia, PA 19181
e-mail: gschmidt@systems.com
Phone/Fax: (484) 879-1177

Günther Schmidt
Computer Systems Analyst
25 State Road
Philadelphia, PA 19181
e-mail: gschmidt@systems.com
Phone/Fax: (484) 879-1177

Günther Schmidt
Computer Systems Analyst
25 State Road
Philadelphia, PA 19181
e-mail: gschmidt@systems.com
Phone/Fax: (484) 879-1177

Günther Schmidt
Computer Systems Analyst
25 State Road
Philadelphia, PA 19181
e-mail: gschmidt@systems.com
Phone/Fax: (484) 879-1177

Günther Schmidt
Computer Systems Analyst
25 State Road
Philadelphia, PA 19181
e-mail: gschmidt@systems.com
Phone/Fax: (484) 879-1177

Günther Schmidt
Computer Systems Analyst
25 State Road
Philadelphia, PA 19181
e-mail: gschmidt@systems.com
Phone/Fax: (484) 879-1177

Gunther Schmidt
Computer Systems Analyst
25 State Road
Philadelphia, PA 19181
e-mail: gschmidt@systems.com
Phone/Fax: (484) 879-1177

Gunther Schmidt
Computer Systems Analyst
25 State Road
Philadelphia, PA 19181
e-mail: gschmidt@systems.com
Phone/Fax: (484) 879-1177

Sales Letter for Tokada Software Solutions

Tokada Software Solutions provides software consulting services to English-speaking companies in Japan. Janet Tokada, the company president, has just met with Aaron Markham, the manager of an American accounting firm in Tokyo. She decides to write him a letter to thank him for their meeting and to inform him of how Tokada Software Solutions can help his business. To create the sales letter you will **Create the Letterhead** and then **Enter and Format the Letter Text**.

activity:

Create the Letterhead

steps:

1. Open a new document, click the **Insert WordArt button** 🖺 on the Drawing toolbar, click the first option in the third row (the object is yellow and orange), then click **OK**
   The WordArt Gallery dialog box appears.

2. Type **Tokada Software Solutions**, select the **Matisse ITC font**, or another if unavailable, then click **OK**

3. Click the **3-D button** 🖺 on the Drawing toolbar, click **3-D Settings**, click the **Direction button** 🖺, click the third 3-D style in the top row, click the **Depth button** 🖺, select the contents of the Custom text box, type **12.00 pt**, as shown in Figure P3-1, then press **[Enter]**

4. Close the 3-D Settings toolbar, drag the object to the top-left of the document, next to the first paragraph marker, click the **Free Rotate button** 🖺 on the WordArt toolbar, point ⌖ over the lower-left corner on the small circle of the WordArt object, click and drag to rotate the object as shown in Figure P3-2, then click 🖺 to turn off rotating

5. Click the **Format WordArt button** 🖺 on the WordArt toolbar, click the **Colors and Lines tab**, click the **Color list arrow**, click **Fill Effects**, click the **Texture tab**, click the texture in the fourth column of the second row (**Granite**), then click **OK**

6. Click the **Size tab**, change the **Height** to **0.5"**, and the **Width** to **4"**, click **OK**, deselect the WordArt object, then save the document as **Letter for Tokada Software Solutions**

7. Click the **Insert Clip Art button** 🖺 on the Drawing toolbar, click in the **Search for clips** text box, type **Computers**, press **[Enter]**, right-click a picture of a computer similar to the picture shown in Figure P3-3, click **Insert**, then close the Insert Clip Art dialog box

8. Right-click the picture, click **Format Picture**, click the **Size tab**, change the Height to **1"**, click the **Layout tab**, click **Square**, click the **Right option button** under Horizontal alignment, then click **OK**

9. Double-click about one-half inch below the WordArt object, enter and format the address information as shown in Figure P3-3, then save the document
   By double-clicking below the WordArt object, you are using the new Click and Type feature. This feature automatically applies the formatting necessary to position the insertion point where you double-clicked.

FIGURE P3-1: **Modifying the 3-D style**

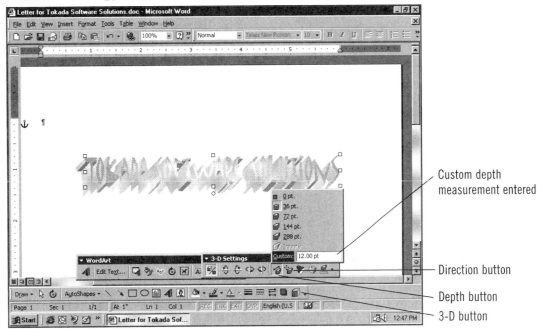

Custom depth measurement entered

Direction button

Depth button

3-D button

FIGURE P3-2: **Rotating the WordArt object**

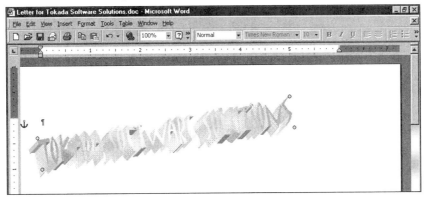

FIGURE P3-3: **Letterhead complete**

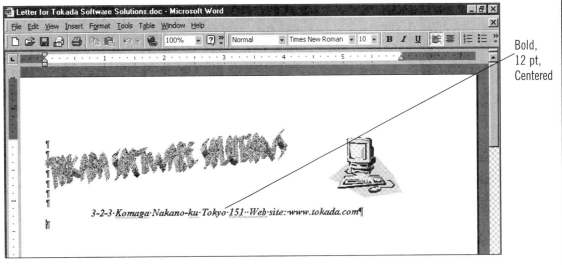

Bold, 12 pt, Centered

activity:

Enter and Format the Letter Text

First, you will use the Click and Type feature to position the insertion point where you want to enter the current date, and then you will type the text for the letter and apply formatting to selected paragraphs.

steps:

Hint

You will find the currency symbol for Japanese Yen (¥) in the (normal text) font in the Symbol dialog box.

1. Double-click at the left margin about 1'' below the address, click **Insert** on the menu bar, click **Date and Time**, select the date format you prefer, then click **OK**

2. Press **[Enter]** twice, then type the text of the letter as shown in Figure P3-4 without including any indents or paragraph numbers

Type the text without formatting. Don't type numbers before each of the three numbered paragraphs and don't worry if your letter extends to two pages. You'll fix this problem later.

3. Click the **Spelling and Grammar button** on the Standard toolbar, and make any necessary corrections

4. Select the descriptions of the three options, then click the **Numbering button** on the Formatting toolbar

When you want to enter a series of numbered paragraphs, you should first type the paragraphs without numbering, and then select them and click the Numbering button. This method allows you to leave unnumbered lines between individual paragraphs.

Time To

✓ **Save**

5. Select **Basic Software Setup**, click the **Bold button** on the Formatting toolbar, then double-click the **Format Painter button** on the Standard toolbar

6. Refer to the completed letter shown in Figure P3-4, apply **Format Painter** to the text that appears in bold, then click to turn it off when you have finished formatting the selected text

7. Click the **Zoom Control list arrow** on the Standard toolbar, click **Whole Page**, click **File** on the menu bar, click **Page Setup**, change the **Left** and **Right Margins** to 1'' and the **Top Margin** to .9'', then click **OK**

The letter may still not fit on one page.

8. Return to **100%** view, hold down **[Ctrl]** and press **[Home]** to move to the top of the page, then use your mouse to slightly adjust the sizes and positions of the Picture and the WordArt object so that they appear as shown in Figure P3-4

You may also need to remove one or two hard returns so that the entire letter fits on one page.

9. Click the **Print button** on the Standard toolbar to print a copy of the letter, then save and close your document

TOKADA SOFTWARE SOLUTIONS

3-2-3 Komaga, Nakano-ku Tokyo 151 Web site: www.tokada.com

December 3, 2001

Mr. Aaron Markham
Manager
Tokyo American Accounting, Inc.
3-3-1 Hongo, Bukyo-ku
Tokyo 143

Dear Mr. Markham:

Thank you for meeting with me last week to discuss how Tokada Software Solutions can help your company maximize its efficiency. As we discussed, Tokada Software Solutions offers the following three packages to meet the needs of Tokyo American Accounting, Inc.

1. **Basic Software Setup**: Purchase and installation of the latest version of AccPac accounting software on your office computers and one day of staff training for **¥120,000** ($1,000 US).

2. **Custom Software Setup**: Design and installation of software customized for all the accounting and office management needs of Tokyo American Accounting, Inc., for **¥600,000** ($5,000 US).

3. **Software Maintenance Plan**: 24-hour-a-day support, monthly staff training sessions, and annual software updating for a monthly fee of **¥25,000** ($200 US).

As you have just recently established your business, Mr. Markham, I feel that a combination of Packages 1 and 3 would be most suitable. Within days, your office will be up and running with AccPac and your staff given some basic training. Our 2-hour support and monthly staff training sessions will provide your staff with all the backup they need to get the most out of your AccPac installation.

The enclosed brochure describes Packages 1 and 3 in more detail. If you have any questions regarding the packages, please call me at 3755 1786 or send me an e-mail at jtokada@tokada.com. You may also wish to explore our new Web site at www.tokada.com.

Thank you for your interest in Tokada Software Solutions. I hope we may look forward to serving you soon.

Sincerely,

Janet Tokada
President

Encl.

Independent Challenges

INDEPENDENT CHALLENGE 1

Create and enhance your own resume. To help determine the information required for your resume, fill in the boxes below, enter the resume text, modify or create a variety of styles, then enhance and print your resume.

1. Determine your objective. What kinds of positions are you looking for that will match your qualifications and experience? Enter your objective in the box below:

Resume Objective: ....
....

2. In the table below, list the components related to your educational background, starting with your most recent school or college. Note the name of the institution, the certificate or degree you received, and a selection of the courses relevant to the type of work you are seeking.

Year(s):	Institution:	Certificate/Degree:	Courses:

3. In the table below, list the details related to your work experience. Use **parallel structure** when listing your responsibilities; that is, make sure that each element uses the same grammatical structure. For example, you can start each point with a verb, such as "maintain," "manage," or "use," and then follow it with the relevant object, for example, "maintain company records" and "use Microsoft Word 2000 to create promotional materials."

Year(s):	Institution:	Certificate/Degree:	Courses:

4. In the table below, describe any volunteer experience you have, awards you have received and, if you wish, your hobbies and interests.

Volunteer Experience	
Awards	
Hobbies/Interests	

5. Set up your resume in Word as follows:

    a. Type all the text required for your resume. Use a table form to enter the information for Education, Work Experience, and Volunteer Experience (if appropriate). Remember to use the Copy and Paste features to save time.

    b. Modify the Normal style so that the text shows the font and font size you prefer.

    c. Create styles for the resume headings. If you wish, you can modify the Resume Heading Style you created in Project 1.

    d. Apply the styles then modify them, if necessary.

    e. Use Format Painter to add other enhancements such as bold, italics, and bullets to selected text.

    f. View your resume in Whole Page view, change the margins, if necessary, and make any other changes required to fit the resume attractively on one or two pages. If your resume extends to two pages, include a header at the top of Page 2 that contains your name and the page number.

    g. Save your resume as "My Personal Resume", then print a copy.

INDEPENDENT CHALLENGE 2

Use the Business Card label sheet to create a sheet of business cards for yourself. Here are some tips for creating your business cards:

1. Select Business Cards from the list of available label sheets in the Label Options dialog box, click OK, then click New Document.
2. Click above the text and create an attractive WordArt logo from your own initials.
3. Reduce the size of the logo and position it attractively on the business card.
4. Save the document as "My Business Cards".
5. Align the business cards in the Address box as you want them to appear when you print.
6. Apply the font styles and sizes you want to the various lines of business card text.
7. Print your sheet of business cards.

INDEPENDENT CHALLENGE 3

Adapt the sales letter you created in Project 3 to promote a product for a company of your choice. For example, you could choose to describe aquarium products for a company called Fish Fantasies or promote Internet services for a company called OnLine OnTime. Once you have decided on a company and product, open the letter for Tokada Software Solutions, delete the current letterhead, create your own letterhead (use WordArt and insert an appropriate picture), then adapt the content to suit your product and company. Save the letter as "Sales Letter for (Your Company Name)", and print the completed letter.

INDEPENDENT CHALLENGE 4

Type the text for the confirmation letter in Figure IC-1, then enhance the letter as directed. Note that the purpose of a confirmation letter is to confirm arrangements related to a specific event or agreement made between two companies or organizations. In the confirmation letter below, Step One Communications confirms a seminar they are hosting for employees of the Midland Counties Bank.

1. Type the text as shown in Figure IC-1. Note that you will find the £ symbol in the (normal text) font in the Symbol dialog box.
2. Use WordArt to create an attractive letterhead, then add a picture if you wish.
3. Modify the Normal style to change the font and font size to the settings you prefer, then apply the style to the entire document.
4. Use your own judgment to enhance the letter so that it appears attractive and fits on one page.
5. View the letter in Whole Page view, then make any spacing or formatting adjustments required.
6. Save the letter as "Confirmation Letter for Challenge 4", and print a copy.

FIGURE IC-1: Text of confirmation letter

Step One Communications, Inc.

[Current Date]

John Shackleton
Personnel Manager
Midland Counties Bank: Basingstoke Branch
24 London Road
Basingstoke, Berkshire
M1K 3P3, UK

Dear Mr. Shackleton:

Thank you for your letter of [specify a date one week prior to the current date] confirming a one-day communications seminar at the Basingstoke Branch of the Midland Counties Bank. My colleague, Ms. Jenna White, will be conducting the seminar and supplying all the materials the participants will require.

Here again are the seminar details:

    Date: [specify a date one month after the current date]
    Time: 0900 to 1700
    Location: 2nd Floor, Administration Building, Reading University, Whiteknights Campus
    Cost: £1,000 for 20 participants

As we discussed, the communications seminar will include the following activities:

1. Warm-up exercises to stimulate a relaxed atmosphere and to determine the general level of communications skills among the participants.

2. Analysis of various communications situations to assess writing strengths and weaknesses.

3. Intensive "hands-on" practice in the communication of clear and effective sales, training, and informational presentations.

I'm very much looking forward to an exciting seminar. Thank you again, Mr. Shackleton, for your interest in Step One Communications. If you have any further questions, please call me at 877045.

Sincerely,

[Your Name]
President

Visual Workshop

Create the letterhead shown in Figure VW-1 in a document named "Letterhead Practice." For the WordArt object, select the Style in the 3rd column, 2nd row, select the Elephant font and the Wave 1 shape, set the Fill Color on the Drawing toolbar at Brown, remove semi-transparent, remove the Line color, set the Height to .5" and the Width to 4", and remove the Shadow. If you can't find the lion picture shown, choose a similar picture. Change the Layout for the picture to square and right-aligned.

FIGURE VW-1: Letterhead

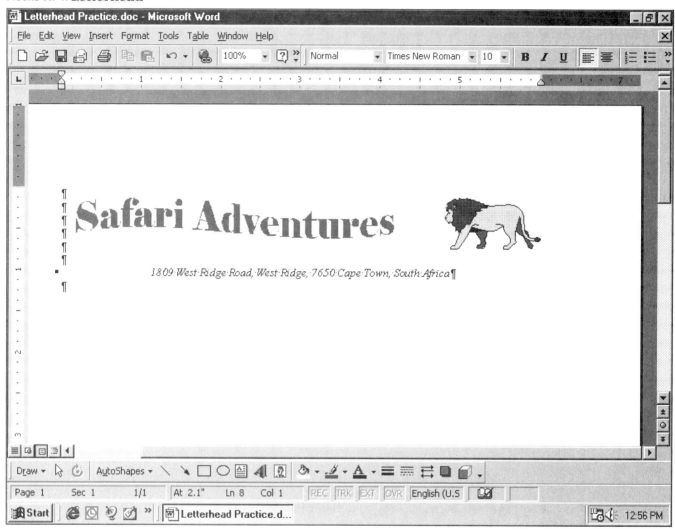

Microsoft ► Excel Projects

Worksheet Building

In This Unit You Will Create:

PROJECT 1 ► Projected Budget

PROJECT 2 ► Course Grades Analysis

PROJECT 3 ► Planning Budget

Microsoft Excel provides you with the tools you need to make effective planning decisions. For example, suppose you want to take a two-week vacation to Hawaii and you have allocated $2,000 for all your trip expenses. To find out if you have enough money to cover your expenses, you can set up a simple worksheet that will list all your expenses for airfare, accommodations, food, entertainment, etc. Once you have totaled all your expenses, you may find that they exceed your $2,000 budget. Rather than cancel your trip, you could then try to determine which expenses you can decrease. You could decide to stay at a less expensive hotel or allocate a reduced amount for your shopping needs. When you use a worksheet as a planning tool, you identify and evaluate different courses of action and then select the actions that will best meet your personal or business needs. In this unit, you will learn how to build arithmetic formulas, use functions in calculations, view a worksheet on a Web browser, and, most important, ask relevant "What if?" questions designed to help you develop worksheets that you can then use as planning tools.

Projected Budget for Cape Cod Arts Council

The Cape Cod Arts Council is a small, nonprofit organization that teaches arts and crafts classes in a converted boathouse located in the Cape Cod area. You will create the Cape Cod Arts Council's budget for the first six months of 2001, based on figures obtained from the 2000 budget, and then ask a series of "What if?" questions to determine realistic planning goals for the second half of 2001.

The following four activities are required to complete the six-month budget for the Cape Cod Arts Council:

Project Activities

Enter and Enhance Labels

You can quickly present worksheet data in an attractive and easy-to-read format. In Figure P1-1, the labels in the top five rows are centered across columns and enhanced with various font styles and sizes, while a white-on-black effect is used to highlight two of the worksheet titles.

Calculate Totals

You can either use the AutoSum button or enter a formula when you need to add values in a spreadsheet. You use the AutoSum method when you want to add the values in cells that appear consecutively in a column or row and when you are entering the total directly below or to the right of the added values. You enter a formula when you want to calculate values that do not appear in consecutive or adjacent cells. For example, you would enter the formula =A1+A3 if you wished to add the values in cells A1 and A3. You can also use the SUM function. For example, you would enter the formula =SUM(A1:A6) if you wished to add all the values in cells A1 through A6 and enter the result in a nonadjacent cell.

Ask "What if?" Questions

One of the most useful tasks you can perform with a spreadsheet program is to change values in a worksheet to see how the totals are affected. For example, you can ask yourself: "*If we spend $2,000 a month on payroll instead of $4,500, how much money will we save over six months?*" As soon as you change the values entered in the Payroll row, the totals are automatically updated. To complete Project 1, you will ask three "What if?" questions.

Format and Print the Budget

You will use a variety of the features in the Page Setup dialog box to produce an attractive printed version of your budget that includes a customized header.

When you have completed the activities above, your budget will appear as shown in Figure P1-1.

FIGURE P1-1: Cape Cod Arts Council projected budget

Cape Cod Arts Council

Six-Month Budget

January to June 2001

Labels centered across columns

Currency style

Comma style

Header text

White text on black background

Border styles

Cape Cod Arts Council

North Shore Boathouse, R.R. #2, Mattapoisett, MA 02739

Projected Budget
January to June 2001

5/6/99

	January	February	March	April	May	June	Totals
Income							
Course Fees	$ 26,041.67	$ 26,041.67	$ 26,041.67	$ 26,041.67	$ 33,854.17	$ 33,854.17	$ 171,875.00
Grants	1,000.00	1,000.00	1,000.00	1,000.00	1,000.00	1,000.00	6,000.00
Donations	400.00	400.00	400.00	400.00	400.00	400.00	2,400.00
Total Income	$ 27,441.67	$ 27,441.67	$ 27,441.67	$ 27,441.67	$ 35,254.17	$ 35,254.17	$ 180,275.00
Expenses							
Payroll	$ 5,520.83	$ 5,520.83	$ 5,520.83	$ 5,520.83	$ 5,520.83	$ 5,520.83	$ 33,125.00
Lease	600.00	600.00	600.00	600.00	600.00	600.00	3,600.00
Course Supplies	1,200.00	1,200.00	1,200.00	1,200.00	1,200.00	1,200.00	7,200.00
Maintenance	400.00	400.00	400.00	400.00	400.00	400.00	2,400.00
Computer Lease	400.00	400.00	400.00	400.00	400.00	400.00	2,400.00
Advertising	700.00	700.00	3,000.00	700.00	700.00	700.00	6,500.00
Total Expenses	$ 8,820.83	$ 8,820.83	$ 11,120.83	$ 8,820.83	$ 8,820.83	$ 8,820.83	$ 55,225.00
Profit	$ 18,620.83	$ 18,620.83	$ 16,320.83	$ 18,620.83	$ 26,433.33	$ 26,433.33	$ 125,050.00

January to June 2001

activity:

Enter and Enhance Labels

You need to enter and enhance the name and address of the organization, the worksheet title, the current date, and the first series of labels.

Hint

If a button does not appear on the Formatting toolbar, click the More Buttons button 》 on the toolbar to view a list of additional buttons.

steps:

1. Start Excel, open a new worksheet, click the blank box to the left of the **A** at the top left corner of the worksheet to select the entire worksheet, click the **Font Size list arrow**, then click **12**

   A font size of 12 is selected for the entire worksheet.

2. Click cell **A1**, type **Cape Cod Arts Council**, press **[Enter]**, type the remaining labels as shown in Figure P1-2, then save your worksheet as **Projected Budget for Cape Cod Arts Council** on the disk where you plan to store all the files for this book

3. Click cell **A1**, click the **Font list arrow** on the Formatting toolbar, select **Comic Sans MS**, if it is available, or select **Britannic Bold**, click the **Font Size list arrow** on the Formatting toolbar, then select **24**

4. Select cells **A4** and **A5**, click the **Font Size list arrow**, then select **18**

   Although the text extends into columns B and C, you only need to select cells A4 and A5 — the place where the text originated.

5. Select cells **A1** to **H5**, as shown in Figure P1-3, **right-click** the selection, click **Format Cells**, click the **Alignment tab**, click the **Horizontal list arrow**, click **Center Across Selection**, click **OK**, select cells **A4** to **H5**, click the **Fill Color list arrow** on the Formatting toolbar, click the **black box**, then click away from the cells to deselect them

   You can no longer see the labels in cells A4 and A5.

6. Select cells **A4** and **A5**, click the **Font Color list arrow** on the Formatting toolbar, then click the **white box**

7. Click cell **A7**, click the **Paste Function button** 𝑓ₓ on the Standard toolbar, select **Date & Time** from the list under Function category, select **Today** from the list under Function name (you'll need to scroll down), click **OK**, click **OK** again, select cells **A7** to **H7**, then click the **Merge and Center button** 🔳 on the Formatting toolbar

8. Click cell **B9**, type **January**, press **[Enter]**, click cell **B9** again, position the mouse pointer over the fill handle in the lower right corner, drag the ╋ to cell **G9**, then click the **Center button** 🔳 on the Formatting toolbar

   The six months from January to June appear and are centered.

9. Click cell **A10**, enter the labels required for cells **A10** to **A25** and cell **H9**, as shown in Figure P1-4, click the **Spelling and Grammar button** 🔤 on the Standard toolbar, correct any spelling errors, then save your worksheet

FIGURE P1-2: Labels for cells A1 to A5

Your Excel 2000 toolbar may look different

Click here to select the whole worksheet

Formatting toolbar More Buttons button

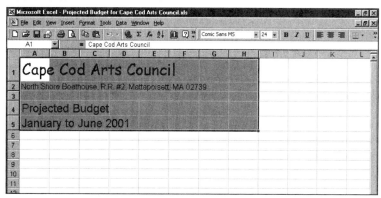

FIGURE P1-3: Cells A1 to H5 selected

Cape Cod Arts Council

North Shore Boathouse, R.R. #2, Mattapoisett, MA 02739

Projected Budget

January to June 2001

FIGURE P1-4: Labels for cells A10 to A25 and H9

Enter "Totals" in cell H9

Labels for cells A10 to A25

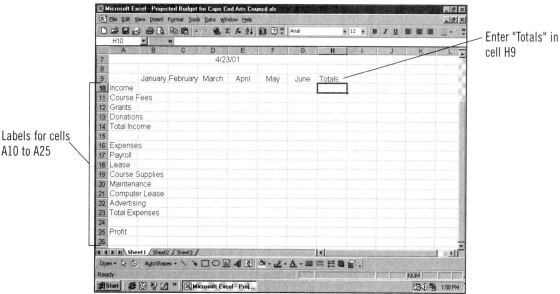

Clues to Use

Merging Cells

A merged cell *is a single cell created by combining two or more cells. The cell reference for the merged cell is the upper-left cell in the original selected range. When you merge a range of cells, only the data in the upper-left cell of the range is included in the merged cell. You use the Alignment tab in the Format Cells dialog box to center several rows of data across columns and you use the Merge and Center button on the Formatting toolbar when you want to center the data in only one cell across several columns.*

activity:

Calculate Totals

You now need to enter the income and expenses that the Cape Cod Arts Council expects in 2001. After you have entered the values, you will calculate the average monthly course fees collected and then the total income and expenses.

steps:

1. Position the mouse pointer on the column divider line between **A** and **B** on the worksheet frame so it changes to ╂, double-click to increase the width of column A to fit all the labels in cells A10 to A25, click cell **B12**, then enter the values for January as shown in Figure P1-5

2. Select cells **B12** to **B22**, position the mouse pointer over the fill handle in the lower-right corner of cell **B22**, then drag across to cell **G22**

   The values in cells B12 to B22 appear in cells C12 to G22.

3. Double-click the **Sheet1 tab** at the bottom of your worksheet, type **Budget**, press **[Enter]**, double-click the **Sheet2 tab**, type **Fees**, then press **[Enter]**

   In the year 2000, you know that approximately 5,000 people took courses in three payment categories: adults, children/seniors, and school groups. You use a new blank worksheet to calculate the average course fee in each category for 2001, based on the total fees collected in 2000. You use a new worksheet to avoid cluttering the current worksheet with data that won't be printed. You named the two worksheets you will be using.

4. Enter and enhance the labels and values in the Fees worksheet, as shown in Figure P1-6

   You will need to use your mouse to widen column A so that the labels are clearly visible and then center and bold the labels in cells A1 to E1.

5. Click cell **E2**, enter the formula **=B2*C2*D2**, then press **[Enter]**

   You should see 110000 in cell E2. If not, check your formula and try again.

6. With cell **E2** selected, drag the fill handle down to cell **E4**, click cell **E5**, then double-click the **AutoSum button** Σ on the Standard toolbar

   The course fees collected should be 156250 or $156,250.

7. Click the **Budget tab**, click cell **B11**, enter the formula **=Fees!E5/6**, press **[Enter]**, then drag the fill handle of cell **B11** across to cell **G11**

   Ooops! Cells C11 through G11 contain zeroes. Why? If you click cell C11 and look at the formula entered in the formula bar at the top of the worksheet, you will see =Fees!F5/6. But cell F5 of Fees! worksheet does not contain a value! You need to enter a formula that designates cell E5 as an absolute value. By doing so, you ensure that the formula always contains a reference to cell E5 no matter where in the worksheet the formula is copied.

8. Click cell **B11**, drag I across **E5** in the formula bar, press **[F4]**, press **[Enter]**, then fill cells **C11** to **G11** with the new formula

   You will see 26042 in cells B11 to G11. Don't worry if decimal places appear. You will format the cells in a later activity.

9. Select cells **B11** to **H14**, click Σ, select cells **B17** to **H23**, then click Σ again

   The total income in cell H14 is 164650, and the total expenses in cell H23 are 46800, as shown in Figure P1-7.

FIGURE P1-5: Values for cells B12 to B22

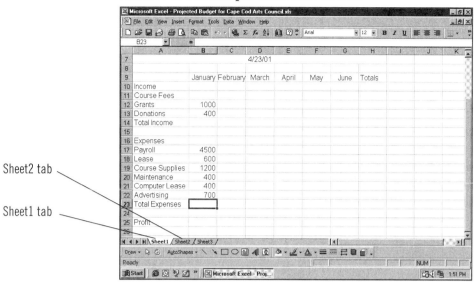

Sheet2 tab

Sheet1 tab

FIGURE P1-6: Fees sheet labels and values

Labels centered
and bold

Column A widened

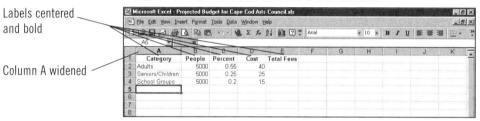

FIGURE P1-7: Worksheet completed with totals

	A	B	C	D	E	F	G	H	I	J	K
7				4/23/01							
8											
9		January	February	March	April	May	June	Totals			
10	Income										
11	Course Fees	26042	26042	26042	26042	26042	26042	156250			
12	Grants	1000	1000	1000	1000	1000	1000	6000			
13	Donations	400	400	400	400	400	400	2400			
14	Total Income	27442	27442	27442	27442	27442	27442	164650			
15											
16	Expenses										
17	Payroll	4500	4500	4500	4500	4500	4500	27000			
18	Lease	600	600	600	600	600	600	3600			
19	Course Supplies	1200	1200	1200	1200	1200	1200	7200			
20	Maintenance	400	400	400	400	400	400	2400			
21	Computer Lease	400	400	400	400	400	400	2400			
22	Advertising	700	700	700	700	700	700	4200			
23	Total Expenses	7800	7800	7800	7800	7800	7800	46800			
24											
25	Profit										
26											

Total income

Total expenses

Clues to Use

Relative and Absolute References

By default Microsoft Excel considers all values entered in formulas as relative values. That is, Excel will change all cell addresses in a formula when you copy it to a new location. If you do not want Excel to change the cell address of a value when you copy it, you must make the value absolute. To do this, you enter a dollar sign ($) before both the column and row designation in the address. You can also press [F4] to insert the symbol. For example, $C$26 tells Excel that the reference to cell C26 must not change, even if you copy the formula to a new location in the worksheet.

activity:

Ask "What if?" Questions

You need to calculate the profit you expect to make in each of the first six months of 2001, then perform the calculations required to answer two "What if?" questions.

steps:

1. Click cell **B25**, enter the formula **=B14-B23**, press **[Enter]**, then copy the formula across to cell **H25**, as shown in Figure P1-8

   The total profit for the first six months of 2000 is 117850 in cell H25.

2. Click the **Fees tab**, click cell **D2**, type **60**, press **[Enter]**, then click the **Budget tab**

   The first "What if?" question is, "What if you raise the adult course fee to $60? The answer is that your total profit in cell H25 is 172850. Good news!

3. Click the **Fees tab**, click cell **B2**, enter the formula **=5000-(5000*.2)**, press **[Enter]**, copy cell **B2** to cells **B3** and **B4**, as shown in Figure P1-9, then click the **Budget tab**

   A course fee increase could result in a 20% drop in the number of students you can expect in 2000. You entered a formula in the Fees sheet that subtracts 20% of 5000 from the total number of adult course fees (5000). The new profit is 130600 — quite a reduction from 172850! Perhaps you shouldn't raise the adult course fees to $60, if the result is a 20% drop in the number of people who take courses!

4. Return to the Fees sheet, change the cost of the adult course fee to **40** and the number of people in cells **B2** to **B4** to **5000**, then return to the Budget sheet

   The results of the first "What if?" question led you to return to your original profit of 117850 in cell H25. To enter new values in a cell that already contains values, just click on the cell and type the new data. Excel will automatically replace the existing values.

5. Click cell **D22** in the Budget sheet, type **3000**, then press **[Enter]**

   The question is, "What if you launch a $3,000 advertising campaign in March?" Your total profit for the six months (cell H25) is now reduced to 115550 from 117850.

6. Click cell **F11**, click at the end of the formula entered on the formula bar, type ***1.3**, press **[Enter]**, then copy the formula to cell **G11**

   A major advertising campaign launched in March could lead to a 30% increase in revenue from course fees in May and June. You edited the formula in cells F11 and G11 to reflect this projected 30% increase. The new total profit in cell H25 is 131175.

7. Click cell **B17**, enter the formula **=(24500/12)+4500**, press **[Enter]**, then copy the formula across to cell **G17**

   The "What if?" question is, "What if you hire a full-time administrative assistant for $24,500 per year?" You divide this amount by 12 to determine the monthly rate, then add the total to the values entered in the Payroll row. Your total profit is now 118925.

8. Change the formula in cell **B17** so that it adds **4500** to half of **24500** divided by **12**, press **[Enter]**, copy the formula across to cell **G17** and compare your worksheet with Figure P1-10

   The value in cell B17 will be 5520.8, and the total profit in cell H25 will be 125050. If your results are different, ensure that your formula in cell B17 adds 4500 to 24500 divided by 2 and 12.

FIGURE P1-8: Formula in cell B25 copied to cell H25

Formula in cell B25

Total profit

	A	B	C	D	E	F	G	H	I	J	K
							=B14-B23				
21	Computer Lease	400	400	400	400	400	400	2400			
22	Advertising	700	700	700	700	700	700	4200			
23	Total Expenses	7800	7800	7800	7800	7800	7800	46800			
24											
25	Profit	19642	19642	19642	19642	19642	19642	117850			
26											
27											
28											
29											
30											
31											
32											

FIGURE P1-9: Formula in cell B2 copied to cells B3 and B4

Formula copied to cells B3 and B4

Formula in cell B2

B2 = =5000-(5000*.2)

	A	B	C	D	E	F	G	H	I	J	K
1	Category	People	Percent	Cost	Total Fees						
2	Adults	4000	0.55	60	132000						
3	Seniors/Children	4000	0.25	25	25000						
4	School Groups	4000	0.2	15	12000						
5					169000						
6											
7											
8											
9											
10											
11											
12											

FIGURE P1-10: Worksheet with completed budget

H25 = =H14-H23

	A	B	C	D	E	F	G	H	I	J	K
7				4/23/01							
8											
9		January	February	March	April	May	June	Totals			
10	Income										
11	Course Fees	26042	26042	26042	26042	33854	33854	171875			
12	Grants	1000	1000	1000	1000	1000	1000	6000			
13	Donations	400	400	400	400	400	400	2400			
14	Total Income	27442	27442	27442	27442	35254	35254	180275			
15											
16	Expenses										
17	Payroll	5520.8	5520.8	5520.8	5520.8	5520.8	5520.8	33125			
18	Lease	600	600	600	600	600	600	3600			
19	Course Supplies	1200	1200	1200	1200	1200	1200	7200			
20	Maintenance	400	400	400	400	400	400	2400			
21	Computer Lease	400	400	400	400	400	400	2400			
22	Advertising	700	700	3000	700	700	700	6500			
23	Total Expenses	8820.8	8820.8	11121	8820.8	8820.8	8820.8	55225			
24											
25	Profit	18621	18621	16321	18621	26433	26433	125050			
26											

Budget / Fees / Sheet3

Draw ▾ AutoShapes ▾

Ready NUM

Start Microsoft Excel - Proj... 2:04 PM

activity:

Format and Print the Budget

Now you need to format values in the Currency or Comma Styles, add border lines to selected cells, use a variety of Page Setup features, and then print a copy of your budget.

steps:

1. Select cells **B11** to **H11**, then click the **Currency Style button** $ on the Formatting toolbar
   The widths of columns B to H automatically increased.

2. Select cells **B12** to **H13**, click the **Comma Style button** , on the Formatting toolbar, select cells **B14** to **H14**, then click $

3. Format cells **B18** to **H22** as **Comma Style**, and format cells **B17** to **H17**, **B23** to **H23**, and **B25** to **H25** as **Currency Style**
   Refer to Figure P1-13 as you work.

4. Select cells **B14** to **H14**, click the **Borders list arrow** on the Formatting toolbar, then select the **Top and Double Bottom Border** style, as shown in Figure P1-11
   A single line appears above cells B14 to H14, and a double line appears below them. Note that you need to deselect the cell to see the borders.

5. Add the **Top and Double Bottom Border** style to cells **B23** to **H23**, then add the **Bottom Double Border** style to cells **B25** to **H25**

6. Center and bold the heading "Totals" in cell **H9**, press and hold the **[Ctrl]** key, select cells **B9** to **G9**, click cells **A10, A14, A16, A23**, and cells **A25** to **H25** to select all of them at once, then click the **Bold button** B on the Formatting toolbar
   Using the [Ctrl] key to select multiple non-adjacent cells saves you time.

7. Click the **Print Preview button** on the Standard toolbar, click **Setup**, click the **Landscape option button** and the **Fit to 1 page option button**, then click the **Margins tab**
   You select a variety of options in the Print Preview mode from the Print Setup dialog boxes in order to format your budget attractively on the printed page.

8. Click the **Horizontally** and **Vertically check boxes**, click the **Header/Footer tab**, click **Custom Header**, enter the text for the header as shown in Figure P1-12, click **OK**, click **OK** again, then compare your print preview screen with Figure P1-13

9. Click **Print**, then save and close the workbook
   The budget for the Cape Cod Arts Council is complete.

FIGURE P1-11: **Border styles**

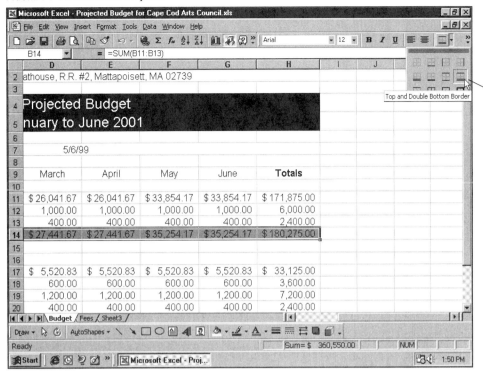

Border Style selected

FIGURE P1-12: **Custom header**

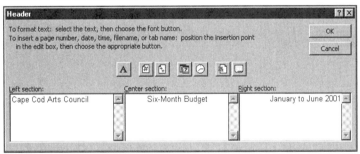

FIGURE P1-13: **Completed worksheet**

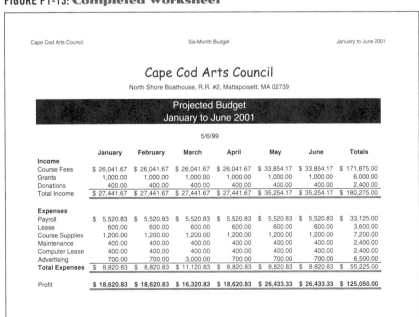

Course Grades Analysis for Marketing 200

As the instructor of Marketing 200, a college-level course in which 20 students are enrolled, you have used an Excel worksheet to record all the scores earned by the students throughout the term. Now you need to calculate a final grade for each student and then create a variety of charts that will help you analyze how well your students have performed. To complete the Course Grades Analysis, you need to **Calculate Totals and Grades, Create a Pivot Table and Column Chart**, and then **Format the Course Grades Analysis**.

Project Activities

Calculate Totals and Grades

To calculate a student's mark for the course, you enter totals for each grade category (Assignments, Quizzes, and Exams), and then enter a formula to *weigh* the grades earned by the students according to type. Assignments are worth 50%, quizzes 15%, and exams 35%.

steps:

1. Open a new workbook, set up the worksheet so that it appears as shown in Figure P2-1, then save the workbook as **Course Grades Analysis**

2. Click cell **I4**, then type **=(B4+D4+G4)/(B20+D20+G20)*I21**

You can also use the "point and click" method to enter cell references in a formula. Just enter the equals sign (=) and open bracket and then click the first cell reference, which is B4 for this formula. You can then type a plus sign (+), click the next cell reference (D4), and so on.

3. Click **B20** in the formula, press **[F4]**, click **D20**, press **[F4]**, click **G20**, press **[F4]**, click **I21**, then press **[F4]**

You used the [F4] command to insert the dollar signs ($) because you want to make the values in cells B20, D20, and G20 absolute. When you copy the formula for the rest of the students, you want each formula to divide the total assignment score by the values in row 21.

4. Press **[Enter]**, copy the formula down to cell **I18**, then click the **Comma Style button** ![comma] on the Formatting toolbar

Khairta Abdela earned a score of 45.63 out of a possible total of 50 on assignments.

5. Click cell **J4**, enter the formula **=(C4+E4)/(C20+E20)*J21**, make cells **C20, E20**, and **J21** absolute, press **[Enter]**, copy the formula down to cell **J18**, then click ![comma]

6. Click cell **K4**, enter the formula that calculates the weighted score for exams, copy the formula down to cell **K18**, then click ![comma]

Khairta earned 15.00 for quizzes and 32.67 for exams.

Hint

Remember to divide the total exam score by the correct absolute values in rows 20 and 21 and then multiply the result by .35.

7. Click cell **L4**, type an **equals sign (=)**, click cell **I4**, type a **plus sign (+)**, click cell **J4**, type a **plus sign (+)**, click cell **K4**, press **[Enter]**, copy the formula down to cell **L18**, then click the **Decrease Decimal button** ![decrease decimal] on the Formatting toolbar **twice** so that no decimal places appear after the values in cells L4 to L18

8. Double-click the **Sheet1 tab**, type **Grades**, press **[Enter]**, double-click the **Sheet2 tab**, type **Lookup**, press **[Enter]**, set up the Lookup worksheet so that it appears as shown in Figure P2-2, then save the workbook

A lookup table in Excel will look up the correct letter grade earned by each student, depending upon the total score entered in column L. The lookup table lists the grades earned according to the total score.

FIGURE P2-1: Course Grades worksheet

Center across columns A to N

Apply Bold and center

Apply Bold and right-align

Apply Bold and 20 pt

Double-click between columns to decrease or increase column widths

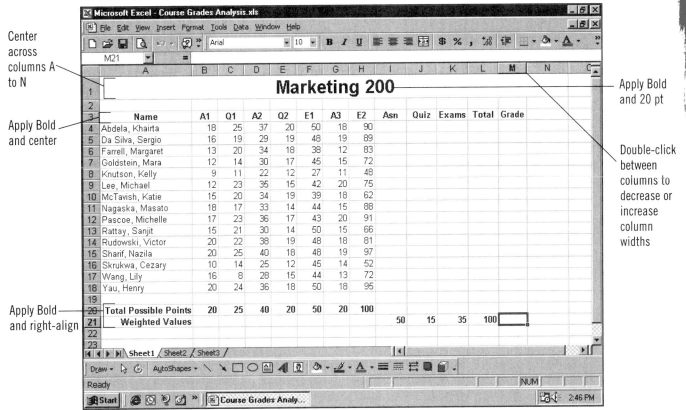

	Name	A1	Q1	A2	Q2	E1	A3	E2	Asn	Quiz	Exams	Total	Grade
4	Abdela, Khairta	18	25	37	20	50	18	90					
5	Da Silva, Sergio	16	19	29	19	48	19	89					
6	Farrell, Margaret	13	20	34	18	38	12	83					
7	Goldstein, Mara	12	14	30	17	45	15	72					
8	Knutson, Kelly	9	11	22	12	27	11	48					
9	Lee, Michael	12	23	35	15	42	20	75					
10	McTavish, Katie	15	20	34	19	39	18	62					
11	Nagaska, Masato	18	17	33	14	44	15	88					
12	Pascoe, Michelle	17	23	36	17	43	20	91					
13	Rattay, Sanjit	15	21	30	14	50	15	66					
14	Rudowski, Victor	20	22	38	19	48	18	81					
15	Sharif, Nazila	20	25	40	18	48	19	97					
16	Skrukwa, Cezary	10	14	25	12	45	14	52					
17	Wang, Lily	16	8	28	15	44	13	72					
18	Yau, Henry	20	24	36	18	50	18	95					
19													
20	Total Possible Points	20	25	40	20	50	20	100					
21	Weighted Values								50	15	35	100	

Marketing 200

FIGURE P2-2: Lookup Table

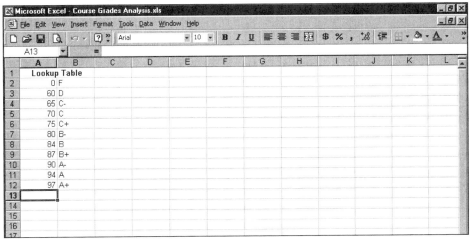

	A	B
1	Lookup Table	
2	0	F
3	60	D
4	65	C-
5	70	C
6	75	C+
7	80	B-
8	84	B
9	87	B+
10	90	A-
11	94	A
12	97	A+

activity:

Create a Pivot Table and Column Chart

Your first step is to enter a formula that will refer to the Lookup Table, which references each student's grade. You will then create a Pivot table that will *count* the number of times that each letter grade appears in column N. A Pivot Table is an interactive table that you can use to quickly summarize large amounts of data. You use a Pivot Table when you want a quick way to sort, subtotal, and total a series of figures. Once you have completed the Pivot table from the list of student grades, you will create a Column Chart that compares how many students earned each letter grade. Figure P2-5 shows the completed Column Chart.

steps:

1. Click the **Grades tab**, click cell **M4**, click the **Paste Function button** 𝑓ₓ on the Standard toolbar, select **Lookup & Reference** from the list of function categories, click **LOOKUP**, then click **OK**

2. Click **lookup_value array**, click **OK**, type **L4**, then press **[Tab]**
   You've entered the cell address of the value that the lookup table will find. This value represents Khairta's total score out of 100 for the course.

3. Click the **Lookup tab** to show the Lookup worksheet, press **[F4]**, then click the **Collapse button** ▬ next to **Array**, select cells **A2** to **B12**, click the **Expand button**, ➕ (compare the Lookup dialog box to Figure P2-3), then press **[F4]**

4. Click **OK**, copy the formula in cell **M4** down to cell **M18**, click the **Center button** ▤ on the Formatting toolbar, then save the workbook

5. Select cells **M3** to **M18**, click **Data** on the menu bar, click **PivotTable and PivotChart Report**, click **Next**, click **Next**, then click **Finish**
   A new worksheet appears.

6. As shown in Figure P2-4, click and drag **Grade** to the **Drop Row Fields Here** section of the table, click and drag **Grade** again to the **Drop Data Items Here**, then close the PivotTable toolbar
   The PivotTable appears in cell A3 of Sheet1. As you can see, the "A+" entry appears below the "A" entry. You need to move the "A+" entry from cell A7 up to cell A5.

7. Click the **row 7** indicator to select all of row 7, point ⟡ just above cell A7, then click and drag row 7 up to row 4 so that the "A+" entry appears above the "A" entry

8. Select cells **B5** to **B13**, then click the **Chart Wizard button** 📖 on the Standard toolbar
   A column chart appears in a new worksheet called Chart1, as shown in Figure P2-5.

FIGURE P2-3: Lookup dialog box

Collapse button

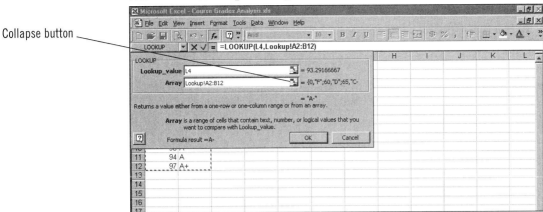

FIGURE P2-4: Pivot Table worksheet

Drop Data Items Here section

Drop Row Fields Here section

Grade

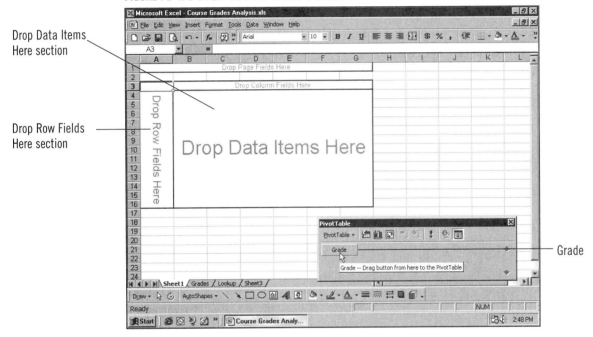

FIGURE P2-5: Column Chart created

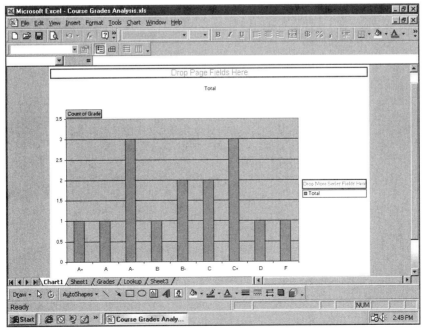

Excel

PROJECT 2

activity:

Format the Course Grades Analysis

Now that you have created a Column Chart that shows the breakdown of grades for the students in Marketing 200, you need to copy the chart into the Grades worksheet, and format the worksheet for printing. Your completed Course Grades Analysis will appear as shown in Figure P2-6.

steps:

1. Click **Total** above the chart, type **Breakdown of Final Grades**, press **[Enter]**, click the **Font Size List Arrow** on the Formatting toolbar, click **24**, then click the **Bold button** **B** on the Formatting toolbar

2. Click **Total** in the Legend to the right of the chart, then press **[Delete]**

3. Click the **Copy button** 📋 on the Standard toolbar, click the **Grades tab**, click cell **A24**, click the **Paste button** 📋 on the Standard toolbar, then move the chart so that its upper-left corner starts in cell **A24**

4. Click away from the chart to deselect it, click **View** on the menu bar, then click **Page Break Preview**

   As you can see, the worksheet will currently print over more than one page.

5. Click the **Print Preview button** 🔍 on the Standard toolbar, click **Setup**, click the **Page tab** (if necessary), click the **Fit to option button**, then click **OK**

   Now all the data fits on the sheet.

6. Click **Normal View**, select cells **A3** through **M21**, click **Format** on the menu bar, click **AutoFormat**, click the **Classic 3** format, then click **OK**

   Your worksheet is looking readable and quite snazzy.

7. Click **View** on the menu bar, click **Zoom**, click the **50% option button**, click **OK**, click the **Column Chart** to select it, drag it back up and over to approximately cell **A24**, then click and drag the lower-right corner handle up to approximately cell **M47**

8. Click away from the chart to deselect it, click the **Print Preview button** 🔍, click **Setup**, click the **Margins tab**, click the **Horizontally** checkbox, then add a **Header** as shown in Figure P2-6

9. Print a copy of the worksheet, then save and close the workbook

   Your printed worksheet should appear similar to Figure P2-6.

Marketing 200   [Your Name]

Marketing 200

Name	A1	Q1	A2	Q2	E1	A3	E2	Asn	Quiz	Exams	Total	Grade
Abdela, Khairta	18	25	37	20	50	18	90	45.63	15.00	32.67	93	A-
Da Silva, Sergio	16	19	29	19	48	19	89	40.00	12.67	31.97	85	B
Farrell, Margaret	13	20	34	18	38	12	83	36.88	12.67	28.23	78	C+
Goldstein, Mara	12	14	30	17	45	15	72	35.63	10.33	27.30	73	C-
Knutson, Kelly	9	11	22	12	27	11	48	26.25	7.67	17.50	51	F
Lee, Michael	12	23	35	15	42	20	75	41.88	12.67	27.30	82	B-
McTavish, Katie	15	20	34	19	39	18	62	41.88	13.00	23.57	78	C+
Nagaska, Masato	18	17	33	14	44	15	88	41.25	10.33	30.80	82	B-
Pascoe, Michelle	17	23	36	17	43	20	91	45.63	13.33	31.27	90	A-
Rattay, Sanjit	15	21	30	14	50	15	66	37.50	11.67	27.07	76	C+
Rudowski, Victor	20	22	38	19	48	18	81	47.50	13.67	30.10	91	A-
Sharif, Nazila	20	25	40	18	48	19	97	49.38	14.33	33.83	98	A+
Skrukwa, Cezary	10	14	25	12	45	14	52	30.63	8.67	22.63	62	D
Wang, Lily	16	8	28	15	44	13	72	35.63	7.67	27.07	70	C-
Yau, Henry	20	24	36	18	50	18	95	46.25	14.00	33.83	94	A
Total Possible Points	20	25	40	20	50	20	100					
Weighted Values								50	15	35	100	

Breakdown of Final Grades

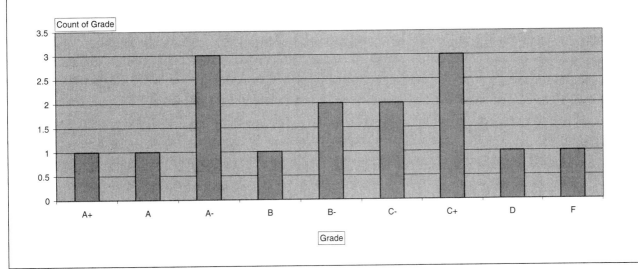

PROJECT 3   OVERVIEW

Planning a Budget for a European Vacation

You are planning a five-week trip to Europe with a friend. Your budget for the trip is $5,000. Before you buy your plane ticket, you need to determine how much you can spend on airfare, accommodations, food, entertainment, and transportation. You may *want* to stay in first-class hotels, but your $5,000 budget may not extend that far. What kind of trip can you really afford? For this project you will **Set Up a Vacation Planning Budget** that you will use to create a spreadsheet, which will help you to plan a European vacation you will remember for a lifetime.

Project Activities

Set Up a Vacation Planning Budget

steps:

Hint

To right align the labels in cells D13 to D15, type the labels in these cells, then select them and click the Align Right button on the Formatting toolbar.

1. Set up your worksheet so that it appears as shown in Figure P3-1, then save your budget as **Europe Trip**
2. Select cells **B4** to **E4**, **right-click**, click **Format Cells**, click the **Alignment tab**, make sure **Right** is selected in the Horizontal section, select **Top** in the Vertical section, drag the **red diamond** in the Orientation section down so the spin box shows -90 Degrees, as shown in Figure P3-2, then click **OK**
3. Click cell **E5**, enter the formula **=C5*D5**, press **[Enter]**, then copy the formula down to cell **E11**
   Resize Column E if necessary.
4. Click cell **E13**, then double-click the **AutoSum button** Σ on the Standard toolbar to calculate the Subtotal ($5707.00)
5. Click cell **E14**, calculate a **15%** contingency on the Subtotal (the contingency will be $856.05), then click cell **E15** and add the **Subtotal** to the **Contingency** to determine your Total Expenses
   Your total expenses in cell E15 are $6,563.05. You are $1,563.05 over your budget of $5,000.
6. Perform the calculations required to answer the following questions:

#	Question	Total Expenses
1	What if you reduce your sightseeing allowance to $20 a day?	$6,361.80
2	What if you book a charter flight that costs $200 less than the current airfare?	$6,131.80
3	What if you lease a car for four weeks at a cost of $435.72 per week, do not buy a train pass, and share the cost of the car lease with a friend?	$6,328.96
4	What if you stay at campsites for 20 days ($22/night for two), stay in youth hostels for 10 days ($28.50/night for one), and then stay in hotels for the remaining 5 days ($120/night for two)?	$5,242.21
5	What if you buy and cook your own food on the days that you camp, thereby reducing your food costs on those days to $25 a day?	$4,897.21
6	If you lease a car, you will split gas costs with your friend during the four weeks that you have the car. You plan to drive approximately 1,500 kilometers; the car you plan to rent gets 12 kilometers to the liter; gas in Europe costs approximately $2.00 a liter.	$5,040.96

As you perform the calculations in Steps 1 through 6, check the total in cell E15 against the totals provided. You will need to think carefully about the calculations required. For some steps you will need to insert new rows. Note that each change you make builds upon the change you made before. As a result, you must make the changes in the order presented.

7. Change the font size to **14** for cells **A4** to the end of the data, adjust the column widths, click cell **A1**, click the **Fill Color button** list arrow on the Drawing toolbar, select a light gray, then add border lines to the selected cells, as shown in Figure P3-3
8. View the worksheet in **Print Preview**, center it **horizontally** and **vertically**, so it appears as shown in Figure P3-3, save the worksheet, then print a copy

FIGURE P3-1: **Worksheet setup**

Font size: 24pt

Font size: 14pt

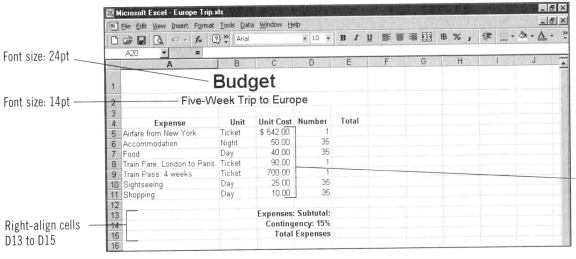

Display the value in cell C5 in the Currency Style and the values in cells C6 to C11 in the Comma Style

Right-align cells D13 to D15

FIGURE P3-2: **Format Cells dialog box**

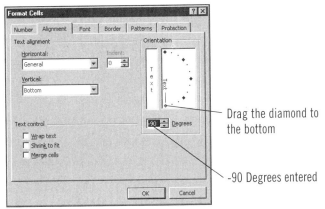

Drag the diamond to the bottom

-90 Degrees entered

FIGURE P3-3: **Completed Trip Planning Budget in Print Preview**

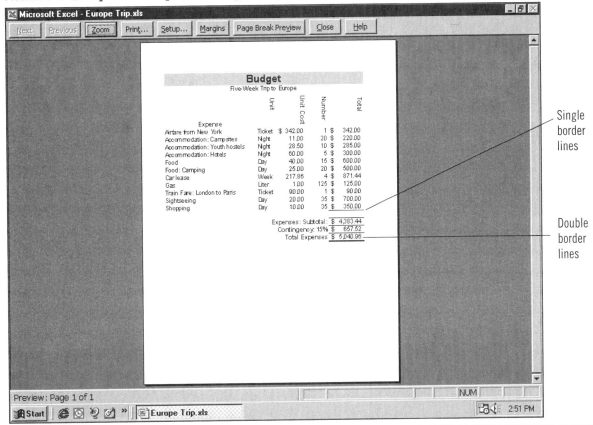

Single border lines

Double border lines

Independent Challenges

INDEPENDENT CHALLENGE 1

Create your own personal budget for the next six months, then ask a series of "What if?" questions to help you make decisions regarding how you will spend your money. Fill in the boxes below with the required information, then set up your budget in an Excel worksheet, and perform the calculations required to answer several "What if?" questions.

1. You need to determine the goal of your budget. Even a personal budget should be created for a specific purpose. For example, you may wish to save for a vacation or to buy a car, or you may just want to live within a set income. Identify the goal of your budget in the box below:

   Budget goal: ....
   ....

2. Determine your sources of income. You may receive money from a paycheck, from investment dividends, or from a student loan. Each income source requires a label and a row on your budget worksheet. In the box below, list the income labels you will require:

   Income labels: 3. ....

   1. ....   4. ....

   2. ....   5. ....

3. Determine your expenses. At the very least, you will probably need to list your rent, food, utilities, and phone. You may also need to list transportation costs such as car payments, gas, insurance, and bus fares. In addition, include labels for entertainment, incidentals, and savings. In the box below, list the expense labels you have identified:

   Expense labels:

   1. ....   6. ....

   2. ....   7. ....

   3. ....   8. ....

   4. ....   9. ....

   5. ....   10. ....

4. Set up your budget in Excel as follows:
   a. Enter and enhance a title for your budget in cell A1.
   b. Enter the current date (use the Today function).
   c. Enter the Income and Expense labels in column A.
   d. Determine the time frame of your budget (e.g., monthly, weekly, annual), then enter the appropriate labels starting in column B.
   e. Enter the values required for your income and expenses. Adjust expenses according to the time of year. For example, your utilities costs will probably be less in the summer than in the winter, while your entertainment and holiday expenses may rise in the summer.
   f. Calculate your total income and expenses.

g. Ask yourself at least five "What if?" questions, and then make the calculations required to answer them. Here are some sample "What if?" questions:

- What if I move in March to a new apartment where my rent is 30% more than the current rent?
- What if I eat out in restaurants only twice a month?
- What if I take the bus or subway to work twice a week?
- What if I join a fitness club with monthly dues?
- What if I buy a car with payments of $250/month? Remember to factor in costs for insurance and gas.
- What if I start taking violin lessons?

Try to formulate questions that will help you plan your finances to achieve the goals you have set.

h. Save your worksheet as "Personal Budget".

i. Format and print a copy of your budget.

INDEPENDENT CHALLENGE 2

You have been working all term as a teaching assistant for a course of your choice. The instructor you work for has given you the grade sheet she has kept "by hand" and has asked you to transfer it to Excel and then calculate each student's grades. Complete the steps below to create a course grades analysis for a course of your choice.

1. Determine the name of the course. For example, the course could be English 100, Psychology 210, or International Business 301.
2. Determine the grade categories and the percentage of scores allocated to each category. For example, you could allocate 40% of the total grades to Assignments, 30% to Exams, and 30% to Oral Presentations. Allocate at least three grade categories and make sure the percentages you assign add up to 100%.
3. Set up the worksheet called Grades with the name of the course, a list of at least 20 students, and labels for the various assignments, exams, quizzes, etc. You determine the number of items in each of the three grade categories you have selected.
4. Determine the total scores possible for each item in each score category and enter the totals one row below the list of names. To check the set up of your Course Grades Analysis, refer to the Course Grades Analysis you created for Project 2.
5. Enter the points for each student. Make sure you refer to the totals you entered to ensure that each score you enter for each student is equal to or less than the total points possible.
6. Calculate the total points for each score category, divide the total points by the total of the possible points, then multiply the result by the percentage you assigned to the mark category. The formula required is: Sum of Student's Points/Sum of Total Points*Percentage. For example, if the Assignment points are entered in cells C4, D4, and F4, the total possible points are entered in cells C25, D25, and F25, and the percentage of Assignments is 40%, the formula required is:
   =(C4+D4+F4)/($C$25+$D$25+$F$25)*.4
7. Calculate the total points out of 100 earned by the first student on your list.
8. Copy the formulas you used to calculate the first student's weighted score in each category for the remaining students.
9. Sort the list of students alphabetically by name.
10. Create a Lookup table in a worksheet called Lookup that lists the letter grades and ranges.
11. Enter the LOOKUP formula in the appropriate cell in the Grades worksheet, then copy the formula down for the remaining students.
12. Create a Pivot table that counts the number of times each letter grade appears.
13. Create a Column chart from the data in the Pivot table to show the breakdown of scores by letter grade.
14. Copy the Column chart to the Grades sheet.
15. Save the workbook as Course Grades Analysis for [Course Name], format the Grades sheet and Column chart attractively, print a copy, then save and close the workbook.

INDEPENDENT CHALLENGE 3

Create a planning budget to help you determine your expenses for a vacation of your choice. The following tasks will help get you started.

1. Before you create the worksheet in Excel, answer the questions listed below:
   a. Where do you plan to go for your vacation?
   b. What is your proposed budget?
   c. How long is your planned vacation?
   d. What kind of activities do you plan to do on your vacation (e.g., sightseeing, guided tours, horseback riding, skiing, etc.)?
2. Set up your worksheet with labels for transportation costs (airfare, car rental, train fares, etc.), accommodations, food, sightseeing, shopping, and any other expense categories appropriate to the kind of vacation you plan to take.
3. Include a contingency amount for emergency expenses that is 10% to 15% of your total expenses.
4. Try to make your budget as realistic as possible. You can choose to base your budget on a vacation you have already taken or on a vacation you hope to take.
5. Save your vacation planning budget as "My Vacation Plan", then format and print a copy.

INDEPENDENT CHALLENGE 4

Create the worksheet in Figure IC-1, then perform the calculations required to answer the questions provided.

FIGURE IC-1: **Personal budgeting worksheet**

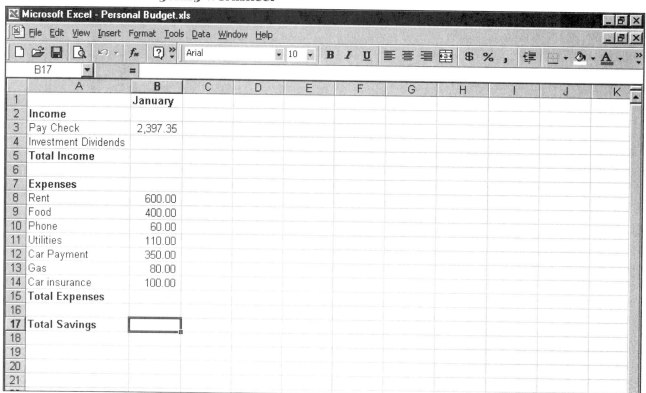

1. Use the AutoFill function to fill in the months from February to June.
2. Copy the values for January across to June.
3. Save the workbook as "Budget Practice."
4. Add a column labeled "Totals," then calculate the row totals and format all the values in the Comma Style.
5. Calculate the Monthly and Total Income and the Monthly and Total Expenses. Your total income is 14,384.10, your total expenses are 10,200.00, and your total savings are 4,184.10.
6. Copy cells A1 to H17 to Sheet2 and then again to Sheet3.
7. Name the Sheet1 tab Vacations, the Sheet2 tab Auto, and the Sheet3 tab Savings.
8. Format the cells in the Auto and Savings worksheets in the Comma style.
9. Click the Vacations tab, then make the calculations required to answer the following two questions:
    a. If you take a vacation in February that costs $2,200.00, how much money will you have left?
    b. If you instead take a vacation in February that costs $1,500.00, how much money will you have left?
10. Click the Auto tab, then make the calculations required to answer the following two questions:
    a. What would your total losses be if, in April, you traded your car for a car that required payments 15% higher than your current payments for the remaining months including April?
    b. If you buy a new car in April, your gas costs will increase by 30% for the remaining months including April. What would your total losses be?
11. Click the Savings tab, then make the calculations required to answer the following three questions:
    a. What if you received investment dividends of $100 a month beginning in January?
    b. What if you took a new job at the beginning of May that paid 20% more than your current job?
    c. If you take a new job, you will need to move to a new apartment in a new city. The rent for the new apartment will be $800/month.
12. When you have completed the questions required for each of the three worksheets, format each sheet attractively, then print a copy of each sheet.
13. Save and close the workbook.

Visual Workshop

Create the six-month budget as shown in Figure VW-1 for Web Spinners, a new company that provides Internet users with quick and easy access to the World Wide Web. Save the budget as "Web Spinners Budget" on your disk, then answer the following questions.

1. In July, you estimate that 1000 Internet subscribers will join Web Spinners at a price of $30 per subscriber. You project that the subscription revenue generated in July will increase by 5% in August, 10% in September, then 20% for each of the remaining months. Calculate all increases based on July revenue. What is the total revenue in cell H9?

2. In July, you estimate that 50 subscribers will purchase space on the server for their Web sites at a price of $100 each. Each month the revenue increases by 30% over the previous month to December. (Enter =B8*1.3 in cell C8, then copy the formula to cell G8.) What is the total revenue in cell H9?

3. Make the Salaries expense for both November and December $21,000. What is the total Salaries expense? What is the total Advertising expense?

4. Make the Equipment Lease for November and December four times the current Equipment Leases for October. What is the total Equipment Leases expense?

5. What is the total projected profit in cell H19?

6. Format the worksheet attractively, save it, then preview and print.

FIGURE VW-1: Web Spinners worksheet

Microsoft Excel - Web Spinners.xls

File Edit View Insert Format Tools Data Window Help

Arial ▾ 10 ▾ **B** *I* U $ % ,

A21

Web Spinners
Proposed Six-Month Budget: July to September 2001
[Current Date]

	July	August	September	October	November	December	Totals
REVENUE							
Internet access subscriptions							
Server space rentals							
Total Revenue							
EXPENSES							
Salaries	4500	4500	4500	4500	4500	4500	
Rent	1500	1500	1500	1500	1500	1500	
Equipment Leases	1000	1000	1000	1000	1000	1000	
Advertising	150	150	150	150	150	150	
Operating Costs	350	350	350	350	350	350	
Total Expenses							
PROFIT							

Microsoft
► Excel
Projects

Document Linking

In This Unit You Will Create:

PROJECT 1 ► **Linked Invoice and Letter**

PROJECT 2 ► **Guest Survey Results**

PROJECT 3 ► **Price List**

You can perform arithmetic calculations in a Word table and enter text in an Excel spreadsheet. By doing so, however, you do not maximize the integration capabilities of Office. To increase your efficiency, you need to use the program best suited to perform a specific task and then create links between the programs to produce the documents you require. For example, suppose that every few months you want to send your customers a letter that contains a price list you have created and frequently update in Excel. You can create a form letter in Word, switch to Excel, copy the price list, then paste it as a link into the Word letter. Every time you make a change to the price list in Excel, the price list you copied into Word will also change. In this unit, you will learn how to link documents that combine elements created in both Word and Excel. You will also learn how to view Word documents that contain links to Excel workbooks on your Web browser.

Linked Invoice and Letter for Creative Cuisine

Creative Cuisine provides full catering services for weddings, parties, conferences, and other special events. As the owner of Creative Cuisine, you have decided to include a personalized thank-you letter with every invoice you send out to your customers. To save time, you've decided to link each invoice with its accompanying letter so that you can quickly and easily update the letter when changes occur to the invoice. Three activities are required to complete the invoice form and letter for Creative Cuisine:

Project Activities

Create the Invoice in Excel

The invoice form lists the products and services that Ms. Marlene Schwartz purchased from Creative Cuisine for her daughter's wedding. Note that the invoice form consists of four principal types of information: the company name and location, shipping and billing information, a list of the items purchased, and the prices. When you create the invoice form, you will enter a formula in the Amount column that will multiply the Quantity by the Unit Price to determine the total amount owed for each item.

Create the Letter in Word

You will create the letterhead in Word, type the text for the letter, then copy elements of the Word letterhead to the Excel invoice.

Link the Invoice and Letter in Word

You will copy selected prices directly from Excel and paste them into Word as links. When you change the prices in the Excel invoice, the prices in the Word letter will also change.

When you have completed Project 1, your invoice form and letter will appear as illustrated in Figures P1-1 and P1-2.

FIGURE P1-1: Creative Cuisine invoice

Shipping and billing information

Items purchased

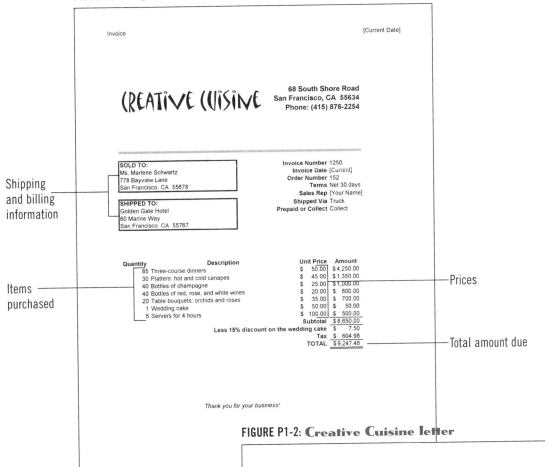

Prices

Total amount due

FIGURE P1-2: Creative Cuisine letter

Linked data from Excel to Word

activity:

Create the Invoice in Excel

You will first create and enhance the Invoice form in Excel and then you will perform the required calculations.

steps:

1. Start Excel

2. Click cell **A12**, enter and enhance the labels for cells **A12** to **A20** to match Figure P1-3, then save your worksheet as **Invoice for Creative Cuisine** on the disk where you plan to save all of your files for this book

You start in cell A12 because you want to leave plenty of room for the heading elements you will later copy from Word.

3. Click cell **G12**, then enter and enhance the labels for cells **G12** to **G18** and cells **H12** to **H18**, as shown in Figure P1-3

4. Click cell **A25**, then enter the labels and values for cells **A25** through **G36**, as shown in Figure P1-3

5. Select cells **A25** to **H25**, click the **Bold button** [B], click the **Center button** [≣], select cells **B25** to **F25**, then click the **Merge and Center button** [⊞] on the Formatting toolbar, select cells **G26** to **H37**, then click the **Currency Style button** [$] on the Formatting toolbar

6. Click cell **H26**, enter the formula **=A26*G26**, press [Enter], increase the column width, click cell **H26** again, then drag the corner handle of cell **H26** down to cell **H32** to copy the formula

You will multiply the Quantity by the Unit Price to determine the total amount due for each item.

7. Click cell **H33**, then double-click the **AutoSum button** [Σ] on the Standard toolbar

You will see $9,075.00 in cell H33.

8. Click cell **H34**, enter the formula **=H31*.15**, press [Enter], enter the formula **=(H33-H34)*.07** in cell **H35**, press [Enter], enter the formula to subtract the discount from the sum of cells **H33** and **H35** in cell **H36**, then press [Enter]

You should see $9,698.21 in cell H36.

Hint

The tooltip on the Borders button may say something different, such as All Borders or Outside Border.

9. Select cells **A12** to **D15**, click the **Borders list arrow** [▦▾] on the Formatting toolbar, click the **Thick Box Border** (last column, last row), apply the same border style to cells **A17** to **D20**, add a **Top and Bottom Border** to cell **H33**, add a **Top and Double Bottom Border** to cell **H36**, then save your workbook

Your worksheet appears as shown in Figure P1-4.

FIGURE P1-3: Worksheet labels and values

Your Excel 2000 toolbar may look different

Click here to select the whole worksheet

Start in cell A12

Bold labels

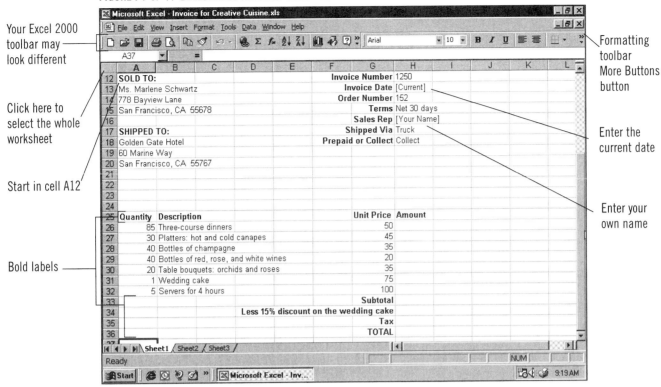

Formatting toolbar More Buttons button

Enter the current date

Enter your own name

FIGURE P1-4: Invoice data calculated and formatted

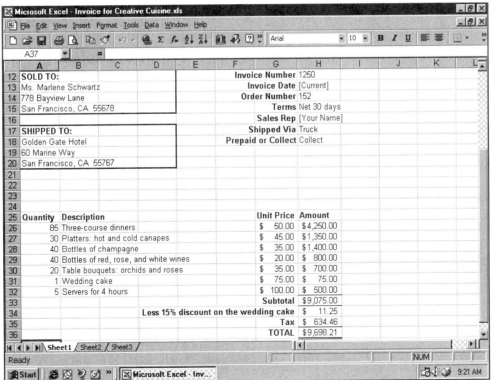

activity:

Create the Letter in Word

You need to modify the document style, create an attractive letterhead for the Word letter, then enter the text for the letter.

steps:

1. Start Word, click **Format** on the menu bar, click **Style**, click **Modify**, click **Format**, click **Font**, select the **Arial** font and a font size of **12**, click **OK**, click **OK** again, click **Apply**, then save the document as **Letter for Creative Cuisine**

2. Click the **Insert WordArt button**  on the Drawing toolbar, select the third WordArt style in the first row, then click **OK**

3. Type **Creative Cuisine**, click the **Font list arrow**, select **Matisse ITC**, or another font if unavailable, then click **OK**

4. Click the **WordArt Shape button** on the WordArt toolbar, then select the **Double Wave 2 shape**

5. Click the **Format WordArt button** on the WordArt toolbar, click the **Layout tab**, click the **Left option button** in the Horizontal alignment section, then click **OK**
   The WordArt object moves to the left margin, but it is too far from the top margin.

6. Click [icon], click **Advanced** in the Layout dialog box, click the **Alignment Option button** in the Vertical section, click the **Relative to list arrow**, click **Margin**, click **OK**, then click **OK** again

7. Double-click to the right of the WordArt object, click the **Align Right button** on the Formatting toolbar, then type the address, as shown in Figure P1-5
   When you use the new Click and Type feature, you need to make sure that you click within the left or right margins.

8. Double-click at the left margin just below the WordArt object, click **Format** on the menu bar, click **Borders and Shading**, click the **Width list arrow**, select **6 pt**, click the **Color list arrow**, select **Gray 25%**, click at the top of the Preview box, then click **OK**

9. Press [Enter] four times, click the Align Left button [icon], if necessary, click **Insert** on the menu bar, click **Date and Time**, select the date format you prefer, click **OK**, press [Enter] twice, enter the text for the letter, as shown in Figure P1-5, then save the document

Trouble

If the Drawing toolbar is not visible, click View on the menu bar, point to Toolbars, then click Drawing.

Hint

If the Office Assistant appears asking if you want help typing the letter, you can either click Cancel or just continue to type the letter without help.

CREATIVE CUISINE

68 South Shore Road
San Francisco, CA 55634
Phone: (415) 876-2254

Right align
all three
lines of the
company
address

Insert a
6-point,
gray 25%,
top border

[Current Date]

Insert the
current date

Ms. Marlene Schwartz
778 Bayview Lane
San Francisco, CA 55678

Dear Ms. Schwartz:

Thank you for choosing Creative Cuisine to provide the food and decorations for
your daughter's wedding on May 2. I hope her special day was everything you
hoped to make it.

Total price
will be
inserted
here

Enclosed is our invoice in the amount of for the total cost of the services we
provided on May 2. As we discussed, I have included a 15% discount of on the
wedding cake.

Discount will
be inserted
here

Thank you again, Ms. Schwartz, for asking our company to cater your daughter's
wedding. I hope you consider using our services for the Silver Wedding
Anniversary celebration you and your husband are planning next year.

Sincerely,

[Your Name]
President

activity:

Link Invoice and Letter in Word

You will need to switch back and forth between the letter in Word and the invoice in Excel. To do this, you can click on the Microsoft Word or Microsoft Excel buttons at the bottom of the screen or you can also press [Alt][Tab] to switch between the programs. First, you will copy the elements of the letterhead from Word to Excel, and then you will copy selected amounts from Excel and paste them as links into Word.

steps:

1. In the Word letter, click the **WordArt** object, click the **Copy button** 📋 on the Standard toolbar, switch to Excel, right-click cell **A1**, click **Paste**, position the pointer on the WordArt object so it changes to 🔖, then drag the object as far to the left and top of the worksheet as possible

2. Switch to Word, select the three lines of the company address, click 📋, switch to Excel, right-click cell **H2**, click **Paste**, right align all three lines if necessary, then click the **Bold button** **B** on the Formatting toolbar

3. Point the mouse between the **10** and **11** on the worksheet frame, drag the mouse up to reduce the height of row 10 to approximately 4.50, as shown in Figure P1-6, select cells **A10** to **H10**, click the **Fill Color list arrow** 🎨 ▾ on the Drawing toolbar, then click the **Gray 25% box**

4. Click cell **H36**, click 📋, switch to Word, then click after the first occurrence of the word "of" in the second paragraph of the letter, as shown in Figure P1-7

5. Click **Edit** on the menu bar, click **Paste Special**, click the **Paste link option button**, click **Unformatted Text**, click **OK**, delete the extra space after the word "of," then save the document
   You use the Paste Special command to paste the price as a link because you cannot use the Paste button to create links. The value in cell H36 ($9,698.21) appears.

6. Switch to Excel, click cell **H34**, click 📋, switch to Word, click after "15% discount of" of in the second paragraph, paste the value as a **link (Unformatted Text)**, then delete the extra space before the link

7. Switch to Excel, reduce the unit price for the champagne to **$25.00**, reduce the price for the wedding cake to **$50.00**, note the new totals, then switch to Word
   The new total amount is $9,247.48, and the new discount is $7.50, as shown in Figure P1-7.

8. Switch to Excel, type **Thank you for your business!** in cell A44, format it with italics, then center it across cells **A44** to **H44**, click **File**, click **Page Setup**, select the **Horizontally** and **Vertically check boxes** on the Margins tab, create a **Custom Header**, as shown in Figure P1-8, on the Header/Footer tab, then print a copy
   The text for the header appears in Figure P1-8.

Time To
✓ Save all documents
✓ Close

9. Switch to Word, view the letter in **Whole Page view**, add some blank lines above the date to center the letter attractively on the page, as shown in Figure P1-7, then print a copy

FIGURE P1-6: Row 10 height reduced

Click here and drag up

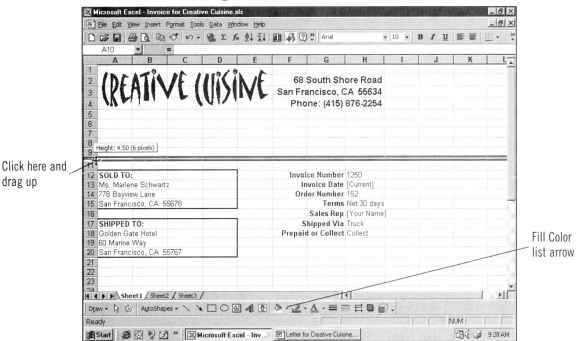

Fill Color list arrow

FIGURE P1-7: Completed letter

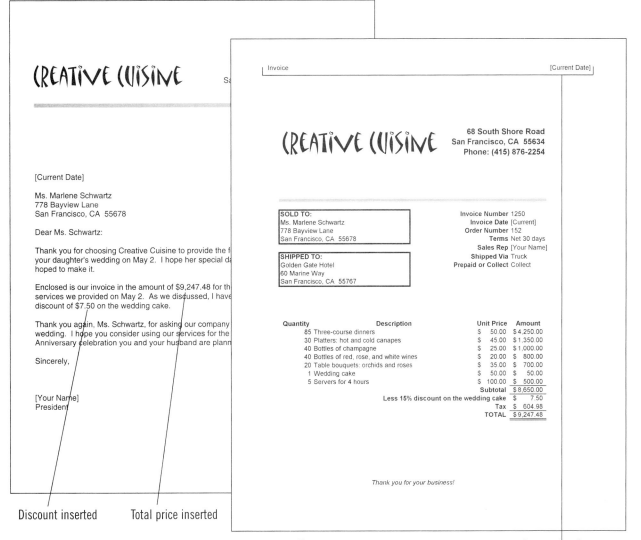

Discount inserted

Total price inserted

FIGURE P1-8: Completed invoice

Custom header

Guest Survey Results for Coral Sands Resort

As the manager of the Coral Sands Resort in the Bahamas, you have compiled the results of a Guest Satisfaction Survey completed by 2,000 guests. You want to use Excel to organize these results into charts. You then want to create a one-page summary of the results in a Word document that includes the charts you created in Excel. Finally, you will add hyperlinks to the selected text in the Word document and preview the document in your Web browser. To create the Guest Survey Results you will **Create Charts in Excel, Create the Summary in Word,** and then **Preview the Word Summary in a Web Browser.**

activity:

Create Charts in Excel

steps:

Hint

To wrap the text in cells B3 to F3, select cells B3 to F3, right-click, click Format Cells, click the Alignment tab, click the Wrap text check box, then click OK

1. Open a new blank workbook in Excel, set up the Survey Results worksheet, as shown in Figure P2-1, then save it as **Coral Sands Survey Charts**

2. Select cells **B4** to **F8**, then click the **AutoSum button** on the Standard toolbar
   You will see 2000 in cells B8 to F8. The values entered in cells B4 to F7 represent the total number of responses to each of the four criteria in each category.

3. Select cells **A3** to **F7**, click the **Copy button** 🖺 on the Standard toolbar, click cell **A10**, click the **Paste button** 🖺 on the Standard toolbar, click cell **B11**, enter the formula **=B4/$B$8*100%**, then press **[Enter]**
   You will see 0.31 in cell B11.

4. Click cell **B11**, drag the corner fill handle down to cell **B14**, drag the corner fill handle of cell **B14** across to cell **F14**, then click the **Percent Style button** 🔣 on the Formatting toolbar

5. Select cells **A10** to **F14**, click the **Chart Wizard button** 📊 on the Standard toolbar, click **Next** to accept the Column chart, then click **Next** to accept the selected data range

6. Enter **Guest Survey Results** as the Chart title, **Guest Facilities** as the X-axis title, and **Response Percentages** as the Y-axis title, click **Next**, click **Finish**, use the mouse to move and resize the chart so it occupies **B21** through **G40**, right-click on any x-axis label such as "Room Cleanliness," click **Format Axis**, click the **Font tab**, change the font size to **8 pt**, then click **OK**

7. Click any cell outside the Column chart, click 📊, click **Pie** under Chart type, click **Next**, click the **Collapse dialog box button** 🔳 at the end of the Data range text box, select cells **A11** through **A14**, type a comma (,), select cells **F11** through **F14**, click the **Restore dialog box button** 🔼 in the Source Data window, then compare your screen to Figure P2-2

8. Click **Next**, enter **Overall Rating Breakdown** as the chart title, click **Next**, then click **Finish**

9. Drag and resize the pie chart so it occupies approximately the range **H21** through **M35**, as shown in Figure P2-3

Time To
✓ **Save**

FIGURE P2-1: Worksheet setup

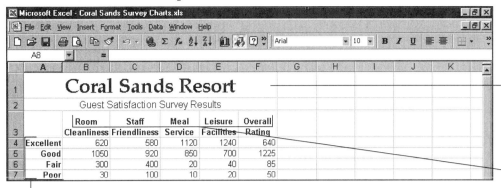

Enhance cell A1 with 24pt. Book Antiqua font and center it across cells A1 to F1

Wrap text in cells B3 to F3, bold and center text, adjust column widths, and adjust the row height

Right-align and bold text in cells A4 to A7

FIGURE P2-2: Data range selected in the Chart Wizard

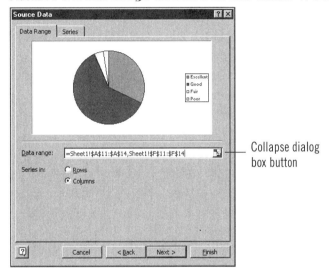

Collapse dialog box button

FIGURE P2-3: Completed column and pie charts

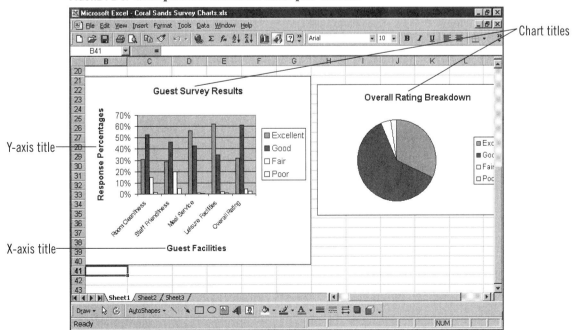

Chart titles

Y-axis title

X-axis title

activity:

Create the Summary in Word

To create an attractive summary in Word, you will first change the margins and select landscape orientation, then you will create a text box and enter the title of the document, and finally you will turn on columns and enter the text.

Trouble

If an alert box appears warning you that a margin is set outside the printable area of the page, click fix to correct the problem and close the alert box.

steps:

1. Switch to a blank document in Word, click **File** on the menu bar, click **Page Setup**, click the **Margins tab**, change all four margins to **.5"**, click the **Paper Size** tab, click the **Landscape option button** under Orientation, then click **OK**

2. Click the **AutoShapes menu button** on the Drawing toolbar, point to **Basic Shapes**, select the **Rounded Rectangle** (first column, second row), drag to create a rectangle about .5" high by 4.5" wide, then save your document as **Coral Sands Resort Survey Results**

3. Click the **Text Box button** 📰 on the Drawing toolbar, click in the rectangle you just drew, change the font to **Arial** and the font size to **18**, click the **Bold button** **B** on the Formatting toolbar, type **Coral Sands Resort Survey Results**, click the **Center button** ▤ on the Formatting toolbar, then widen the rectangle if necessary

4. With the text box still selected, click the **Fill Color list arrow** 🎨 on the Drawing toolbar, click one of the **Light Gray boxes**, then click outside the text box to deselect it
Your text box looks quite snazzy, as shown in Figure P2-4.

5. Double-click below the text box, click **Format** on the menu bar, click **Columns**, select the **Two Column** format, click the **Line between check box**, click the **Apply to list arrow**, click **This point forward**, then click **OK**

6. Type the text for the first column, as shown in Figure P2-5, then press **[Enter]** twice
Make sure you add bullets where indicated in Figure P2-5.

Time To
√ Save

7. Click **Insert** on the menu bar, click **Break**, click the **Column break option button**, click **OK**, then type and format the text for column 2, as shown in Figure P2-5
You will need to leave three blank lines after paragraph 2 in column 2. Note that the line between the columns will not appear until you start entering the text for column 2.

FIGURE P2-4: Completed text box

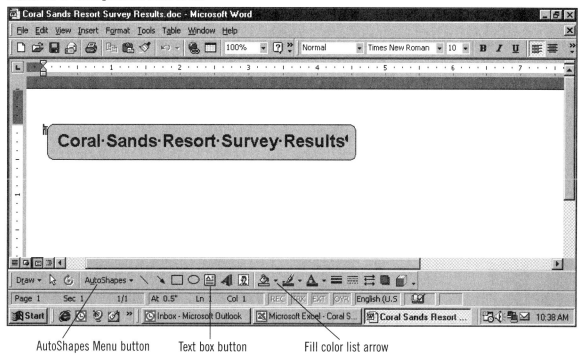

AutoShapes Menu button   Text box button   Fill color list arrow

FIGURE P2-5: Text for columns 1 and 2

Coral Sands Resort Survey Results

The Coral Sands Resort is proud to announce the results of its annual survey. This year, 2,000 guests participated in the survey. The guests were asked to rate the following categories of service in terms of four criteria: Excellent, Good, Fair, and Poor.

- Room Cleanliness
- Staff Friendliness
- Meal Service
- Leisure Facilities
- Overall Rating

As displayed in the column chart below, our Leisure Facilities received the highest rating. However, a significant percentage of our guests rated Staff Friendliness as Poor. The Coral Sands Resort will initiate a series of staff training seminars to ensure that next year's survey shows a more favorable rating.

The pie chart displayed below breaks down the Overall Rating in terms of the four rating criteria: Excellent, Good, Fair, and Poor.

We can be proud that an overwhelming majority of our guests rated the Coral Sands Resort as either Excellent or Good.

Category Descriptions
To earn a rating of Excellent, a category must conform to the standards described below.

- **Room Cleanliness:** The room must be completely free of dust, lint, smudges, smears, and sand particles.
- **Staff Friendliness:** The staff must be courteous, offer assistance, and act towards guests as they would toward an honored friend.
- **Meal Service:** Meals must be of an exceptionally high standard, comparable with the best 5-star restaurants and served with impeccable attention to each guest's comfort.
- **Leisure Facilities:** The pool and leisure center facilities must be spotlessly clean, well equipped, and efficiently run.

Column break
inserted here

GUEST SURVEY RESULTS FOR CORAL SANDS RESORT

activity:

Link the Excel Charts with the Word Summary

You need to copy the column chart and the pie chart from Excel and then paste them as links into Word. You will then update the chart information in Excel and add hyperlinks to selected text in the Word document.

steps:

Trouble

If the column chart appears at the top of column 2, drag the handles to reduce the chart size slightly so that it appears at the bottom of column 1. If this doesn't work, you might have inserted the chart after the column break. Try again.

1. In Word, click **View** on the menu bar, click **Zoom**, click the **Whole page option button**, then click **OK**

2. Switch to Excel, click the **Column chart** to select it, click the **Copy button** 🖺 on the Standard toolbar, switch to Word, click below **more favorable rating** in column 1, press **[Enter]**, click **Edit** on the menu bar, click **Paste Special**, click the **Paste link option button**, then click **OK**

3. Switch to Excel, click the **Pie chart** to select it, then copy and paste it as a link below the second paragraph in column 2 in the Word document, as shown in Figure P2-6
Now that you've copied the charts into Word, you've discovered that the Overall Rating results are incorrect. Fortunately, you linked the survey data in the Excel charts with the Word summary. When you change the values related to the charts in Excel, the charts in Word will also be updated.

4. Look at the pie chart in Word, switch to Excel, change the value in cell **F5** to **800** and the value in cell **F6** to **510**, then switch back to Word
As you can see, the "Fair" slice in the pie chart has increased considerably as a result of the new values you entered in Excel.

5. Click the **Zoom list arrow** on the Standard toolbar, click **100%**, select the **Category Descriptions** heading under the Pie chart, click **Insert** on the menu bar, then click **Bookmark**
You need to assign a name to the bookmark.

6. Type **Category**, then click **Add**

7. Select the bulleted list from **Room Cleanliness** through **Leisure Facilities** in column 1, click **Insert** on the menu bar, click **Hyperlink**, click **Place in This Document**, click **Category**, then click **OK**
The bulleted list now appears in as blue and underlined text.

8. Click the **Room Cleanliness** hyperlink
The Web toolbar appears and the list of descriptions underneath the pie chart appears. Don't worry if your charts appear to disappear, they will print out correctly and you can view them again in Whole Page view.

9. Click the **Print button** 🖨 on the Standard toolbar
Your Coral Sands Resort Survey Results document is complete.

Clues to Use

Understanding Hyperlinks

You create local hyperlinks to move quickly from one location in a document or on a Web page to another location in the same document or Web page. The hyperlink you created in this project is a local hyperlink. You can also create a hyperlink to a remote location such as another document saved on your system or another Web page anywhere on the World Wide Web.

FIGURE P2-6: Completed Survey results viewed in Whole Page view

Coral Sands Resort Survey Results

The Coral Sands Resort is proud to announce the results of its annual survey. This year, 2,000 guests participated in the survey. The guests were asked to rate the following categories of service in terms of four criteria: Excellent, Good, Fair, and Poor.

- Room Cleanliness ————— Hyperlinks
- Staff Friendliness
- Meal Service
- Leisure Facilities
- Overall Rating

As displayed in the column chart below, our Leisure Facilities received the highest rating. However, a significant percentage of our guests rated Staff Friendliness as Poor. The Coral Sands Resort will initiate a series of staff training seminars to ensure that next year's survey shows a more favorable rating.

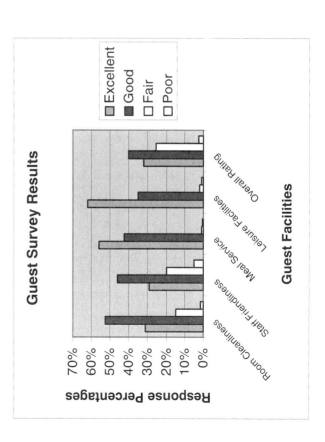

The pie chart displayed below breaks down the Overall Rating in terms of the four rating criteria: Excellent, Good, Fair, and Poor.

We can be proud that an overwhelming majority of our guests rated the Coral Sands Resort as either Excellent or Good.

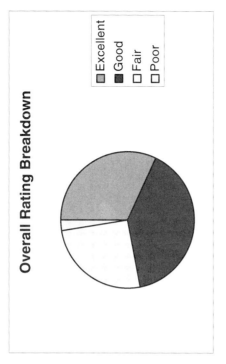

Category Descriptions

To earn a rating of Excellent, a category must conform to the standards described below.

- **Room Cleanliness**: The room must be completely free of dust, lint, smudges, smears, and sand particles.

- **Staff Friendliness**: The staff must be courteous, offer assistance, and act towards guests as they would toward an honored friend.

- **Meal Service**: Meals must be of an exceptionally high standard, comparable with the best 5-start restaurants and served with impeccable attention to each guest's comfort.

- **Leisure Facilities**: The pool and leisure center facilities must be spotlessly clean, well equipped, and efficiently run.

Price List for Spiral Bath Products

You are the owner of Spiral Bath Products, a small, home-based business in Auckland, New Zealand, that sells uniquely scented bath salts in 100-gram and 1 kilo packages. You distribute your bath salts to gift shops, department stores, and bath specialty stores all over New Zealand. You have now decided to advertise your bath salts to stores around the world via the World Wide Web. On your new Web page, you will create a price list that you have created in Word that includes a worksheet created in Excel. First you will **Create the Price List in Excel** and then you will **Set Up the Price List in Word**.

activity:

Create the Price List in Excel

As you create the price list in Excel, you will take advantage of the AutoComplete feature to save you from typing similar labels more than once.

steps:

1. Open a blank Excel workbook, type **Product** in cell A1, type **Size** in cell B1, type **Price** in cell C1, then save your worksheet as **Spiral Bath Products Price List**

2. Click cell **A2**, type **Raspberry Swirl**, press [Tab], type **100 grams**, press [Tab], type **4.5**, then widen column A and format row 1, as shown in Figure P3-1

3. Click cell **A3**, type **R**, press [Tab], type **1 kilo**, press [Tab], type **=C2*10**, then press [Enter]
   The formula in cell C3 multiplies the value in cell C2 by 10 to determine the cost of 1 kilo of the Raspberry Swirl bath salts, because 100 grams multiplied by 10 is equal to 1 kilo. Therefore, the cost of 1/10 kilo of Raspberry Swirl is 10 times the cost of 100 grams.

4. Click cell **C3** then drag the corner handle down to cell **C17**
   Some of the cells contain values appearing in scientific notation because the formula has continually multiplied the value in cell C2 by 10. Don't worry! As you enter the 100-gram price for each of the products, these numbers will change to the correct amounts.

5. Click cell **A4**, type **Citrus Heaven**, press [Tab], type **100 g**, press [Tab], type **3.75**, then press [Enter]
   "100 grams" appears in cell B4 thanks to the handy AutoComplete feature. Also note that the 1 kilo price (37.5) appears in cell C5. Pressing [Enter] moves the active cell to the next empty cell in the table.

6. Enter the remaining data for the price list, as shown in Figure P3-1
   Note that you still need to enter the 100 gram prices in column C. The 1 kilo prices appear automatically.

7. As shown in Figure P3-1, format cells **C2** to **C17** in the **Currency style**, **Bold** and **Center** the labels in row 1, **widen** the columns where necessary, then save the worksheet

8. Open a new blank document in Word, type and enhance the text, as shown in Figure P3-2, then save the document as **Spiral Bath Products Price List**

FIGURE P3-1: **Price list data in Excel**

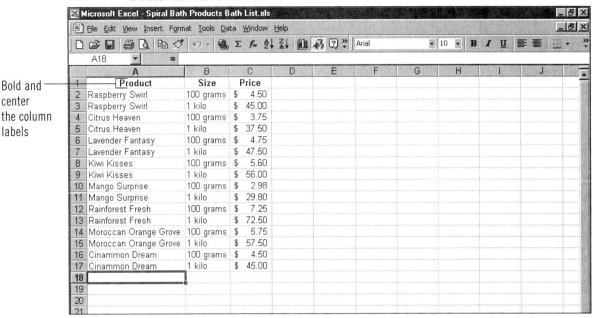

Bold and center the column labels

FIGURE P3-2: **Text for the Word document**

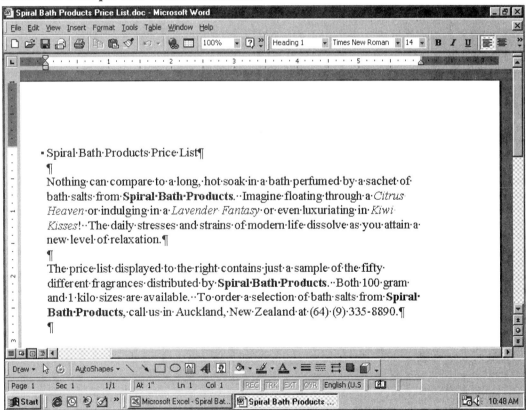

AutoComplete Feature

When you start to type a label into a cell, Excel checks the surrounding cells for similar data. If Excel finds similar data, it automatically completes the entry for you. For example, if you have entered "Bath Salts" in cell A1, then type "B" in cell A2, Excel immediately enters "Bath Salts" in cell A2.

activity:

Set Up the Price List in Word

You need to copy the price list from Excel to Word, then use the Word Table AutoFormat features to format the price list information attractively. You will then add a theme to the document, find an appropriate clipart picture from Microsoft's Clip Gallery Live, and then save the document as a Web page.

Hint

[Ctrl][C] is the Copy command used in all Windows applications.

steps:

1. In the Spiral Bath Products Price List worksheet, select cells **A1** to **C17**, then press **[Ctrl][C]**

2. In the Spiral Bath Products Price List document, double-click about 1" below the last paragraph, click **Edit** on the menu bar, click **Paste Special**, click the **Paste link option button**, click **Formatted text (RTF)**, then click **OK** and save your document
   The Excel worksheet appears in the Word document.

3. Click anywhere in the table, click **Table** on the menu bar, click **Table AutoFormat**, click **Contemporary** (you will need to scroll down), then click **OK**, move your mouse over the table so the ⊞ appears as shown in Figure P3-3, click ⊞, right-click the table, click **Table Properties**, under text wrapping, click **Around**, under alignment, click **Right**, then click **OK**

Hint

If necessary, click Install to install the Spiral theme. If you can't install the Spiral theme, select another theme.

4. Drag the table up so that its top row appears between paragraphs 1 and 2, as shown in Figure P3-3, click **Format** on the menu bar, click **Theme**, scroll down the list of themes, click **Spiral**, then click **OK**
   The document is automatically formatted with the Spiral theme.

5. Click at the top of the document, click the **Insert ClipArt button** 🖼 on the drawing toolbar, click **Clips Online**, click **OK**, connect to the Internet if requested, then click **Accept**
   You need to make Internet Explorer your default Web browser in order to perform step 5.
   In a few moments, Microsoft's Clip Gallery Live will appear.

6. Click in the Search box, type **bath**, press **[Enter]**, then click the **Download This Clip Now button** 📥 of an appropriate picture, as shown in Figure P3-4
   The picture appears in the Insert ClipArt dialog box.

7. Right-click the picture in the Insert ClipArt dialog box, click **Insert**, close the Insert ClipArt dialog box, return to the Word document, then reduce the size of the image so that it is about 1" high
   You may want to disconnect from the Internet now.

8. Click **File** on the menu bar, click **Web Page Preview**, compare your screen to Figure P3-5, then print a copy of the Web page from your browser

Time To

✓ **Save**
✓ **Close all documents**

9. Return to Word, click **File** on the menu bar, click **Save as Web Page**, type **s** to display **spiral_files** in the File name box, click **Save**, click in the File name box, type **prices**, then click **Save**
   The document is saved as prices.htm in a new folder called spiral_files. This folder also includes the clip art image. If you have an Internet Service Provider and your own Web site, you can now post the files in the spiral_files folder to the World Wide Web.

FIGURE P3-3: **Table moved above paragraph 2**

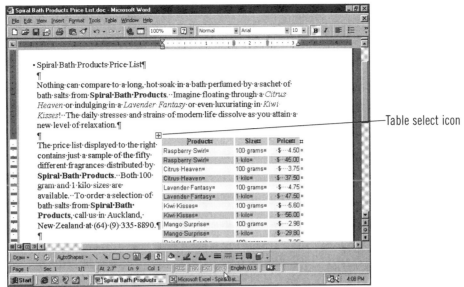

Table select icon

FIGURE P3-4: **Downloading a clip art picture from the Clip Gallery Live**

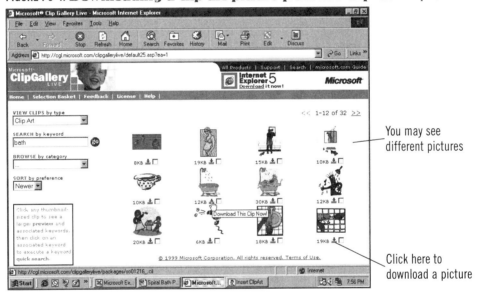

You may see
different pictures

Click here to
download a picture

FIGURE P3-5: **Completed price list viewed on the Web Browser**

Your picture may
be different

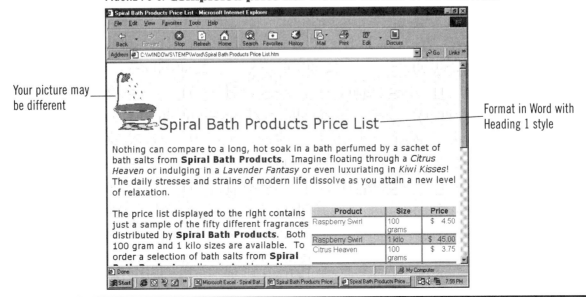

Format in Word with
Heading 1 style

In Iepen Ient Cha llen ges

INDEPENDENT CHALLENGE 1

Create an invoice in Excel, and then link it to a letter you create in Word. Fill in the boxes below with the required information, then set up your invoice in an Excel worksheet, create a letter in Word, copy some of the graphics, such as a picture or a WordArt object, in the Word letter to Excel, then copy some of the values in Excel, and paste them as links into the Word letter.

1. Determine the company name and type of business that will send the invoice. The type of company you select will determine the kinds of items you will list on the invoice form. For example, a ski touring company called Powder Trails could list items such as skis, boots, and poles, and services such as ski waxing and ski touring lessons. In the box below, write the name of your company and five items or services that it sells:

Company name: ....

Items to sell: ....

1. ....

2. ....

3. ....

4. ....

5. ....

2. In the box below identify the name and address of the company that has purchased the products or services listed in your invoice. You can include a different address under Shipped to: if the products will not be sent directly to the purchaser.

Sold to: ....

Shipped to: ....

3. Set up your invoice in Excel as follows:

   a. Leave about ten rows blank at the top of the invoice so that you can paste in elements from the letterhead you will create in Word.

   b. Right-align the labels in the billing section of your invoice.

   c. Enter the formulas required to make the following calculations:

   • Multiply the Quantity values by the Unit Price values, and put the results in the Amount column.

   • Add the values in the Amount column to determine the subtotal.

   • Calculate a 15% discount on one of the items.

   • Calculate tax as 7% of the Subtotal value.

   • Add the Subtotal and Tax values.

   • Subtract the discount from the Subtotal and add Tax to determine the Total Amount Due.

   d. Save the invoice as "Invoice for [Company Name]" on your disk.

   e. Switch to Word, create an attractive letterhead (use WordArt and insert a picture, if you wish), then create and format a letter similar to the letter you created for Project 1.

   f. Switch to Excel, copy the total amount, then switch to Word, and paste the amount into the appropriate sentence in the letter.

   g. Copy elements of the WordArt letterhead to Excel.

   h. Save the letter as "Letter for [Company Name]" on your disk, then print a copy of both the Invoice and the Letter.

INDEPENDENT CHALLENGE 2

Create a Survey Results Summary for a company or organization of your choice. Refer to the summary you created in Project 2 for formatting ideas. Here are some tips for creating your summary:

1. Set up a Survey Results worksheet in Excel. Select categories appropriate to your company or organization. For example, if your company is a neighborhood restaurant, you could select such categories as Food Quality, Selection, Service, and Ambiance, or, if you choose to analyze a course you're taking at college, you could select such categories as Instructor Presentation, Relevance of Assignments, Course Materials, and Grading System. You can use the rating criteria used in Project 2 (i.e., Excellent, Good, Fair, and Poor) or select different rating criteria.
2. Convert the values that represent the total number of responses to each of the criteria in each category to percentages.
3. Create a column chart or a line chart based on the data in your worksheet.
4. Create a pie chart that shows the breakdown of responses in the Overall Rating column.
5. Switch to Word, create a WordArt object and a text box in the heading, then enter three or four paragraphs of text that describe the survey and its results. Refer to Project 2 for ideas. Include text that describes each category evaluated in the survey you did in Project 2.
6. Copy the charts from Excel into the Word summary. Remember to paste the charts as links into Word.
7. Make some changes to the data in the Excel worksheet. The charts copied into Word will also change.
8. Format the Word summary in Whole Page view, then add an appropriate picture, if you wish.
9. Make the list of categories a hyperlink to their description.
10. Save and view the summary in your Web browser, then print a copy.
11. Save both the Excel worksheet and the Word summary as "Survey Results for [Company Name]". The appropriate extension (i.e., XLS or DOC) will be added automatically to differentiate between the two files.

INDEPENDENT CHALLENGE 3

Create a price list in Excel for a selection of products sold by a company of your choice. As you create the price list, let the AutoComplete feature help minimize your typing time. When you have completed the price list, set up a Word document as you did in Project 3. Make sure you include a theme. Copy the Excel price list, and paste it as a link into Word. Format the Word price list attractively, include a WordArt object and a picture, and use the Table AutoFormat feature to attractively present the data in the Excel price list. Add one of the preset themes to the document and then insert an appropriate picture from Microsoft's Clip Gallery Live. View the document in your Web browser, then print a copy. Save the Excel file as "Price List for [Company Name]".

INDEPENDENT CHALLENGE 4

Create an Excel worksheet with the projected income and expenses for Elysian Landscaping, a small home-based landscaping business in Phoenix. You will then use the data in the worksheet to create two charts, which you will link to a Projected Sales Summary you will create in Word. Finally, you will add hyperlinks and a ClipArt picture, and then you will view the completed Word document in your Web browser.

1. Open a blank workbook in Excel, then set up a worksheet using data from the worksheet in Figure IC-1. Note that the heading in cell A1 is formatted with the Forte font and a font size of 20-point. To save time, copy the values entered in column B across to column E.
2. Save the workbook as Elysian Landscaping Projected Sales Summary.
3. Enter and copy the formulas required to calculate the following amounts:
   a. Total monthly and four month Income (cells B7 to F6).
   b. Cost of Sales: Value of Sales multiplied by 60% (i.e., B6*.6).

c. Total monthly and four-month Expenses (cells B16 to F16).

d. Total Profit (cells B18 to F18): subtract the total expenses from the total income for each month. When you have completed all the calculations, you should see $28,000.00 in cell F18.

4. Create a pie chart that shows the breakdown of expenses by total amount. You will need to click the Chart Wizard button, select the pie chart type, and then select cells A10 to A15 and cells F10 to F15 as the data range. Remember to insert a comma between the two ranges in the Source Data dialog box and be sure that the columns radio button is selected under Series in the step 2 of 4 dialog box of the Chart Wizard. Call the pie chart "Breakdown of Expenses", and move the chart below the worksheet.

5. Create a column chart that compares the projected monthly income with the projected monthly expenses. Call the chart "Projected Income and Expenses".

6. Remove the chart legend by clicking on it and pressing [Delete].

7. Switch to Word, then enter the text for the Sales Summary, as shown in Figure IC-2. Note the spaces you will leave for amounts that will be pasted as links form the Excel worksheet.

8. Save the document as "Elysian Landscaping Projected Sales Summary".

9. Copy the pie chart, the column chart, and any totals required from Excel, and paste them as links into Word. Note that you paste the totals as unformatted text.

10. Switch to Excel, increase the salaries expense for April to 10,000 and decrease it to 2,000 for July, then increase the sales income for June to 12,000. Note the changes to the pie chart and the column chart.

11. Switch to Word, then apply the theme of your choice.

12. Enhance the Projected Expenses and Projected Income headings with the Heading 3 style, then insert the title in the Heading 1 style, as shown in Figure IC-3.

13. Insert a ClipArt picture from Microsoft's Clip Gallery Live similar to the picture shown in Figure IC-3.

14. Make the Projected Expenses heading a bookmark called Expenses and the Projected Income heading a bookmark called Income.

15. Make a hyperlink from "income" in paragraph 1 to the Projected Income bookmark, then make a hyperlink from "expenses" in paragraph 1 to the Projected Expenses bookmark.

16. Preview the page in your Web browser, as shown in Figure IC-3, then print a copy.

FIGURE IC-1: Elysian Landscaping Projected Sales Summary worksheet

FIGURE IC-2: Text for Elysian Landscaping Projected Sales Summary

Margaret O'Leary, our accountant at Elysian Landscaping, has projected the income and expenses for our landscaping business for the months of April through July.

Projected Expenses
The total projected expenses for April through July, 2001, are. A breakdown of expenses by total amount is displayed in the pie chart below:

In order to help decrease our expenses, Jason Bream, one of our own staff members, will create a series of brochures to advertise our products and services, thereby cutting our advertising expenses by 25%.

Projected Income
The total projected income for April through July, 2001, is . The projected profit for Elysian Landscaping from April through July, 2001, is . We plan to increase sales by charging a higher rate for our landscaping services in June and July, our busiest months.

The column chart displayed below compares our projected monthly income to our projected monthly expenses.

FIGURE IC-3: Completed sales summary for Elysian Landscaping shown in the Web browser

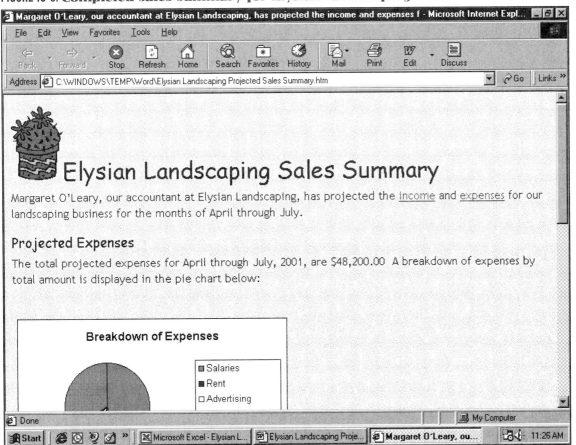

Excel

Visual Workshop

Create the Price List shown in Figure VW-1 in Excel, calculate the prices where indicated, paste the worksheet as a link (Formatted Text (RTF)) into Word, then modify the Word document so that it appears as shown in Figure VW-2. You will need to add the Citrus Punch theme to the document and the Grid 8 Table AutoFormat to the price list. Add a similar picture and move the table as shown in Figure VW-2. Print a copy of the price list. Save the worksheet and document as "Price List for Sara's Gourmet Heaven", then close all files.

FIGURE VW-1: **Price List worksheet**

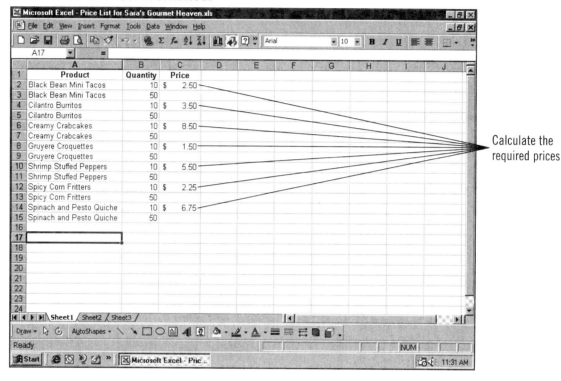

Calculate the required prices

FIGURE VW-2: **Price List for Sara's Gourmet Heaven**

Heading 1 Style

Heading 3 Style

Microsoft
► Access
Projects

Database Creation

In This Unit You Will Create:

PROJECT 1 ► **Inventory**

PROJECT 2 ► **Artist Profiles**

PROJECT 3 ► **Sales Information**

To survive and compete in the contemporary business world, companies and organizations need reliable information about their products or services, their customers, their suppliers, and their personnel. Suppose you run a fitness center and have decided to offer a special incentive plan to all the clients who joined the center in January of 2001. You could comb through all your paper files to find the clients, or you could use a relational database program, such as Access, to print out a list of all the clients who joined your center in January of 2001 or during any other time period you choose. A relational database program stores information in related tables that you can link to find the information you need to answer questions. To create a database, you first identify the attributes or fields that define the entity you are describing, such as customers or inventory, and then you formulate queries or questions to retrieve the information you need. In this unit, you will learn how to use Microsoft Access to set up a variety of databases and then ask questions to find the information you need to perform specific tasks.

Inventory for Global Crafts

Global Crafts is a non-profit organization based in Montreal that sells crafts made by artisans all over the world. The profits from the sales are invested back into the artisans' communities to be used to build schools and hospitals, finance agricultural projects, and operate social programs. You are in charge of monitoring the inventory levels and placing orders with the suppliers who work directly with the artisans to distribute their products. For this project, you will create a small database consisting of a Products table that contains 15 records and a Suppliers table that contains four records. Your principal goal in this project is to find out which products you need to order and the supplier you need to contact to place the order. Four activities are required to build an inventory database for Global Crafts and then produce a list of the products to order.

Project Activities

Set Up Products Table

The Products table shown in Figure P1-1 lists 15 of the products sold by Global Crafts. This table consists of seven fields, including a field for Units in Stock. You will use the Table Wizard to create the Products table.

Set Up Suppliers Table

The Suppliers table lists the four suppliers who obtain the products from the artisans and then ship them to Global Crafts. You will use the Form Wizard to enter the data required for the Suppliers table. Figure P1-2 shows a form created to enter the data for one of the suppliers.

Create Queries

You will create queries to find information listed in the Products table and Suppliers table of the Global Crafts database. You will be most concerned with the data entered in the Units in Stock field.

Format and Print an Order Report

You will create a query that lists all the products that you need to order, along with the distributors you need to contact. You will then create and format a report that presents this information in an easy-to-read and attractive format. Figure P1-3 shows the Order report you will create.

Clues to Use

Database Design

A "real" database for a viable company such as Global Crafts would, of course, contain considerably more records because the company would need to sell more than 15 products to stay in business. However, the number of products has been reduced to minimize the amount of time you need to spend entering data.

FIGURE P1-1: **Datasheet View of Products table for Global Crafts Database**

Field names —

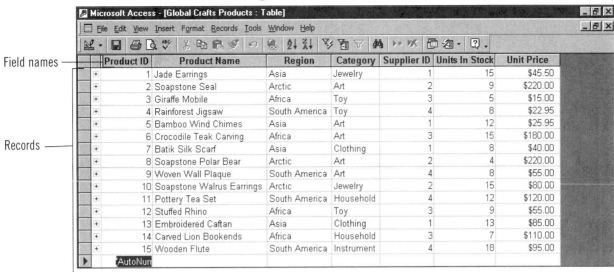

Records —

	Product ID	Product Name	Region	Category	Supplier ID	Units In Stock	Unit Price
+	1	Jade Earrings	Asia	Jewelry	1	15	$45.50
+	2	Soapstone Seal	Arctic	Art	2	9	$220.00
+	3	Giraffe Mobile	Africa	Toy	3	5	$15.00
+	4	Rainforest Jigsaw	South America	Toy	4	8	$22.95
+	5	Bamboo Wind Chimes	Asia	Art	1	12	$25.95
+	6	Crocodile Teak Carving	Africa	Art	3	15	$180.00
+	7	Batik Silk Scarf	Asia	Clothing	1	8	$40.00
+	8	Soapstone Polar Bear	Arctic	Art	2	4	$220.00
+	9	Woven Wall Plaque	South America	Art	4	8	$55.00
+	10	Soapstone Walrus Earrings	Arctic	Jewelry	2	15	$80.00
+	11	Pottery Tea Set	South America	Household	4	12	$120.00
+	12	Stuffed Rhino	Africa	Toy	3	9	$55.00
+	13	Embroidered Caftan	Asia	Clothing	1	13	$85.00
+	14	Carved Lion Bookends	Africa	Household	3	7	$110.00
+	15	Wooden Flute	South America	Instrument	4	18	$95.00

FIGURE P1-2: **Form for Supplier 1**

FIGURE P1-3: **Completed Order report**

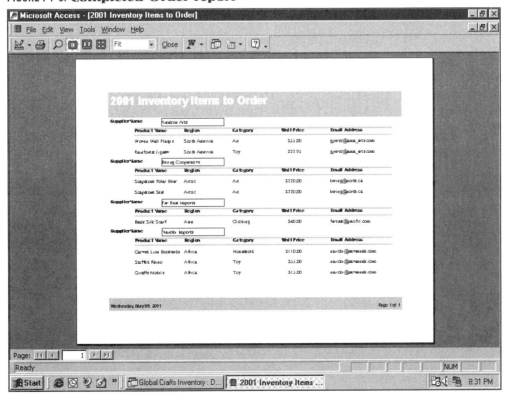

activity:

Set Up Products Table

You first need to enter the data required for the Products table.

steps:

1. Start Access, click the **Blank Access database option button** in the Microsoft Access dialog box, click **OK**, find the directory containing your disk (if necessary), type **Global Crafts Inventory** in the File name box, then click **Create**

2. Double-click **Create table by using wizard**

   You could go directly to a blank datasheet; however, the Table Wizard automatically enters selected fields into your table, thereby saving you time.

3. Click **Products** in the Sample Tables list box, make sure **ProductID** is selected in the **Sample Fields** list box, then click the **Select Single Field button** `>`

   The ProductID field appears in the "Fields in my new table" list box.

4. Click `>` to select **ProductName**, click **CategoryID**, click `>`, click **Rename Field** under the Fields in my new table list box, type **Region**, click **OK**, then select the following fields: **SupplierID**, **UnitsInStock**, and **UnitPrice**

   If you select the wrong field, click the Remove Single Field button `<` to return the field to the Sample Fields list.

5. Click **Next**, type **Global Crafts Products** for the table name, accept the default to let the Wizard set a primary key, click **Next**, accept the default to enter data directly into the table, then click **Finish**

   The Datasheet View appears. At present, no data appears in the six fields.

6. Press **[Tab]**, type **Jade Earrings**, press **[Tab]**, type **Asia**, then press **[Tab]**

   A warning message appears because you have entered the wrong kind of data into the Region field. Originally this field was called CategoryID, which Access formats as a field that contains only numbers.

7. Click **OK** to remove the message, press **[Backspace]** until you erase "Asia," click the **View button** on the toolbar to switch to Design View, click **Number** in the Data Type column for Region, click the **Data Type list arrow**, then click **Text**, as shown in Figure P1-4

   You changed the data type of the field in Design view so that you can enter text data.

8. Click the **View button** on the toolbar to switch to Datasheet View, click **Yes** to save the table, press **[Tab]** twice to move to the Region field, type **Asia**, then enter the remaining data for Record 1, as shown in Figure P1-5

   Just type the numbers for the Unit Price field. Access automatically formats the number in the Currency style. Note that you can press [Shift][Tab] if you need to move backwards to a previous cell.

9. Enter the data for records 2 to 15, as shown in Figure P1-5, double-click on each column divider to resize the columns, click **File** on the menu bar, click **Close,** then click **Yes** if a Save message appears

   You can also click the Close button that appears at the top right corner of the Datasheet window.

FIGURE P1-4: **Design View of the Products table**

View button

Primary Key field

Region field

Data Type list arrow

Text data type selected

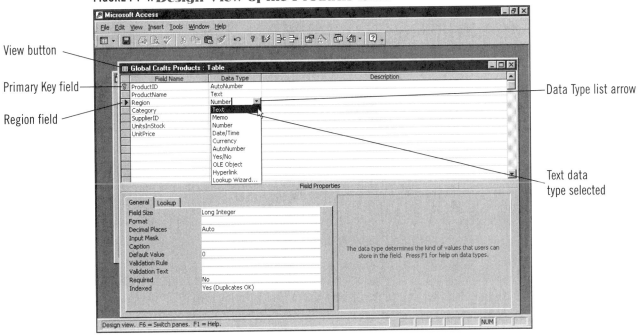

FIGURE P1-5: **Data for records 1 to 15**

Data for record 1

Unit price field formatted automatically as Currency

Product ID	Product Name	Region	Supplier ID	Units In Stock	Unit Price
1	Jade Earrings	Asia	1	15	$45.50
2	Soapstone Seal	Arctic	2	9	$220.00
3	Giraffe Mobile	Africa	3	5	$15.00
4	Rainforest Jigsaw	South America	4	8	$22.95
5	Bamboo Wind Chimes	Asia	1	12	$25.95
6	Crocodile Teak Carving	Africa	3	15	$180.00
7	Batik Silk Scarf	Asia	1	8	$40.00
8	Soapstone Polar Bear	Arctic	2	4	$220.00
9	Woven Wall Plaque	South America	4	8	$55.00
10	Soapstone Walrus Earrings	Arctic	2	15	$80.00
11	Pottery Tea Set	South America	4	12	$120.00
12	Stuffed Rhino	Africa	3	9	$55.00
13	Embroidered Caftan	Asia	1	13	$85.00
14	Carved Lion Bookends	Africa	3	7	$110.00
15	Wooden Flute	South America	4	18	$95.00

To adjust column width, position ←‖→between the field names, then double-click

activity:

Set Up Suppliers Table

The Suppliers table you created for a "real" business would include the address, phone numbers, and even e-mail address of each supplier. For the Global Crafts Suppliers table, you'll save time by including only the name, region, and e-mail address of each of the four suppliers who send you the crafts made by the artisans in their region. You can use the Table Wizard to enter data for a table into a datasheet, or you can use the Form Wizard to enter the data into a form. You will use the Table Wizard to set up the Suppliers table, then use the Form Wizard to enter the data required.

steps:

1. Double-click **Create table by using wizard**

2. Click **Suppliers** in the list of Sample Tables (you will need to scroll down), then add **SupplierID**, **SupplierName**, and **ContactName** to the Fields in my new table list box

3. Click **Rename Field**, type **Region**, click **OK**, add **EmailAddress** to the table, click **Next**, type **Global Crafts Suppliers**, then click **Next**

Access asks you if your new table is related to any other tables in your current database. Tables that contain at least one common field can be related. Both the Products table and the Suppliers table contain two common fields: Region and SupplierID.

4. Click **Relationships**, click **One record in the 'Global Crafts Suppliers' table**, as shown in Figure P1-6, click **OK**, click **Next**, check that the **Enter data directly into the table option button** is selected, then click **Finish**

In a few moments the Datasheet view of the Suppliers table appears.

5. Click **File** on the menu bar, click **Close**, click **Forms** in the Database window, then double-click **Create form by using wizard**

6. Click the **Tables/Queries list arrow**, click **Table: Global Crafts Suppliers**, click the **Select All Fields button** ⏩ , click **Next**, click **Next** to accept the **Columnar** layout, click **Ricepaper**, click **Next**, make sure the **Open the form to view or enter information option button** is selected, then click **Finish**

In a few seconds a blank form appears.

7. Press **[Tab]**, type **Far East Imports** for the Supplier Name, press **[Tab]**, type **Asia**, press **[Tab]**, type **fareast@pacific.com**, then press **[Tab]** twice to move to the Supplier Name field in form 2

8. Enter the data for the next three forms, as shown in Figures P1-7, P1-8, and P1-9

9. Close the last form

You can now view the data for the Global Crafts Suppliers in both individual forms and in a datasheet.

FIGURE P1-6: **Relationships dialog box**

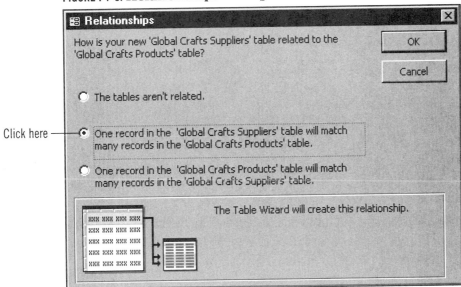

Click here →

Relationships

How is your new 'Global Crafts Suppliers' table related to the 'Global Crafts Products' table?

OK

Cancel

○ The tables aren't related.

◉ One record in the 'Global Crafts Suppliers' table will match many records in the 'Global Crafts Products' table.

○ One record in the 'Global Crafts Products' table will match many records in the 'Global Crafts Suppliers' table.

The Table Wizard will create this relationship.

FIGURE P1-7: **Data for Supplier 2**

Global Crafts Suppliers

Supplier ID: 2

Supplier Name: Bering Cooperative

Region: Arctic

Email Address: bering@north.ca

Record: 2 of 4

FIGURE P1-8: **Data for Supplier 3**

Global Crafts Suppliers

Supplier ID: 3

Supplier Name: Nairobi Imports

Region: Africa

Email Address: nairobi@savannah.com

Record: 3 of 4

FIGURE P1-9: **Data for Supplier 4**

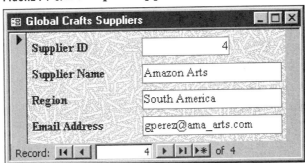

Global Crafts Suppliers

Supplier ID: 4

Supplier Name: Amazon Arts

Region: South America

Email Address: gperez@ama_arts.com

Record: 4 of 4

activity:

Create Queries

Now that you've set up the two tables for the Global Crafts database, you will ask three questions, called **queries** in database language. These queries relate to specific actions you wish to perform using the data stored in the two tables. First you want to make a quick count of the products made in Asia. The fastest method of obtaining this information is to use the Filter tool in the Datasheet view of the Global Crafts Products table.

steps:

1. Click **Tables** in the Database window, double-click **Global Crafts Products** to open it, click the first **Asia** entry in the Region field, then click the **Filter By Selection button** 🍸 on the Standard toolbar

    As you can see, four of the products are made in Asia.

2. Click the **Remove Filter button** ▽

3. Click the **View button** 📐 on the toolbar to switch to Design View, click the row selector to the left of SupplierID, **right-click** the mouse, click **Insert Rows**, click the blank **Field Name cell**, type **Category**, then press **[Tab]**

    The default data type is Text, which is fine in this case. You can always add new fields to a table just by working in Design View.

4. Click the **View button** 🖩 on the toolbar to switch to Datasheet View, click **Yes** to save the table, enter the category for each product, as shown in Figure P1-10, click **File** on the menu bar, then click **Close**

5. Click **Queries** in the Database window, double-click **Create query by using wizard**, click the **Table/Queries list arrow**, click **Table: Global Crafts Products**, click the **Select All Fields button** ⟩⟩ to select all the fields in the Global Crafts Products table, click **Next**, click **Next** to accept a Detail query, click the **Modify the query design option button**, then click **Finish**

    The design grid appears.

6. As shown in Figure P1-11, click the **Region Criteria cell**, type **Africa**, click the **Category Criteria cell**, type **Toy**, then click the **Run button** ⏺

    Two of the products from Africa are toys — the Stuffed Rhino and the Giraffe Mobile.

7. Click **File** on the menu bar, click **Close**, then click **No**

    You don't save the constraints for this query because you will not use it again. Often you create queries to find a specific piece of information that you read off the screen before closing the query. If you need to view the information again, you can easily modify the query.

8. Double-click **Global Craft Products Query**, switch to Design View, scroll to and click the **UnitsInStock Criteria cell**, type **<10**, then click ⏺

    A datasheet listing all the products with fewer than 10 units in stock appears, as shown in Figure P1-12. These are the items that you need to order.

9. Click **File** on the menu bar, click **Close**, then click **No**

FIGURE P1-10: Category records for the Global Crafts Products table

Plus signs indicate that the table is related to the suppliers table

	Product ID	Product Name	Region	Category	Supplier ID	Units In Stock	Unit Price
+	1	Jade Earrings	Asia	Jewelry	1	15	$45.50
+	2	Soapstone Seal	Arctic	Art	2	9	$220.00
+	3	Giraffe Mobile	Africa	Toy	3	5	$15.00
+	4	Rainforest Jigsaw	South America	Toy	4	8	$22.95
+	5	Bamboo Wind Chimes	Asia	Art	1	12	$25.95
+	6	Crocodile Teak Carving	Africa	Art	3	15	$180.00
+	7	Batik Silk Scarf	Asia	Clothing	1	8	$40.00
+	8	Soapstone Polar Bear	Arctic	Art	2	4	$220.00
+	9	Woven Wall Plaque	South America	Art	4	8	$55.00
+	10	Soapstone Walrus Earrings	Arctic	Jewelry	2	15	$80.00
+	11	Pottery Tea Set	South America	Household	4	12	$120.00
+	12	Stuffed Rhino	Africa	Toy	3	9	$55.00
+	13	Embroidered Caftan	Asia	Clothing	1	13	$85.00
+	14	Carved Lion Bookends	Africa	Household	3	7	$110.00
+	15	Wooden Flute	South America	Instrument	4	18	$95.00
	(AutoNum						

FIGURE P1-11: Design grid for Query 2

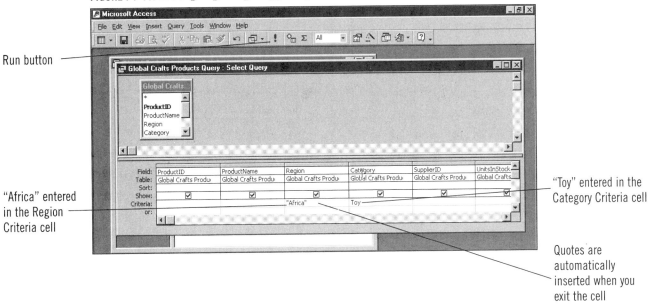

Run button

"Africa" entered in the Region Criteria cell

"Toy" entered in the Category Criteria cell

Quotes are automatically inserted when you exit the cell

FIGURE P1-12: Datasheet view of Query 3 results

	Product ID	Product Name	Region	Expr1	Supplier ID	Units In Stock	Unit Price
▶	2	Soapstone Seal	Arctic		2	9	$220.00
	3	Giraffe Mobile	Africa		3	5	$15.00
	4	Rainforest Jigsaw	South America		4	8	$22.95
	7	Batik Silk Scarf	Asia		1	8	$40.00
	8	Soapstone Polar Bear	Arctic		2	4	$220.00
	9	Woven Wall Plaque	South America		4	8	$55.00
	12	Stuffed Rhino	Africa		3	9	$55.00
	14	Carved Lion Bookends	Africa		3	7	$110.00
*	(AutoNumber)						

Record: 1 of 8

activity:

Format and Print an Order Report

You will create a query from both the Global Crafts Products table and the Suppliers table to list the products you need to order and the names of the suppliers you need to contact, and then you will format and print an Order report.

steps:

1. Double-click **Create query by using wizard**, click the **Tables/Queries list arrow**, click **Table: Global Crafts Products**, click the **Select All Fields button** >> , click the **Tables/Queries list arrow**, click **Table: Global Crafts Suppliers**, then select **SupplierName** and **EmailAddress** for inclusion in the table

2. Click **Next**, click **Next** again, type **Items to Order** as the Query table name, then click **Finish**

3. Switch to **Design View**, click the **UnitsInStock Criteria cell**, type **<10**, click the **SupplierName Sort cell**, click the **Sort Cell list arrow**, click **Ascending**, then click the **Run button** !
   You have your list of eight products to order and the names and e-mail addresses of the suppliers to contact sorted by supplier name. Note that you may need to scroll right to view all the fields in the query table.

4. Click **File** on the menu bar, click **Close**, click **Yes**, click **Reports**, then double-click **Create report by using wizard**

5. Click the **Tables/Queries list arrow**, click **Query: Items to Order**, then select the following fields: **ProductName**, **Region**, **Category**, **UnitPrice**, **SupplierName**, and **EmailAddress**

6. Click **Next**, click **by Global Crafts Products**, if necessary, click **Next**, click **Supplier Name** in the list of groupings, click the **Select Single Field button** > , click **Next**, click **Next** again, click the **Align Left 1 option button**, click the **Landscape option button**, click **Next**, click **Soft Gray**, click **Next**, type **2001 Inventory Items to Order**, then click **Finish**
   The Unit Price field heading appears too far to the right.

7. Click the **Zoom list arrow** on the Print Preview toolbar, then click **Fit**

8. Click the **View button** to switch to Design View, click the **Unit Price** label, press and hold

   [Shift], click the **Unit Price** field, move the mouse over a selected label until the 🖐 appears, then drag the 🖐 to move the two selected labels to the left, as shown in Figure P1-13

9. Click the **Print Preview button** on the Standard toolbar, maximize the report window, check the positioning of the Unit Price labels, as shown in Figure P1-14, click the **Print button** on the Standard toolbar, close the report, click **Yes**, then close the database

Clues to Use

Formatting Reports

If you want to modify the positioning of the Unit Price labels or any other labels, switch back to Design View, make the adjustments required, then view the results in the Print Preview screen. To format a report in Access, you need to switch frequently between Design View and the Print Preview screen.

FIGURE P1-13: **Position of the Unit Price labels in Design View**

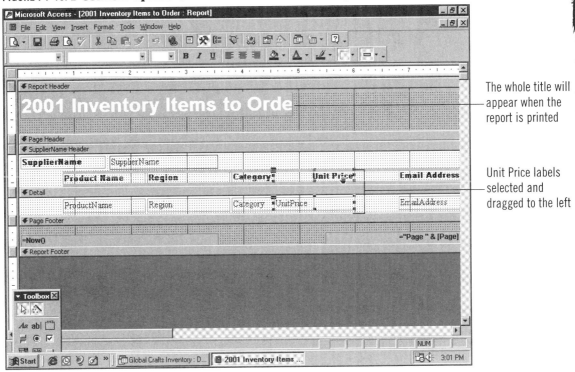

The whole title will appear when the report is printed

Unit Price labels selected and dragged to the left

FIGURE P1-14: **Completed report in the Print Preview screen**

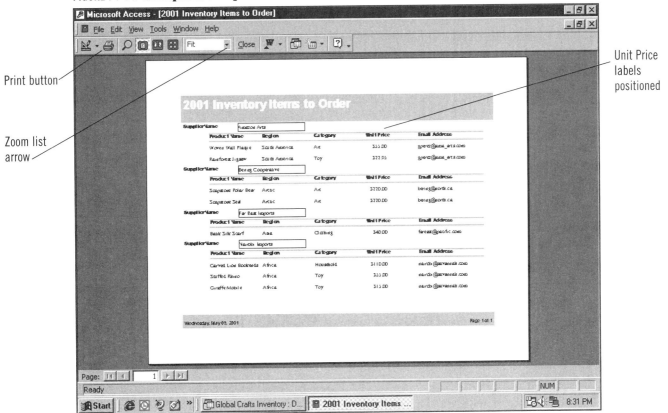

Print button

Zoom list arrow

Unit Price labels positioned

Artist Profiles for London Road Art Gallery

The London Road Art Gallery in Reading, England, exhibits paintings by local and international artists. As the manager of the London Road Art Gallery, you decide to set up a database that you can use to identify the artists who have sold the most paintings, the most popular styles of art purchased, and which artists sold paintings for more than €5,000 in the new Euro currency. You will **Create the Painting Sales and Artists Tables**, **Create and Modify a Query**, and then **Format and Print a Report**.

activity:

Create the Painting Sales and Artists Tables

Your first task is to create the two tables in the London Road Art Gallery Client Database.

steps:

1. Click **File** on the menu bar, click **New**, click **Database**, click **OK**, save the database as **London Road Art Gallery Client Database**, then click **Create**

2. Double-click **Create table in Design view**, then enter the following field names: **Painting Title**, **Artist Name**, **Buyer Name**, and **Price**
   Access automatically assigns Text as the data type for each field.

3. Click **Text** next to the Price field, click the **Data Type list arrow**, click **Currency**, click **Currency** next to Format on the General tab, click the **list arrow**, then select the **Euro** as shown in Figure P2-1

4. Switch to **Datasheet View**, save the table as **Painting Sales**, click **Yes** to create a Primary Key, then enter the data and increase the column widths, as shown in Figure P2-2

5. Click **Artist Name**, then click the **Sort Ascending button** on the Standard toolbar

6. Click the **Artist Name** field, click the **Copy button** on the Standard toolbar, close the table, click **Yes** to save changes, then double-click **Create table by entering data**

7. Click the **Field1** field, click the **Paste button** on the Standard toolbar, click **Yes**, double-click **Field1**, type **Artist Name**, press [Enter], then widen the column so that you can see all the names

8. Right-click the row selector to the left of the second occurrence of Bess Davidson, click **Delete Record** on the pop-up menu, click **Yes**, then repeat the process to delete duplicate occurrences of the remaining artists, as shown in Figure P2-3
   Note that you can select more than one row at a time to delete.

9. Rename Field2 **Style**, enter the style for each artist, as shown in Figure P2-3, close the table, click **Yes** to save the changes, name the table **Artists**, then click **Yes** to create a Primary key

FIGURE P2-1: **Euro currency format selected**

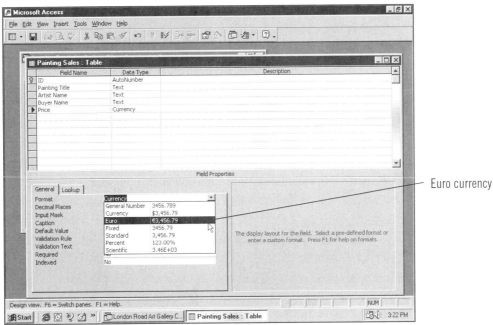

Euro currency

FIGURE P2-2: **Records for the Painting Sales table**

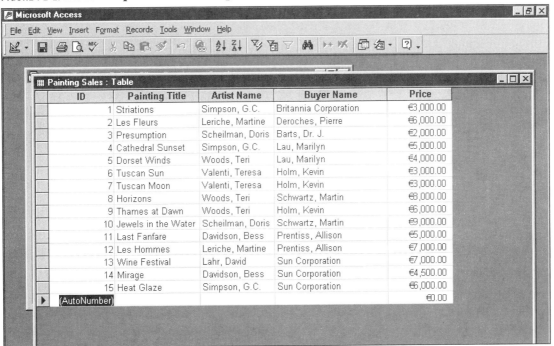

ID	Painting Title	Artist Name	Buyer Name	Price
1	Striations	Simpson, G.C.	Britannia Corporation	€3,000.00
2	Les Fleurs	Leriche, Martine	Deroches, Pierre	€6,000.00
3	Presumption	Scheilman, Doris	Barts, Dr. J.	€2,000.00
4	Cathedral Sunset	Simpson, G.C.	Lau, Marilyn	€5,000.00
5	Dorset Winds	Woods, Teri	Lau, Marilyn	€4,000.00
6	Tuscan Sun	Valenti, Teresa	Holm, Kevin	€3,000.00
7	Tuscan Moon	Valenti, Teresa	Holm, Kevin	€3,000.00
8	Horizons	Woods, Teri	Schwartz, Martin	€8,000.00
9	Thames at Dawn	Woods, Teri	Holm, Kevin	€6,000.00
10	Jewels in the Water	Scheilman, Doris	Schwartz, Martin	€9,000.00
11	Last Fanfare	Davidson, Bess	Prentiss, Allison	€5,000.00
12	Les Hommes	Leriche, Martine	Prentiss, Allison	€7,000.00
13	Wine Festival	Lahr, David	Sun Corporation	€7,000.00
14	Mirage	Davidson, Bess	Sun Corporation	€4,500.00
15	Heat Glaze	Simpson, G.C.	Sun Corporation	€6,000.00
(AutoNumber)				€0.00

FIGURE P2-3: **Records for the Artists table**

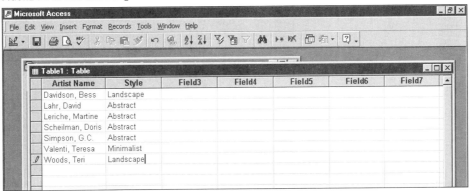

Artist Name	Style	Field3	Field4	Field5	Field6	Field7
Davidson, Bess	Landscape					
Lahr, David	Abstract					
Leriche, Martine	Abstract					
Scheilman, Doris	Abstract					
Simpson, G.C.	Abstract					
Valenti, Teresa	Minimalist					
Woods, Teri	Landscape					

ARTIST PROFILES FOR LONDON ROAD ART GALLERY

activity:

Create and Modify a Query

You need to create a query to determine the most popular style of art purchased and then modify this query to list only those artists who sold paintings for more than €5,000. Before you can create the query, you need to establish a relationship between the Painting Sales and Artists tables.

steps:

1. Click **Tools** on the menu bar, click **Relationships**, click **Add** in the Show Table dialog box to add the Artists table, click **Painting Sales** in the Show Table dialog box, click **Add**, then click **Close**

2. Click **Artist Name** in the Artists table, drag it across to **Artist Name** in the Painting Sales table, then click **Create** in the Edit Relationships dialog box that appears
   A link now exists between the two tables, as shown in Figure P2-4.

3. Click the **Close button** ☒ in the Relationships window, then click **Yes** to save the changes

4. Click **Queries**, double-click **Create query by using wizard**, click the **Tables/Queries list arrow**, click **Table: Painting Sales**, then click the **Select All Fields button** ⟩⟩ to insert all the fields

5. Click the **Tables/Queries list arrow**, click **Table: Artists**, add the **Style** field to the selected fields, click **Next**, click **Next** again, name the query **Top Sales**, click the **Modify the query design option button**, then click **Finish**

6. Click the **Style Sort cell** (you may need to scroll to view it), click the **Sort cell list arrow**, click **Ascending**, then click the **Run button** ⏯ on the toolbar
   The abstract style is by far the most popular, as shown in Figure P2-5.

7. Click the **View button** 📐 on the toolbar to switch to Design View, click the **Price Criteria cell**, type **>5000**, then click ⏯
   Seven paintings match the criteria.

8. Switch to **Design View**, click the **Price Sort cell**, click the **Price Sort list arrow**, click **Ascending**, click the **ID Show cell** to remove the check mark, click ⏯, then compare your screen with Figure P2-6

9. Click the **Close button** ☒ in the Query Results window, then click **Yes** to save the modified query

FIGURE P2-4: Creating the table relationship

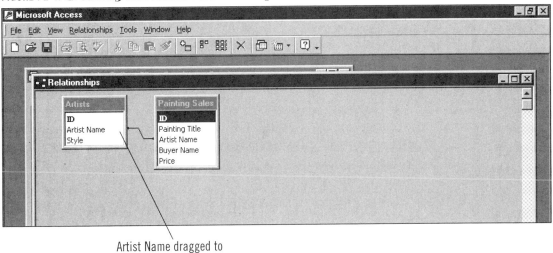

Artist Name dragged to
the Painting Sales table

FIGURE P2-5: Results of the Most Popular Styles query

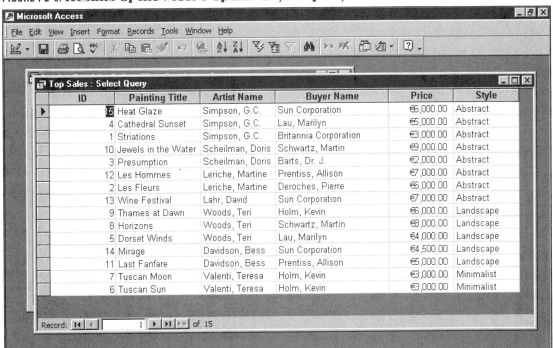

FIGURE P2-6: Results of the Top Sales query

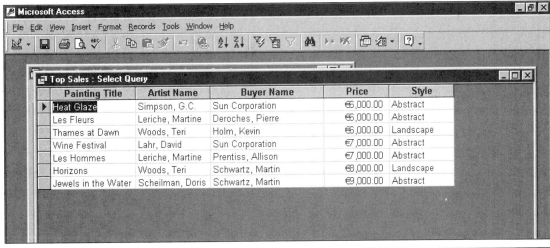

activity:

Format and Print a Report

You need to create the report that appears as shown in Figure P2-7.

steps:

1. Click **Reports**, double-click **Create report by using wizard**, click the **Tables/Queries list arrow**, click **Query: Top Sales**, then click the **Select All Fields button** >>

2. Click **Next**, click **Artist Name**, click the **Select Single Field button** > to insert Artist Name as a header, click **Next**, click **Summary Options**, click the **Sum Check** box, then click **OK**

3. Click **Next**, click the **Align Left 2 option button**, click **Next**, click **Casual**, click **Next**, type **London Road Art Gallery Top Sales**, then click **Finish**

4. Click the **View button** , click the **Artist Name** label in the Artist Name Header, press and hold **[Shift]**, click the **Artist Name** field, click the **Font Size list arrow** on the Formatting toolbar, then click **14**

5. Click the **Print Preview button** on the Standard toolbar, change the Zoom to **75%**, then scroll down to view the report

   As you can see, part of the price data is cut off and the Price and Style labels appear too close together.

6. Click **Close** on the Print Preview toolbar, use [Shift] to select the two **Price** boxes and the two **Sum** boxes, click **Format** on the menu bar, click **Size,** click **To Fit**, then click the **Align Right button** on the Formatting toolbar

7. Select the two **Style** boxes, then click the **Center button** on the Formatting toolbar

8. Click , compare your report to Figure P2-7, then make any adjustments required in Design View

9. Click the **Print button** , close and save the report, then close the database

London Road Art Gallery Top Sales

Artist Name Lahr, David

Painting Title	Buyer Name	Price	Style
Wine Festival	Sun Corporation	€7,000.00	Abstract

Summary for 'Artist Name' = Lahr, David (1 detail record)

Sum €7,000.00

Artist Name Leriche, Martine

Painting Title	Buyer Name	Price	Style
Les Hommes	Prentiss, Allison	€7,000.00	Abstract
Les Fleurs	Deroches, Pierre	€6,000.00	Abstract

Summary for 'Artist Name' = Leriche, Martine (2 detail records)

Sum €13,000.00

Artist Name Scheilman, Doris

Painting Title	Buyer Name	Price	Style
Jewels in the Water	Schwartz, Martin	€9,000.00	Abstract

Summary for 'Artist Name' = Scheilman, Doris (1 detail record)

Sum €9,000.00

Artist Name Simpson, G.C.

Painting Title	Buyer Name	Price	Style
Heat Glaze	Sun Corporation	€6,000.00	Abstract

Summary for 'Artist Name' = Simpson, G.C. (1 detail record)

Sum €6,000.00

Artist Name Woods, Teri

Painting Title	Buyer Name	Price	Style
Thames at Dawn	Holm, Kevin	€6,000.00	Landscape
Horizons	Schwartz, Martin	€8,000.00	Landscape

Summary for 'Artist Name' = Woods, Teri (2 detail records)

Sum €14,000.00

Grand Total €49,000.00

Thursday, June 17, 1999

Page 1 of 1

Sales Information for Castaway Cruises

Castaway Cruises offers clients in the Chicago area a wide variety of cruise trip packages. As the Sales Manager of Castaway Cruises, you have decided to set up a database that contains information about all the cruises sold during March of 2001. You want to use the information in the database to print a report based on the results of three queries. You will **Create the Database, Queries, and Report**.

activity:

Create the Database, Queries, and Report

steps:

1. Create a database called **Castaway Cruises**, then double-click **Create table in Design view**
2. Type **Cruise Name**, press **[Tab]** three times, type **Date**, then enter the remaining field names, as shown in Figure P3-1
3. Designate the **Duration** field as a **Number** field, the **Cruise Cost** field as a **Currency** field, and the **Bookings** field as a **Number** field
4. Switch to Datasheet View, click **Yes** to save the table, enter **March Cruise Sales** as the table name, click **OK**, click **Yes** to create a primary key, enter the data for the table, as shown in Figure P3-1, then close the table

   Press [Ctrl]['] to enter duplicate information.
5. Using the Query Wizard, select all the fields from the **March Cruise Sales table**, call the query table **Cruises from $4,000**, modify the query design by entering **>=4000** in the **Cruise Cost Criteria cell**, run the Query, then close and save it

   Nine of the cruises cost $4,000 or more.
6. Using the Query Wizard, select all the fields in the **Cruises from $4,000** query, call the query **European Cruise Sales**, modify the query design by entering **European Odyssey** in the **Cruise Name Criteria cell**, type **Greek Isles** in the **or: cell** and **>10** in the **Bookings Criteria cell** on both rows, then run the query

   Note that three of the European cruises that cost $4,000 or more have bookings of more than 10.
   The greater than 10 entry must appear on both of the criteria rows (next to both "European Odyssey" and "Greek Isles").
7. Return to Design View, sort the Bookings field in **Ascending** order, run the query, then close and save the European Cruise Sales query table
8. Use the Report Wizard to create a report named **European Cruise Sales** from the European Cruise Sales query that appears similar to the report shown in Figure P3-2

   You will need to use Cruise Name as a grouping level, select Sum for the Bookings field, select the Stepped layout, Landscape orientation, the Corporate format, and adjust the layout in Design View. Note that you will need to center some of the headings and fields.
9. Print the report and close the database

   Your report is complete.

Time To
✓ Save
✓ Close
✓ Exit

FIGURE P3-1: **Field names and records for March Cruise Sales table**

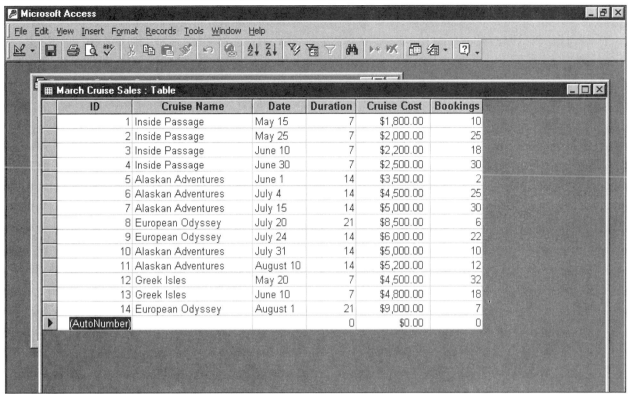

FIGURE P3-2: **Completed European Cruise Sales report**

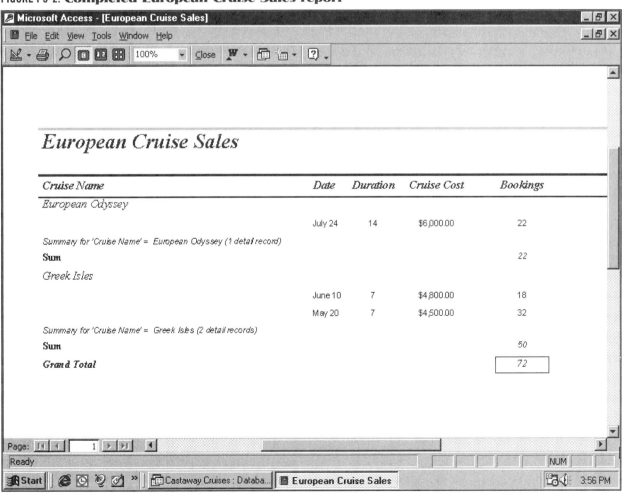

Independent Challenges

INDEPENDENT CHALLENGE 1

Create a report based on tables that contain information about 20 to 30 products stocked by a company of your choice. For example, you could create a report for a small company that sells classic videos or gourmet coffee. Follow the steps provided to create the database, create a Products table and a Suppliers table, make two or three queries, then create a report.

1. You need to know the name of your company and the type of products it sells. For example, you could call your company Waves and describe it as a retail operation that sells water sports equipment, such as surfboards, bathing suits, and inflatable water toys. Write the name of your company and a brief description of it in the box below:

Company name: ....

Description: ....

2. Create a database called [Company name] Inventory.
3. Create a Products table. Use the Table Wizard to create a Products table similar to the table you created for Project 1. Include at least six fields, including the UnitsInStock field. If necessary, rename some of the fields to match the type of data you plan to enter.
4. Create a Suppliers table. Use the Form Wizard to enter the data for a Suppliers table. Include at least four or five fields. Make sure that at least one of the fields in the Suppliers table is the same as a field in the Products table. Use the Copy and Paste commands to minimize typing time.
5. Create relationships between the two tables.
6. In the box below, write four queries you plan to make based on the Products and Suppliers tables. For example, you could ask which products are handled by a certain supplier, which products conform to a specific category, and which suppliers are located in a specific area. The queries you make will depend upon the type of data you included in your Products and Suppliers tables and the relationships you have created between the two tables.

Query 1: ....

Query 2: ....

Query 3: ....

Query 4: ....

7. Use the Query Wizard to create the queries. Make sure you specify the criteria for each query in Design View.
8. Select the query table that you will use to create your Inventory Report.
9. Use the Report Wizard to create your report. Experiment with the many features available in Report Design view. Remember that you will need to switch frequently between Report Design view and the Print Preview screen to check your progress.
10. Print the report then close the database.

INDEPENDENT CHALLENGE 2

Create an Event database that contains information about an event of your choice. For example, you could create tables that contain information about a concert or a conference that you are helping to organize. Plan and then create the database as follows:

1. Create a database called [Event Name]. For example, a database for a local computer users conference could be called "Seattle Computer Users Conference."

2. Open the Table Wizard and select the Events sample table.

3. Plan your database on paper:

   a. Write down the fields from the Events sample table that you plan to include in a table.

   b. Determine additional fields for a second table.

   c. List a few of the records you plan to include in the two tables.

   d. Determine two or three queries that you could make based on the data in the two tables.

   e. Identify the information that you would like to show in a report. For example, you could create a report that lists the total amount of money made at the event from three categories of people who attended (e.g., adults, seniors, and students). Spend a fair bit of time planning your Events database so that when you begin working in Access, you will know exactly what kinds of fields and records you need to enter in order to create the type of report you require.

4. Create the tables required for your database.

5. Establish relationships between the tables.

6. Make two or three queries based on the data in the two tables.

7. Create and print an attractively formatted report based on one of the query tables you created.

INDEPENDENT CHALLENGE 3

Create a database that contains information about all the sales made in the past month by a company of your choice. Suppose, for example, that you owned a pet store. You could create three tables related to sales: Pet Sales, Buyers, and Accessories. The Pet Sales table, for example, could look similar to the table shown in Figure IC-1.

Spend some time designing your Sales Information database, then create three tables, make two or three queries, and create a report based on one of the queries. Use your imagination and Access skills to create a database that you can use to produce an informative and useful report regarding some aspect of your product sales. Refer to the database you created for Castaway Cruises in Project 3 for ideas.

FIGURE IC-1: **Pet Sales table**

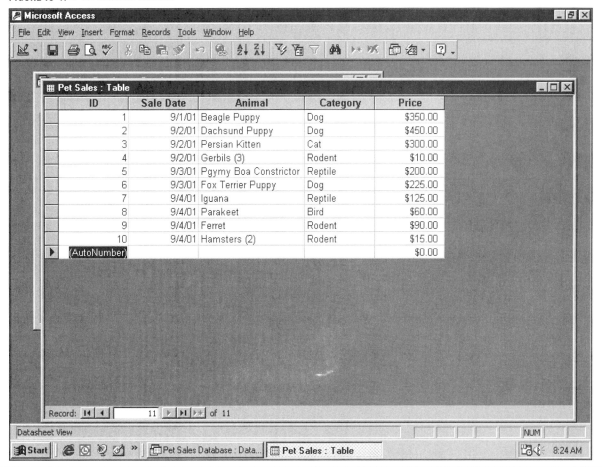

INDEPENDENT CHALLENGE 4

You are a freelance travel photographer with a large collection of slides and photographs that you want to sell to various travel magazines. To help you determine which magazines would be interested in your photographs, you've decided to create a database consisting of two tables: Picture File and Magazines. The Picture File table will contain data about your photographs, such as subject, location, and format, and the Magazines table will contain data related to the type of photographs purchased (e.g., preferred subjects, locations, and formats). Once you have completed the two tables, make three queries designed to help you choose which magazines may be interested in your photographs.

1. Create a database called Photography Database.
2. Enter the fields for the Picture File and Magazines tables in Design View and the data in Datasheet View, as shown in Figures IC-2 and IC-3. Make sure you click Yes when Access asks you to create a Primary Key so that you can create relationships between the two tables.
3. Fill in the boxes below with your answers to the following queries:
   Query 1: Which magazine(s) want monochrome photographs of mountains?
   (HINT: Insert all the fields from the Magazines table; enter "Monochrome" in the Format Criteria cell and "Mountains" in the Category Criteria cell.)
   Query 2: Which magazines want color slides?
   (HINT: Change the design of Query 1 so that "Color Slide" appears in the Format Criteria cell; delete "Mountains" in the Category Criteria cell.)
   Query 3: *Tips for Travelers* wants color slides of architecture in Italy. Which of your photos would *Tips for Travelers* want?
   (HINT: Run a query from the Picture File table called "Photographs for Tips for Travelers" that finds all the records containing the Country, Category, and Format requirements for *Tips for Travelers*. Save the query as "Photographs for Tips for Travelers".)
4. Create a report from the Photographs for Tips for Travelers query that lists the photographs you plan to send to *Tips for Travelers*. Format the report attractively, then print a copy.
5. Close the Photography database.

FIGURE IC-2: **Picture File table**

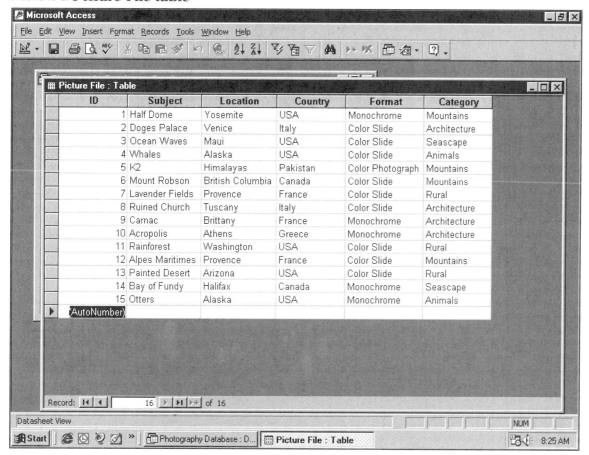

FIGURE IC-3: **Magazines table**

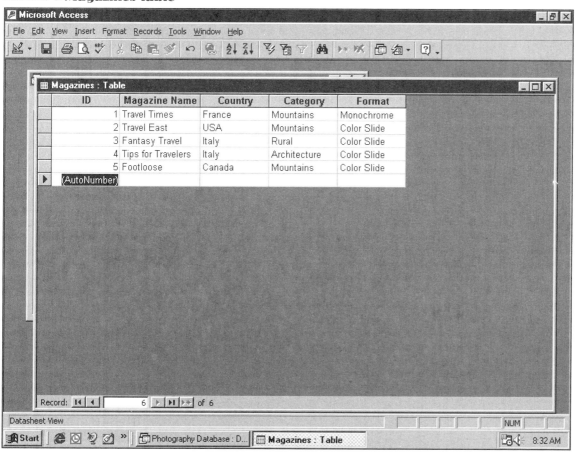

Visual Workshop

Create a database called Staff Travel using the table shown in Figure VW-1. Create a query to find all the staff members who spent more than $3,000 on travel and who traveled to either Europe or Asia, sort the Region field in the query in ascending order, then create a report that appears as shown in Figure VW-2. Use the Outline 1 and Soft Gray formats.

FIGURE VW-1: **Travel Expenses table**

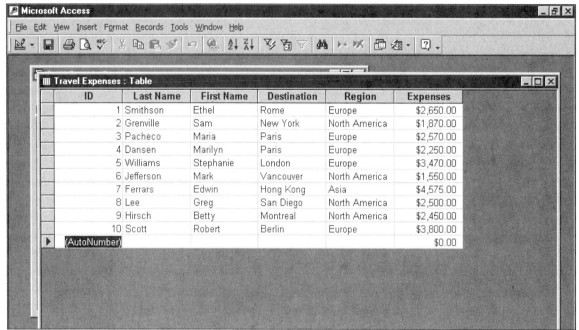

FIGURE VW-2: **Travel Expenses report**

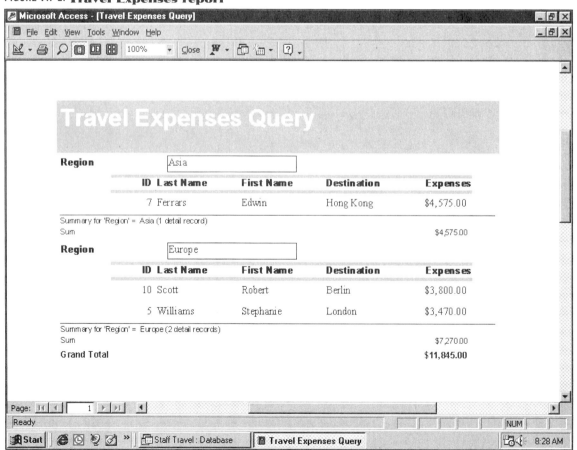

Microsoft
► Word, Excel, and Access
Projects

Task Streamlining

In This Unit You Will Create:

PROJECT 1 ► **Job Search Database**

PROJECT 2 ► **Company Profile**

PROJECT 3 ► **Video Catalogue**

In a typical day as the administrator of a business, you could send out form letters, create sales charts, identify new inventory to order, complete purchase orders, and produce a proposal to secure a new contract—all before lunch. To accomplish such a wide diversity of tasks quickly and easily, you need to use each program in the Office suite to maximum efficiency. You would start by building an extensive Access database that contains the names and addresses of all your customers and suppliers, information about your inventory, and sales records. You would then combine the information in this database with Word to produce mail-outs, labels, and catalogues and with Excel to produce charts and spreadsheets. You can also create data in Word and Excel that you then transfer to Access. In this unit you will create three databases in Access that provide you with the information you need to create business documents in both Word and Excel.

Job Search Database for Don Chan

Don Chan has just graduated from Detroit Community College with a certificate in business administration. He now wants to find a job in the Detroit area as an office manager, sales and marketing coordinator, or management trainee. To coordinate his job search efforts, Don will enter all the names and addresses of his employment contacts in an Access database, which he will then merge with a job application form letter he creates in Word. Finally, Don will analyze the results of his job search efforts by creating a chart in Excel. Three activities are required to complete Don's Job Search Database:

Project Activities

Set Up the Job Search Database

Don uses Access to create two related tables for his Job Search database. The First Contacts table contains the names and addresses of all the employers he has contacted. He will merge this table with the job application form letter he creates in Word. The Search Results table contains information about the responses Don received after sending out the form letters. Figure P1-1 shows the data in the First Contacts table. Don writes to Alice Danby to inquire about the marketing analyst position that he saw advertised in the May 2nd edition of the *Detroit Times*.

Create the Job Application Form Letter

Don switches to Word, creates the job application form letter as a main document, then merges the letter with the names and addresses in the First Contacts table he created in Access. He then prints the form letters. Figure P1-2 shows a portion of the form letter he will send to Ms. Danby, the personnel manager at First Fashions.

Analyze the Job Search Results

Don receives several positive responses to the form letters he sent. He decides to rate each job offer in terms of four criteria: Location, Pay, Benefits, and Advancement. He creates a Ratings table in Access, then switches to Excel, where he creates a pie chart based on the Ratings table. Figure P1-3 shows the Ratings table Don copies into Excel, and Figure P1-4 shows the pie chart he creates from columns B and H.

FIGURE P1-1: First Contacts table for the form letter

The data in the first record appears in the form letter

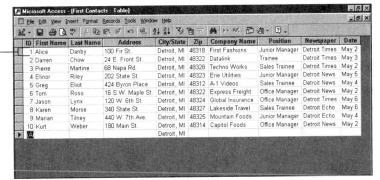

FIGURE P1-2: Form letter created in Word for Ms. Danby

Don Chan
2440 State Street, Detriot, MI 48311
e-mail: dchan@michigan.edu

[Current Date]

Alice Danby
100 Fir Street
Detroit, MI 48318

Dear Alice Danby:

I wish to apply for the position of Junior Manager that was advertised in the Detroit Times on May 2. The enclosed resume details my qualifications and experience.

FIGURE P1-3: Ratings table

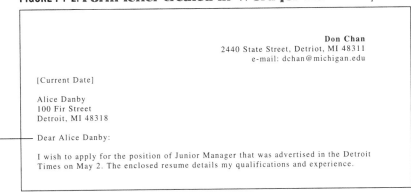

FIGURE P1-4: Pie chart created in Excel

The data in columns B and H appears in the pie chart

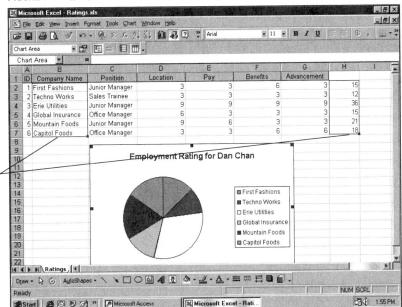

activity:

Set Up the Job Search Database

Don will create the First Contacts and Search Results tables from the data he has for ten employers. He will use the Table Wizard to create the First Contacts table, then create the Search Results table in Datasheet view.

steps:

1. Start Access, click the **Blank Access database option button**, click **OK**, save the database as **Job Search Database** on the disk where you plan to store all your files for this book, then double-click **Create table by using wizard**

2. Click **Contacts** in the Sample Tables list, click **ContactID**, click the **Select Single Field button** [>], click **Rename Field**, type **ID**, click **OK**, then select and rename the following fields for the table:

Sample Field	Rename	Field Name	Rename
FirstName	(Don't Rename)	CompanyName	(Don't Rename)
LastName	(Don't Rename)	Title	Position
Address	(Don't Rename)	Title	Newspaper
City	City/State	LastMeetingDate	Date
PostalCode	Zip		

3. Click **Next**, name the table **First Contacts**, click **Next**, click the **Modify the table design option button**, then click **Finish**

4. Click the **Data Type cell** for Zip, drag your mouse across **00000\-9999** in the current **Input Mask** to select it, press **Delete**, click the **Data Type list arrow** for Date, click **Text**, then delete the current input mask
You change the input mask for the Zip Code so that you can enter 5-digit zip codes. You change the input mask for the Date so that you can enter simple dates such as May 2 instead of 2/05/01.

5. Click the **Data Type** cell for City/State, click in the **Default Value box**, then type "Detroit, MI"
Make sure you include the quotation marks around Detroit, MI. Every company Don has contacted is located in Detroit. He saves time by making Detroit, MI the default value for every record.

Hint

Use [Ctrl]['] to enter duplicate information.

6. Click the **Datasheet view button** 🔲 on the standard toolbar, click **Yes**, then enter the records as shown in Figure P1-5

7. Close and save the **First Contacts** table, double-click **Create table in Design view**, enter the field names as shown in Figure P1-6, close and save the table as **Search Results**, then answer **Yes** to create a Primary Key

8. Double-click **First Contacts**, drag your mouse to select the **Company Name** and **Position** fields, click the **Copy button** 📋 on the Standard toolbar, close the **First Contacts** table, open the **Search Results** table, select the **Company Name** and **Position** fields, click the **Paste button** 📋 on the Standard toolbar, then click **Yes**

9. Enter the remaining data for the Search Results table as shown in Figure P1-7, then close and save the table

FIGURE P1-5: **Records for the First Contacts table**

Adjust column widths

Default value

FIGURE P1-6: **Field names for the Search Results table**

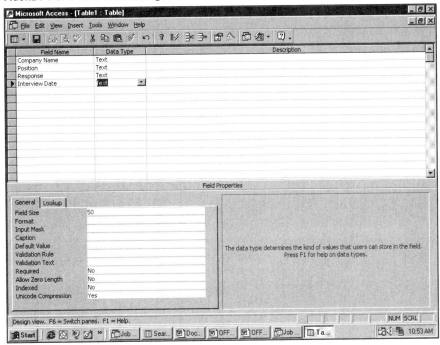

FIGURE P1-7: **Records for the Search Results table**

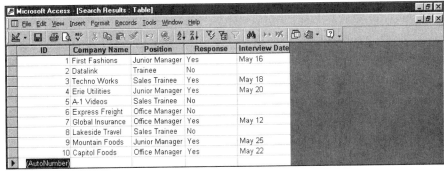

Clues to Use

Using Input Masks

An input mask ensures that the data you enter in a field will fit the format you define. For example, the input mask defined for a zip code requires that you enter only the digits required to make up a 5+4 U.S. zip code. You can change an input mask either by deleting it or by using the Input Mask Wizard to define a new input mask. For example, you may wish to enter a 5-digit zip code or a zip code for another country.

activity:

Create the Job Application Form Letter

steps:

1. Start Word, click **Tools** on the menu bar, click **Mail Merge**, then click **Create**

2. Click **Form Letters**, then click **Active Window**

3. Click **Get Data**, click **Open Data Source**, select the drive containing your files for this book (if necessary), click the **Files of type list arrow**, click **MS Access Databases**, click **Job Search Database**, click **Open**, then click **OK** to select the **First Contacts** table

4. Click **Edit Main Document**, double-click at the right margin, type and enhance the return address of Don Chan, as shown in Figure P1-8, press **[Enter]** three times, then click the **Align Left button** on the Formatting toolbar

5. Click **Insert** on the menu bar, click **Date and Time**, select the date format you prefer, click the **Update automatically check box** to select it, if necessary click **OK**, press **[Enter]** three times, then save the main document as **Job Search Form Letter**
By selecting the Update automatically check box, you ensure that the current date will appear every time you open the form letter.

6. Click **Insert Merge Field** on the Merge toolbar, click **FirstName**, press **[Spacebar]**, click **Insert Merge Field**, click **LastName**, then press **[Enter]**
The name fields are inserted in the letter. You use the same procedure to enter each field required for the form letter.

7. Enter all the fields and type the text for the form letter, as shown in Figure P1-8, then correct any spelling errors

8. Press **[Ctrl][A]** to select all the text, click the **Font Size list arrow** on the Formatting toolbar, click **12**, click the **Start Mail Merge button** Merge... on the Merge toolbar, then click **Merge**
When the merged letters appear, scroll through them to ensure that the records from the First Contacts table appear correctly.

Hint
You don't save merged documents because you can easily re-create them and because they take up unnecessary space on your hard drive or disk.

9. Click **File** on the menu bar, click **Print**, click the **Pages option button** in the Page Range field, type **1,2** and click **OK**, compare the printed pages to Figure P1-9, close the merged letters without saving them, then save and close the main document
Now that you have created the main document and linked it to the First Contacts table in the Job Search Database, you can run the merge at any time and print either all the merged letters or just a few of them, as required.

FIGURE P1-8: Return address, fields, and text for the form letter

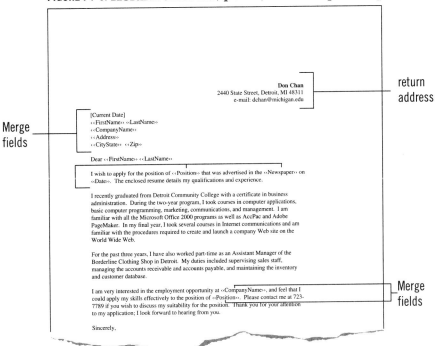

Merge fields

return address

Don Chan
2440 State Street, Detroit, MI 48311
e-mail: dchan@michigan.edu

[Current Date]
‹‹FirstName›› ‹‹LastName››
‹‹CompanyName››
‹‹Address››
‹‹CityState›› ‹‹Zip››

Dear ‹‹FirstName›› ‹‹LastName››

I wish to apply for the position of ‹‹Position›› that was advertised in the ‹‹Newspaper›› on ‹‹Date››. The enclosed resume details my qualifications and experience.

I recently graduated from Detroit Community College with a certificate in business administration. During the two-year program, I took courses in computer applications, basic computer programming, marketing, communications, and management. I am familiar with all the Microsoft Office 2000 programs as well as AccPac and Adobe PageMaker. In my final year, I took several courses in Internet communications and am familiar with the procedures required to create and launch a company Web site on the World Wide Web.

For the past three years, I have also worked part-time as an Assistant Manager of the Borderline Clothing Shop in Detroit. My duties included supervising sales staff, managing the accounts receivable and accounts payable, and maintaining the inventory and customer database.

I am very interested in the employment opportunity at ‹‹CompanyName››, and feel that I could apply my skills effectively to the position of ‹‹Position››. Please contact me at 723-7789 if you wish to discuss my suitability for the position. Thank you for your attention to my application; I look forward to hearing from you.

Merge fields

Sincerely,

FIGURE P1-9: Two merged letters

Don Chan
2440 State Street, Detroit, MI 48311
e-mail: dchan@michigan.edu

[Current Date]

Alice Danby
First Fashions
100 Fir Street
Detroit, MI 48318

DearAlice Danby

I wish to apply for the position of Junior Manager that was advertised in the Detroit Times on May 2. The enclosed resume details my qualifications and experience.

I recently graduated from Detroit Community College with a certificate in business administration. During the two-year program, I took courses in computer applications, basic computer programming, marketing, communications, and management. I am familiar with all the Microsoft Office 2000 programs as well as AccPac and Adobe PageMaker. In my final year, I took several courses in Internet communications and am familiar with the procedures required to create and launch a company Web site on the World Wide Web.

For the past three years, I have also worked part-time as an Assistant Manager of the Borderline Clothing Shop in Detroit. My duties included supervising sales staff, managing the accounts receivable and accounts payable, and maintaining the inventory and customer database.

I am very interested in the employment opportunity at First Fashions, and feel that I could apply my skills effectively to the position of Junior Manager. Please contact me at 723-7789 if you wish to discuss my suitability for the position. Thank you for your attention to my application; I look forward to hearing from you.

Sincerely,

Don Chan

Don Chan
2440 State Street, Detroit, MI 48311
e-mail: dchan@michigan.edu

[Current Date]

Darren Chow
Datalink
24 E. Front St.
Detroit, MI 48322

Dear Darren Chow

I wish to apply for the position of Trainee that was advertised in the Detroit Times on May 3. The enclosed resume details my qualifications and experience.

I recently graduated from Detroit Community College with a certificate in business administration. During the two-year program, I took courses in computer applications, basic computer programming, marketing, communications, and management. I am familiar with all the Microsoft Office 2000 programs as well as AccPac and Adobe PageMaker. In my final year, I took several courses in Internet communications and am familiar with the procedures required to create and launch a company Web site on the World Wide Web.

For the past three years, I have also worked part-time as an Assistant Manager of the Borderline Clothing Shop in Detroit. My duties included supervising sales staff, managing the accounts receivable and accounts payable, and maintaining the inventory and customer database.

I am very interested in the employment opportunity at Datalink, and feel that I could apply my skills effectively to the position of Trainee. Please contact me at 723-7789 if you wish to discuss my suitability for the position. Thank you for your attention to my application; I look forward to hearing from you.

Sincerely,

Don Chan

PROJECT 1

JOB SEARCH DATABASE FOR DON CHAN

activity:

Analyze the Job Search Results

All of the companies that interviewed Don have offered him employment. Now he needs to decide which company to accept. To help himself make a wise decision, Don will create a query table that lists only those companies that interviewed him, then add several new fields that will rank each company in terms of its location, pay, benefits, and opportunities for advancement. Don decides on a rating scale as follows: 3 = Poor; 6 = Good; 9 = Excellent. Once he has completed the table, he will switch to Excel and create a chart that graphically illustrates his overall ranking for each company.

steps:

1. Return to the Job Search Database window, click **Queries**, double-click **Create query by using wizard**, click the **Tables/Queries list arrow**, click **Table: Search Results**, select the **Company Name**, **Position**, and **Response** fields, click **Next**, type **Positive Results** as the query table title, click the **Modify the query design option button**, then click **Finish**

2. Click the **Response Criteria cell**, type **Yes**, then click the **Run button** ! on the toolbar
   All six of the companies that responded positively to Don's form letter appear.

3. Select the **Company Name** and **Position** fields, click the **Copy button** on the Standard toolbar, click the **Close button**, click **Yes** to save changes, click **Tables**, double-click **Create table by entering data**, select **Field1** and **Field2**, click the **Paste button** on the Standard toolbar, then click **Yes** to paste the records

4. Double-click the **Field1** label, type **Company Name**, double-click the **Field2** label, type **Position**, increase the column widths, then enter the labels and records for Fields 3 to 6, as shown in Figure P1-10

5. Click the **Close button**, click **Yes**, save as **Ratings**, click **Yes** to create a Primary Key, click **Ratings**, click the **OfficeLinks list arrow** on the Standard toolbar, then click **Analyze It with MS Excel**
   In a few moments the table appears in Excel.

6. Select cells **D2** to **H7**, click the **AutoSum button** Σ on the Standard toolbar, then click away from the selected cells

7. Click the **Chart Wizard button** on the Standard toolbar, click **Pie**, click **Next**, click the **Collapse Dialog button**, select cells **B2** to **B7**, type a comma (**,**), select cells **H2** to **H7**, click the **Restore Dialog button**, click **Next**, click in the Chart Title text box, type **Employment Rating for Don Chan** as the chart title, click **Next**, then click **Finish**

8. Increase the size of the pie chart so that all the data is clearly visible, as shown in Figure P1-11

9. Print a copy of the worksheet, save and close the worksheet, then close the database
   Don can see at a glance that the job offered by Erie Utilities most closely matches his employment criteria.

Trouble
If you get a message telling you that the worksheet was created in a previous version of Excel, click Yes to save it in the updated format.

FIGURE P1-10: **Records for Ratings table**

New field names and data

Copied records

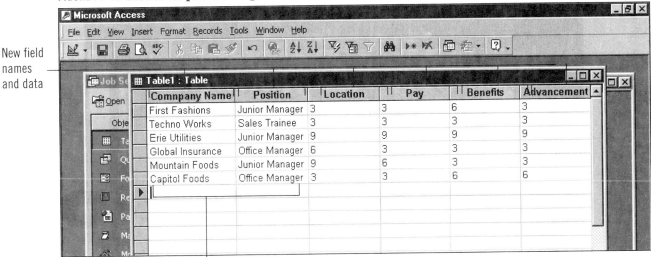

FIGURE P1-11: **Completed pie chart in Excel**

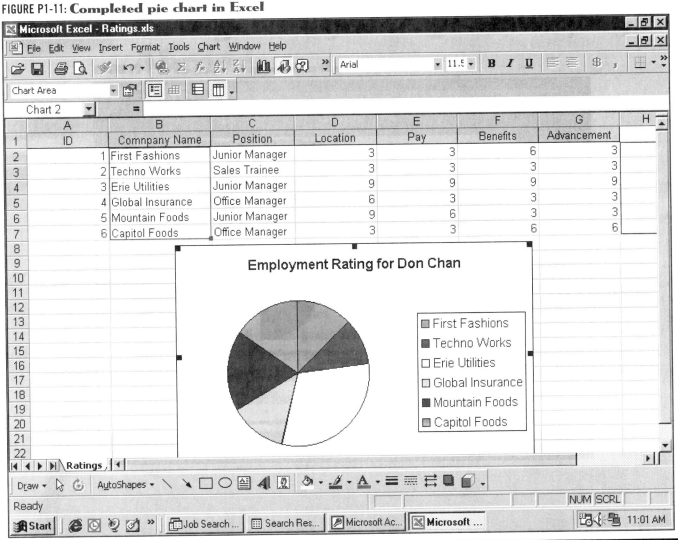

OVERVIEW

Company Profile for Arcadia Designs

As the owner of a small desktop-publishing and Web site design company in Honolulu, Hawaii, you've decided to upgrade your computer system, move into an office, and hire an assistant. Marilyn Wood, one of your clients, is so pleased with your work that she is thinking of lending you $20,000 to finance your expansion. To help her make her decision, she has asked you to put together a two-page profile of your company that includes information about your recent jobs and a pie chart that illustrates the most popular—and profitable—services you offer. You will **Create the Arcadia Designs Database, Create a Pie Chart in Excel,** and then **Create a Company Profile in Word.**

activity:

Create the Arcadia Designs Database

You will create a database that contains information about the contracts completed by Arcadia Designs in September 2001, then you will create a query table that lists all the contracts to design Web sites.

steps:

1. Create a database in Access called **Arcadia Designs Database,** then double-click **Create table in Design view**

2. As shown in Figure P2-1, enter the field names for the table, then change the Data Type for the Date field to **Date/Time** and the Data Type for the Total Cost field to **Currency**

3. Switch to **Datasheet view,** save the table as **September Contracts,** answer **Yes** to create a Primary Key, then enter the records for the September Contracts table, as shown in Figure P2-2

4. Click the **September Contracts table Close** button, click **Yes,** if necessary, click **Queries,** double-click **Create query by using wizard,** select all the fields for the query, click **Next,** click **Next** again, type **Web Site Contracts** as the query title, click the **Modify the query design option button,** then click **Finish**

5. Click the **Job Category Criteria** cell, type **Web site,** then click the **Run button** !

   Seven of the 15 contracts you completed in September involved the designing of Web sites.

6. Click the **Web Site Contracts query Close** button, click **Yes** to save it, click the **OfficeLinks list arrow** 🏭▾ on the Standard toolbar, then click **Analyze It with MS Excel**

7. Click cell **E9,** double-click the **AutoSum button** Σ on the Standard toolbar, press **[Enter],** click cell **D9,** then type **Total Earnings**

8. Format the worksheet so that it appears as shown in Figure P2-3, then save the worksheet

Hint

If a message appears asking you to update the version of the Excel workbook, click Yes.

FIGURE P2-1: Fields and data types for the September Contracts table

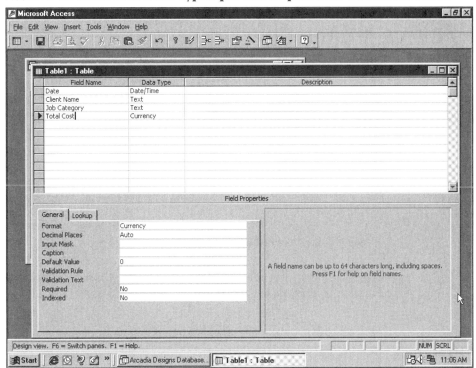

FIGURE P2-2: Records for the September Contracts table

The year that appears in your database may be different

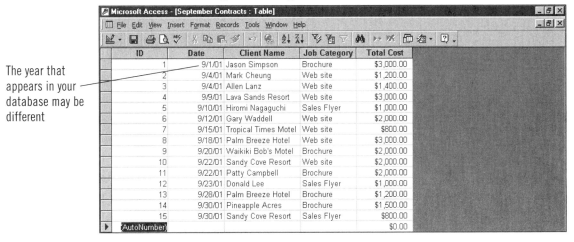

FIGURE P2-3: Completed Web site Contracts worksheet in Excel

Adjust the width of column A

Bold column labels

Center cells D2 to D8

Add borders

Right-align cell D9

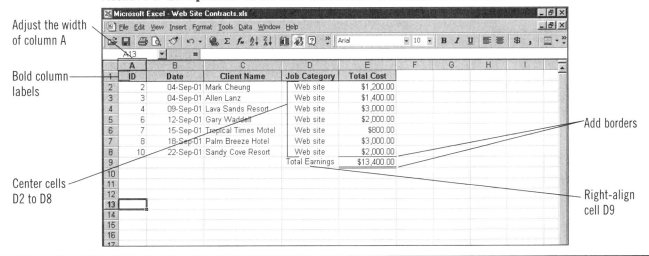

activity:

Create a Cone Chart in Excel

You want to include a cone chart that displays the breakdown of earnings in terms of job category. You will create this chart in Excel from the data entered in the September Contracts table. To simplify the task of creating the cone chart, you will first display the September Contracts table, then sort the Job Category records in alphabetical order. You will then use the Subtotal function to create the cone chart in Excel that shows the total earnings for each job category.

steps:

1. In Access, click **Tables**, double-click **September Contracts** to open it, click **Job Category**, then click the **Sort Ascending button** ⬇ on the Standard toolbar

2. Click the **September Contracts table Close button**, click **Yes**, then click the **Office Links button** 📄
   The September Contracts table appears in a new worksheet in Excel.

3. Select cells **A1** to **E16**, click **Data** on the menu bar, then click **Subtotals**
   The Subtotal dialog box appears. You need to specify that you want the subtotals to appear after each series of jobs.

4. Click the **At Each Change in List arrow**, click **Job Category**, then click the down arrow in the **Add Subtotal box**, make sure **Total Cost** is selected, as shown in Figure P2-4, then click **OK**
   The total revenue from each of the three job categories now appears in your worksheet. For example, you made a total of $9,700.00 on developing brochures in September.

5. Click away from the selected cells to deselect them, click the **Chart Wizard button** 📊 on the Standard toolbar, scroll down the list of chart types, click **Cone**, click **Next**, click the **Collapse Dialog button** 📉

6. Press and hold the [Ctrl] key, click cells **E7**, **E11**, and **E19**, click the **Restore Dialog button** 📇, click the **Series tab**, then click the Category (X) axis labels text box, click the **Collapse Dialog button** 📉, use [Ctrl] to click **D6**, **D10**, and **D18**, then click the **Restore Dialog button** 📇

7. Click **Next**, click the **Chart title box**, type **Breakdown of Earnings by Job Category** as the chart title, then click **Finish** move the chart down so that it begins in cell **A31**, then drag the lower-right corner to cell **E50**

8. Click **Series1** to select it, press **[Delete]**, right-click anywhere on the gray walls of the chart, click **Format Walls**, click **Fill Effects**, click the **Texture tab**, select the **Recycled Paper** texture, as shown in Figure P2-5, click **OK**, then click **OK**
   Your chart appears as shown in Figure P2-6.

9. Click away from the chart to deselect it, then click the **Save button** 💾 on the Standard toolbar

FIGURE P2-4: Subtotal dialog box

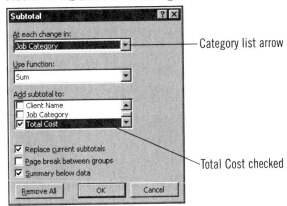

— Category list arrow

— Total Cost checked

FIGURE P2-5: Recycled paper texture selected

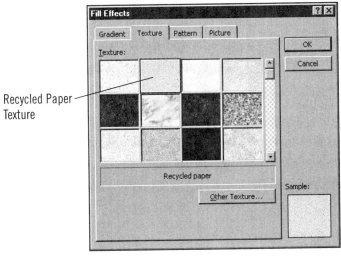

Recycled Paper
Texture

FIGURE P2-6: Completed cone chart in Excel

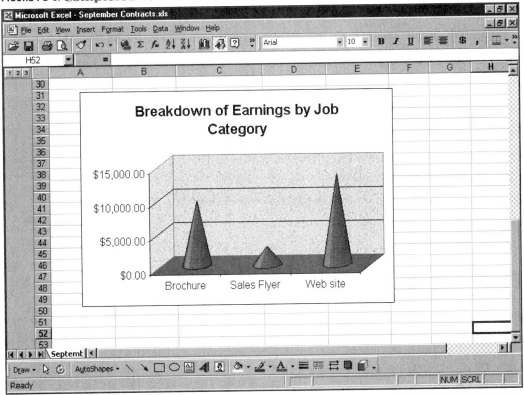

COMPANY PROFILE FOR ARCADIA DESIGNS

activity:

Create a Company Profile in Word

The company profile consists of two pages, as shown in Figure P2-7. You will first create the heading and type the text, and then you will paste the September Contracts table from Access and the cone chart from Excel as links.

Hint

Press [Ctrl][Enter] to insert a hard page break where indicated.

steps:

1. Open a new Word document, type and enhance just the text, as shown in Figure P2-7, paste the total as a link from Excel (**Edit, Paste Special, Paste Link (Unformatted Text)**), then save the document as **Arcadia Designs Company Profile**

   Make sure you press [Enter] three times between the paragraphs where the data from Access and Excel will be pasted.

2. In Access click **Tables**, click **September Contracts**, click the **OfficeLinks list arrow**  on the Standard toolbar, then click **Publish It with MS Word**

3. When the table appears in Word, click **Table** on the menu bar, point to **Select**, click **Table**, press **[Ctrl][C]**, click **Window** on the menu bar, click **Arcadia Designs Company Profile**, click in the **Service Overview** paragraph mark below the second paragraph, then press **[Ctrl][V]**

   The September Contracts table appears in Word. Note that you use the Publish It option when you do not plan to update the table in Access. When you want any changes you made in the Access table to also appear in the table published in Word, you use the Copy, Paste Special, and Paste Link commands.

4. Click the **Table Select button** ⊕ outside the top-left corner of the table, click **Table** on the menu bar, click **Table AutoFormat**, select the **Columns 5** format, click **OK**, then click the **Center button** ▤ on the Formatting toolbar

5. Click the **cone chart** in Excel, click the **Copy button** ▤ on the Standard toolbar, click after the **Service Breakdown** paragraph in the Arcadia Designs Company Profile document, click **Edit** on the menu bar, click **Paste Special**, click **Paste Link**, then click **OK**

Hint

If a floating clipboard appears on your screen, click its Close button.

6. Copy cells **A1** to **E9** from the Web Site Contracts workbook, then paste them as a formatted text link into the Arcadia Designs Company Profile document, as shown in Figure P2-7

7. Use your mouse to center the cone chart between the left and right margins, click ⊕ on the Excel table, then click ▤

   Refer to Figure P2-7 as you work to complete the profile.

8. Click the **View list arrow** on the Standard toolbar, click **Two Pages**, click the **Insert Clip Art button** ▨ on the Drawing toolbar, click **Clips Online**, click **OK** when the Online Clip Gallery appears, click in the **Search box**, type **Tropics**, press **[Enter]**, then insert and size the picture of your choice

   The picture will not appear in the correct location.

9. Right-click the image, click **Format Picture**, click the **Layout tab**, click **Tight**, click **Right**, click **OK**, print a copy of the document, then save and close all files

FIGURE P2-7: Completed Company Profile for Arcadia Designs

36 pt

18 pt

Heading 3 style

Company Profile

Arcadia Designs

Heading 3 style

Description

Arcadia Designs provides desktop publishing and Web site design services to small business owners in the Honolulu area. At present, few other design services in the Honolulu area offer a comprehensive Web site design service. Arcadia Design focuses primarily on providing its clients with an attractive and cost-effective presence on the World Wide Web. In addition, Arcadia Designs assists its clients in setting up effective e-commerce sites that attract and keep customers worldwide.

Body text is 12pt

Service Overview

The table displayed below lists all the contracts performed by Arcadia Designs in September of 2001.

ID	Date	Client Name	Job Category	Total Cost
1	9/1/01	Jason Simpson	Brochure	$3,000.00
2	9/4/01	Mark Cheung	Web site	$1,200.00
3	9/4/01	Allen Lanz	Web site	$1,400.00
4	9/9/01	Lava Sands Resort	Web site	$3,000.00
5	9/10/01	Hiromi Nagaguchi	Sales Flyer	$1,000.00
6	9/12/01	Gary Waddell	Web site	$2,000.00
7	9/15/01	Tropical Times Motel	Web site	$800.00
8	9/18/01	Palm Breeze Hotel	Web site	$3,000.00
9	9/20/01	Waikiki Bob's Motel	Brochure	$2,000.00
10	9/22/01	Sandy Cove Resort	Web site	$2,000.00
11	9/22/01	Patty Campbell	Brochure	$2,000.00
12	9/23/01	Donald Lee	Sales Flyer	$1,000.00
13	9/28/01	Palm Breeze Hotel	Brochure	$1,200.00
14	9/30/01	Pineapple Acres	Brochure	$1,500.00
15	9/30/01	Sandy Cove Resort	Sales Flyer	$800.00

On average, Arcadia Designs completes two contracts a week. In September, Arcadia Designs received orders for an additional seven contracts. At present, its owner completes all the contracts accepted by Arcadia Designs. In order to accept new contracts, Arcadia Designs will need to hire new personnel to assist the owner.

{PAGE }

Insert page break here

Heading 3 style

Service Breakdown

The cone chart below shows the breakdown of contracts in terms of the income generated in September of 2001. The Web Sites cone represents 52% of this income.

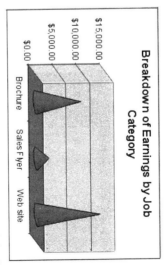

Breakdown of Earnings by Job Category

$15,000.00
$10,000.00
$5,000.00
$0.00

Brochure   Sales Flyer   Web site

Since January of 2001, the Web site design has become the number one priority of Arcadia Designs. The table below lists all the clients who required Web sites in September 2001. A total income of $13,400 was earned from designed Web sites.

ID	Date	Client Name	Job Category	Total Cost
2	04-Sep-01	Mark Cheung	Web site	$1,200.00
3	04-Sep-01	Allen Lanz	Web site	$1,400.00
4	09-Sep-01	Lava Sands Resort	Web site	$3,000.00
6	12-Sep-01	Gary Waddell	Web site	$2,000.00
7	15-Sep-01	Tropical Times Motel	Web site	$800.00
8	18-Sep-01	Palm Breeze Hotel	Web site	$3,000.00
10	22-Sep-01	Sandy Cove Resort	Web site	$2,000.00
			Total Earnings	$13,400.00

Arcadia Designs has outgrown its home-based operation. In January 2002, Arcadia Designs will move to a commercial office space and hire two Web site designers.

{PAGE }

Copy from cell E9 of the Excel workbook "Web Site Contracts" and paste as a link (unformatted text)

Video Catalogue for Home Library

Stacks of videos containing all the movies and documentary programs you have taped over the past six months surround your television set. You have decided that you need to organize these videos into a database that you can then use to produce labels for the videotape spines and create a chart showing the breakdown of videos by category. First, you will **Create the Video Database**, then you will **Create the Labels and Chart**.

activity:

Create the Video Database

You will create the video database in Access.

steps:

1. Create a new database called **Personal Video Library**, then create a table called **Video List** that includes a Primary Key and contains the field names and records as shown in Figure P3-1, then close the table

2. Click **Queries**, double-click **Create query by using wizard**, select the **Video Title** and **Length** fields, click **Next**, name the query **Videotape Labels**, then click **Finish**

3. Click the **View list arrow** , click **Design View**, click the **Video Title Sort cell**, then select **Ascending**

4. Click the **Run button** on the Standard toolbar, then close and save the query

5. Double-click **Create query by using wizard**, click the **Tables/Queries list arrow**, click **Table: Video List**, insert all the fields into the table, click **Next**, name the query **Literary Videos**, click the **Modify the query design option button**, then click **Finish**

6. Complete the design grid so that it appears as shown in Figure P3-2, then click the **Run Button**
   Now you know which videos conform to your favorite genres—drama, movie, or literary. Your screen appears as shown in Figure P3-3.

7. Close and save the query

FIGURE P3-1: Fields and records for the Video List table

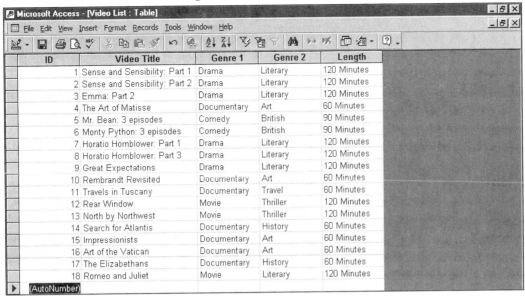

FIGURE P3-2: Design view for Literary Videos query

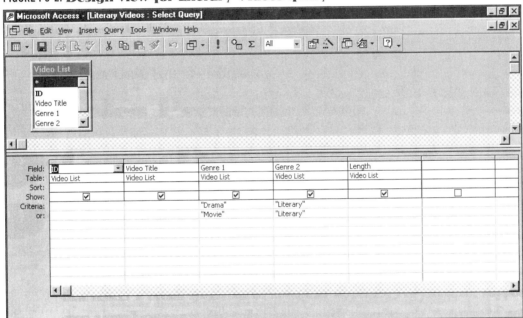

FIGURE P3-3: Completed query table

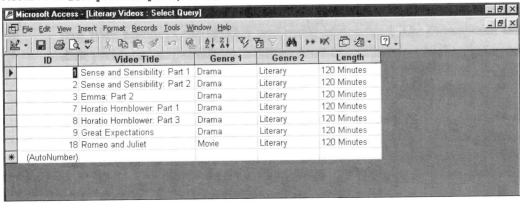

activity:

Create Labels and Chart

You will merge the records in the Videotape Labels query table with Word to create a sheet of videotape labels, then you will display the Video List table in Excel so that you can create a chart that shows the breakdown of videos by genre.

steps:

1. Click Video Tape Labels on the Queries tab, click the OfficeLinks list arrow 🖼️ on the toolbar, click Merge It with MS Word, click the Create a new document and then link the data to it option button, then click OK

2. Maximize the Word window, click Tools on the menu bar, click Mail Merge, click Create, click Mailing Labels, click Change Document Type, then click Setup

The Labels Options dialog box appears.

3. Select 5199-S - Video Spine in the Product number list, then click OK

The Create Labels dialog box appears.

4. Click Insert Merge Field, click Video_ Title, press [Enter], click Insert Merge Field, then click Length

5. Triple-click the Video Title field to select it, right-click, click Font, select the Arial font, Bold Italic, and 16 pt, then click OK

6. Click OK to close the Create Labels dialog box, click Merge, then click Merge again

In a few seconds a sheet of videotape labels appears. Figure P3-4 shows several of the labels that appear on your screen after you have completed the merge.

7. Print a copy of the videotape labels on plain paper, close the document without saving, save the label main document as Videotape Labels, then exit Word

8. In Access, sort the Genre 1 records in the Video List table in ascending order, close and save the table, analyze the table with Excel, select cells A1 through E19, click Data on the menu bar, click Subtotals, click the At each change in list arrow, click Genre1, and make sure Genre 1 is selected under Add subtotal to list arrow

9. Create a Doughnut chart that displays the breakdown of genres, as shown in Figure P3-5, save and print the worksheet, then close all files and exit all programs

Note that the data for the Doughnut chart appears in cells C4, C12, C19, and C3. You can select the category labels from the appropriate cells in the Subtotals list (for example: C3, C11, C18, and C23).

FIGURE P3-4: First six video labels in Word

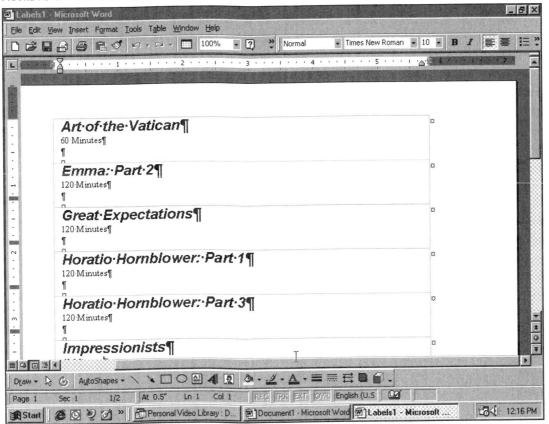

FIGURE P3-5: Video data and doughnut chart in Excel

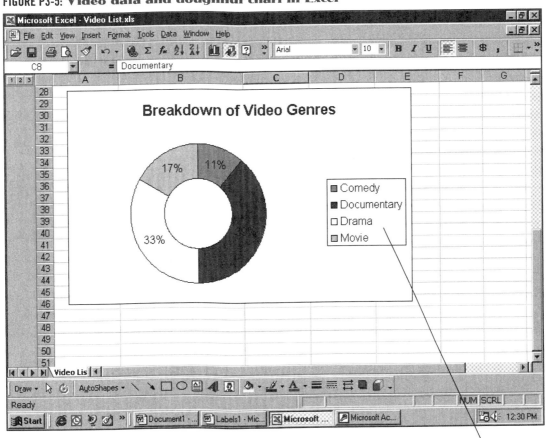

Legend displayed

Independent Challenges

INDEPENDENT CHALLENGE 1

Create a Job Search database similar to the database you created for Project 1 to track your own job search efforts. Even if you are not currently seeking employment, create a "practice" database and accompanying form letter for your dream job. You can then modify these files when you are ready to seek employment. Follow the steps provided to create the database, merge it with a form letter you create in Word, and then create a chart in Excel that graphically displays your ratings of the companies that responded positively to your form letter.

1. Your first task is to determine the type of job position you are seeking and the type of company or organization you would like to work for. For example, you could seek a job as an office manager at real estate or architectural companies. In the box below, write the job position you are seeking and the types of companies you would like to work for.

   Job Position: ....
   Companies: ....

2. You need at least ten employers for your job search database. Look through the employment advertisements in your local paper to find potential employers, or, if you can't find advertisements for the specific job you require, look through the Yellow Pages to find the names and addresses of at least ten companies that you think you would like to work for and that may be interested in an applicant with your qualifications. Try to include as many realistic records in your job search database as possible.
3. Create a database called "My Job Search Database".
4. Create a Contacts table. Use the Table Wizard to create a table similar to the First Contacts table you created for Project 1. Include at least eight fields, including the position you wish to apply for and the name and date of the newspaper advertising the position (if appropriate). Make sure you answer "Yes" to create the primary key.
5. Switch to Word and set up an application form letter. Use the form letter you created in Project 1 to help you determine the information to include. Make sure you fully describe your qualifications and experience. Select the records in the Contacts table as the data source for the form letter, and include the appropriate fields.
6. Merge the data source with the form letter, then print two or three of the letters.
7. Switch back to Access and create a Response table similar to the Search Results table you created in Project 1. Enter positive responses for at least five of the employers.
8. Create a query that lists only the companies that responded positively to your form letter.
9. Copy the Company Name and Position records from the query to a new table called Ratings Table, then enter your ratings for each company in terms of four criteria: Location, Pay, Benefits, and Advancement.
10. Analyze the Ratings table in Excel, then create a pie chart that shows the breakdown of companies according to your ratings. Remember that you will need to add the ratings for each company, and then use the Chart Wizard to create a pie chart that includes only the company names and the total ratings.
11. Print the Excel chart then close all the files and applications.

INDEPENDENT CHALLENGE 2

Create a two-page company profile for a company of your choice. For example, you could create a company profile for a small computer store or a bookkeeping business that you run from your own home. Follow the steps provided to create the data for your company profile and then publish it in Word, along with a chart you create in Excel.

1. Create a database called "[Company Name] Profile" that contains information about all the sales made in the past month by your company. Create a table called "[Month] Sales" (for example, December Sales). Assign a category to each sale. For example, the categories for items sold in a computer store could be PCs, Laptops, Accessories, and Software. For ideas, refer to the September Contracts table you created in Project 2 for Arcadia Designs. Make sure you also include the price of each item. Answer "Yes" to create the primary key.
2. Determine the most popular category of items sold, then create a query table that lists all the sales of items in that category.
3. Analyze the query table in Excel to determine the total amount of sales in the most popular category. Format the Excel worksheet attractively for inclusion in the company profile.
4. Analyze the [Month] Sales table in Excel. Create a cone chart that shows the total sales of items in each category. Refer to the cone chart you created in Project 2 for ideas.
5. Switch to Word, create an attractive heading (use WordArt and insert a picture from the Online Clip Gallery, if you wish), then write text for your company profile similar to the text included in the company profile in Project 2.
6. Publish the [Month] Sales table in the Word summary, then copy the cone chart and worksheet from Excel and paste them as links into the Word summary.
7. Save the Word summary as "[Company Name] Profile".
8. Format your company profile attractively, then print a copy.

INDEPENDENT CHALLENGE 3

Create a database that contains information about your personal collection of CDs, records, tapes, videos, photographs, or a collection of your choice. Plan and create the database as follows:

1. Create a database called "My Collection of [Items]". For example, a database for a vintage comic book collection could be called "My Collection of Vintage Comic Books".
2. Set up a table for your list. Include fields that will differentiate the various records in terms of genre, category, or type, as appropriate. If your table lists all your CDs, for example, you could include fields for Music Genre, Artist, and even Price.
3. Switch to Word and create labels for each item in your collection. Look through the list of labels available in the Labels Options dialog box. You will probably find a label appropriate for the items in your collection. Print your labels.
4. Select the Access table as the data source to merge with your labels, enter the appropriate fields in the label, then run the merge and print a sheet of labels.
5. Switch back to Access, sort one of the genres in the table alphabetically, then analyze it in Excel and create a chart that shows the breakdown of items by genre. Print the Excel chart and worksheet.

INDEPENDENT CHALLENGE 4

You own a small software company that creates imaginative computer games for children and adults. You've decided to analyze the types of customers who have bought your games in the past month in terms of age, occupation, and geographical location. Follow the instructions provided to create a table in Access, analyze it in Excel, publish it in Word, and then update the table in Access so that the data is also updated in Word and Excel.

1. Create a database called "Software Quest Customer Database". Double-click Create a table in Design view, list the fields (except the ID field) as shown in Figure IC-1, save the table as Customer List, answer "Yes" to create a Primary Key, then enter the records as shown in Figure IC-1.
2. Sort the Occupation records in ascending order.
3. Analyze the Customer List with Excel, then create a cylinder chart that shows the breakdown of customers by occupation. You will need to create a Subtotals list to count the number of records in each category in order to create the cylinder chart. Remove the legend from the chart and fill the chart walls with the Bouquet texture. Refer to the chart included in the complete profile, as shown in Figure IC-2.
4. Switch to Word, enter the text as shown in Figure IC-2, then apply similar formatting.
5. Save the document as "Software Quest Customer Analysis".
6. Open the Customer List table in Access, reduce column widths so that the table appears as shown in Figure IC-2.
7. Close and save the table.
8. Click the Copy button, switch to Word, then click below the first paragraph of text.
9. Click Edit, Paste Special, Paste Link (Formatted Text (RTF)), then click OK.
10. Switch to Excel, then copy the cylinder chart and paste it as a link into Word.
11. Add a picture from the Online Clip Gallery to the document, as shown in Figure IC-2. Make sure you format the layout as Tight and Right.
12. Format the pages attractively in Word, print a copy, then save and close all files.

FIGURE IC-1: **Customer List table**

ID	Last Name	First Name	Age	Occupation	State or Province	Product
1	Callaghan	Jake	12	Child	Michigan	Galaxy
2	Leland	Sheila	40	Teacher	Ontario	Knights Alive
3	Hunt	Gary	11	Child	California	Galaxy
4	Gill	Parminder	36	Consultant	California	Voyage to Jupiter
5	Marsh	Angus	22	Student	British Columbia	Galaxy
6	Leigh	Donald	18	Student	British Columbia	Galaxy
7	Van Halen	Richard	12	Child	California	Jungle Jazz
8	Flynn	Catherine	13	Child	New York	Jungle Jazz
9	Leblanc	Michelle	12	Child	New York	Galaxy
10	Powell	William	44	Teacher	California	Voyage to Jupiter
11	Louie	Cheryl	37	Teacher	Washington	Voyage to Jupiter
12	McDowell	Carol	22	Student	Washington	Galaxy
13	Schmidt	Doris	45	Teacher	California	Knights Alive
14	Amin	Zahra	12	Child	California	Galaxy
15	Mah	Betsy	11	Child	British Columbia	Galaxy

FIGURE IC-2: **Completed Customer Analysis**

Software Quest

We have analyzed the types of customers who have bought our computer games during the month of July 2001 in terms of age, occupation, and geographical location. The following table shows the breakdown of customers for July 2001:

ID	Last Name	First Name	Age	Occupation	State or Province	Product
9	Leblanc	Michelle	12	Child	New York	Galaxy
8	Flynn	Catherine	13	Child	New York	Jungle Jazz
7	Van Halen	Richard	12	Child	California	Jungle Jazz
3	Hunt	Gary	11	Child	California	Galaxy
1	Callaghan	Jake	12	Child	Michigan	Galaxy
15	Mah	Betsy	11	Child	British Columbia	Galaxy
14	Amin	Zahra	12	Child	California	Galaxy
4	Gill	Parminder	36	Consultant	California	Voyage to Jupiter
12	McDowell	Carol	22	Student	Washington	Galaxy
6	Leigh	Donald	18	Student	British Columbia	Galaxy
5	Marsh	Angus	22	Student	British Columbia	Galaxy
13	Schmidt	Doris	45	Teacher	California	Knights Alive
11	Louie	Cheryl	37	Teacher	Washington	Voyage to Jupiter
10	Powell	William	44	Teacher	California	Voyage to Jupiter
2	Leland	Sheila	40	Teacher	Ontario	Knights Alive

As shown in the cylinder chart illustrated below, our single biggest occupation group is children under the age of 16. To continue serving this ever-growing market, Software Quest plans to develop a marketing strategy in consultation with contacts at the local school boards. This plan will also bring us into more intensive contact with our second largest occupation group—teachers.

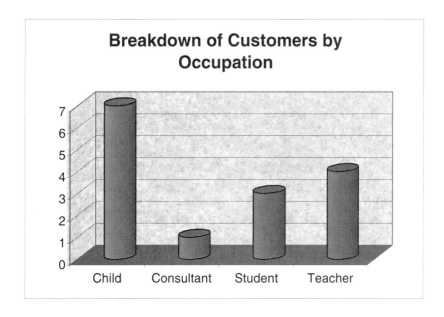

Visual Workshop

Create a database called "New England Computers", create a table called "October Sales", as shown in Figure VW-1, that includes a Primary Key. Analyze the table in Excel, then create a bar chart in Excel, as shown in Figure VW-2. You will need to resize the chart and format the labels. Save and print the Excel worksheet, then close all files.

FIGURE VW-1: **Eastern Sales table**

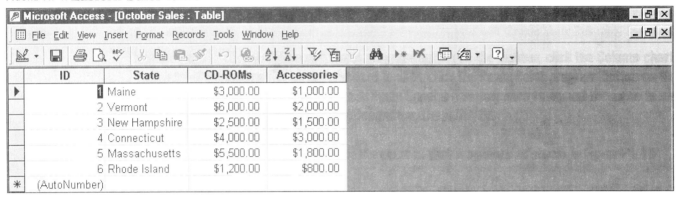

FIGURE VW-2: **New England Sales by State**

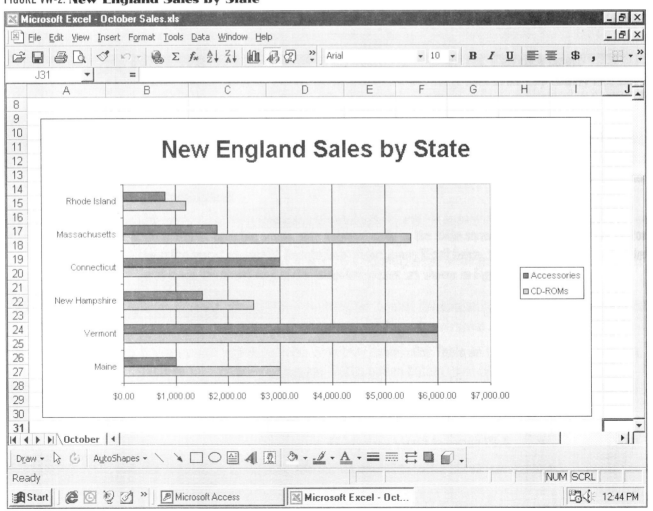

Microsoft
►**PowerPoint**
Projects

Presentation Graphics

In This Unit You Will Create:

PROJECT 1 ► **Training Presentation**

PROJECT 2 ► **Event Poster and Web Page**

PROJECT 3 ► **Lecture Presentation**

You use PowerPoint to create attractively formatted presentations, posters, and flyers that communicate important information to an audience. Suppose you have been asked to present a lecture to your co-workers to describe what you learned at a seminar on how to use Microsoft Access. Your audience will apply the information you give them to develop their own databases. You could, of course, just talk to your audience and perhaps hand out a sheet or two of notes. But imagine how much more compelling your lecture would be if you accompanied it with colorful slides or overheads that provided your audience with a visual backup to your words. People learn best when they can see, hear, and then write down information. You supply the words, and PowerPoint supplies the visual information that your audience can then write down in note form. In this unit, you will learn how to use PowerPoint to create and run presentations and how to use the graphics capabilities of PowerPoint to create posters and flyers.

Training Presentation on Oral Presentation Skills

You have been asked to teach a group of your co-workers how to give an oral presentation. To help emphasize the points you plan to make, you will accompany your lecture with an on-screen presentation that you create in PowerPoint. Four activities are required to complete the training presentation for Project 1:

Project Activities

Choose a Presentation Design and Create the Presentation Outline

A presentation consists of a series of slides. Each slide contains a title and a series of points, often in bullet form. Your first task is to enter the information you would like to display on each slide. You enter this information in the Outline pane. Figure P1-1 shows the Outline of the first four slides for the Oral Presentation Pointers presentation. Notice that the PowerPoint screen is divided into three panes—Outline, Slide, and Notes. As you enter text in the Outline view, it also appears in the Slide View pane, as shown in Figure P1-1.

Modify the Slide Master

Once you have entered all the information you wish to include in your presentation, you need to format each slide attractively. You will make changes to the template in Slide Master view. Any change you wish to make in Slide Master view—for example, reducing the font size of the slide title—will appear on every slide in your presentation.

Modify Individual Slides

Pictures from the ClipArt Gallery and geometric shapes that you draw right on the screen help enliven selected slides and highlight important information. The slide shown in Figure P1-2 includes a clip art image downloaded from Microsoft's Clip Gallery Live and the slide shown in Figure P1-3 includes two geometric shapes.

Edit and Show the Presentation

You will preview the slides in Slide Sorter view so that you can switch the order of selected slides and then preview the presentation in Slide Show view, where you will then learn how to annotate a slide during a slide show.

FIGURE P1-1: Outline of the presentation

Bulleted points

Slide titles

Outline View pane

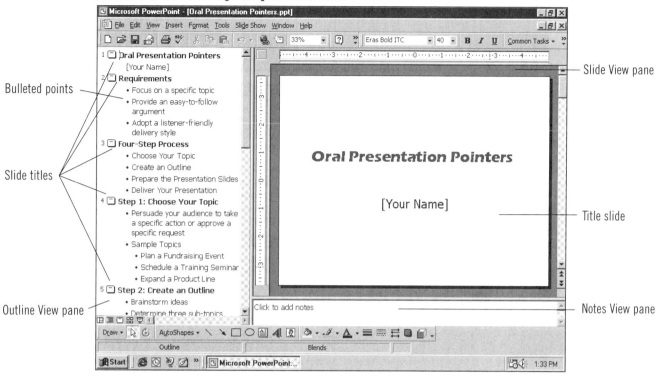

Slide View pane

Title slide

Notes View pane

FIGURE P1-2: Slide with clip art from the Online Clip Gallery

FIGURE P1-3: Slide with geometric shapes

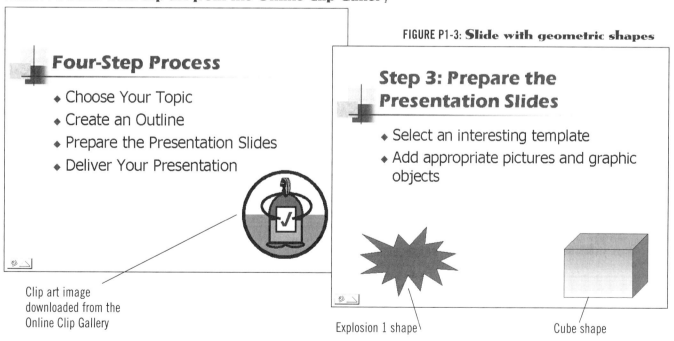

Clip art image downloaded from the Online Clip Gallery

Explosion 1 shape

Cube shape

PowerPoint

TRAINING PRESENTATION ON ORAL PRESENTATION SKILLS

activity:

Choose a Presentation Design and Create the Presentation Outline

You need to access PowerPoint, create a new presentation using a Presentation Design template, then enter the information you wish to display on each of the eight slides in the Oral Presentation Pointers presentation.

steps:

1. Start PowerPoint, click the Design Template option button, click OK, click Blends in the New Presentation dialog box, then click OK
   The New Slide dialog box appears.

2. Click OK to accept the Title Slide AutoLayout

3. Click to the right of the Slide 🔲 in the Outline View pane, type Oral Presentation Pointers, press [Enter], press [Tab], type your name, as shown in Figure P1-4, then save the presentation as Oral Presentation Pointers on the disk where you plan to store all files for this book
   You have entered the information that will be displayed on the first slide in your presentation.

4. Press [Enter], press [Shift][Tab] to start a new slide, type Four-Step Process, press [Enter], press [Tab], then type Choose Your Topic
   As you can see in the Slide View pane, the text you just typed appears as the first bulleted item on the slide titled "Four-Step Process."

5. Press [Enter], type Create an Outline, press [Enter], type Prepare the Presentation Slides, press [Enter], type Deliver Your Presentation, then press [Enter]
   Another bullet appears.

6. Press [Shift][Tab], type Requirements, press [Enter], press [Tab], then type the three points shown for Slide 3 in Figure P1-4
   Remember to press [Enter] after each entry. PowerPoint automatically displays a bullet for the next entry.

7. Press [Enter] after the third point in Slide 3, press [Shift][Tab], type Step 1: Choose Your Topic, press [Enter], press [Tab], type Persuade your audience to take a specific action or approve a specific request, press [Enter], type Sample Topics, then press [Enter]

8. Press [Tab], enter the three items under Sample Topics, as shown in Figure P1-3, press [Enter], then press [Shift][Tab] twice to return to the left margin
   You can also click the Demote (Indent More) button 📇 or the Promote (Indent Less) button 📇 to move the insertion point to the right or left.

9. Enter the information for Slides 5, 6, 7, and 8, as shown in Figure P1-4, click the Spelling button 📇 on the Standard toolbar, make any corrections required, then save the presentation
   Remember to press [Tab] to move the insertion point to the right and [Shift][Tab] to move the insertion point to the left.

1. ❏ **Oral Presentation Pointers**

    [Your Name]

2. ❏ **Four-Step Process**
   - Choose Your Topic
   - Create an Outline
   - Prepare the Presentation Slides
   - Deliver Your Presentation

3. ❏ **Requirements**
   - Focus on a specific topic
   - Provide an easy-to-follow argument
   - Adopt a listener-friendly delivery style

4. ❏ **Step 1: Choose Your Topic**
   - Persuade your audience to take a specific action or approve a specific request
   - Sample Topics
     - Plan a Fund-raising Event
     - Schedule a Training Seminar
     - Expand a Product Line

5. ❏ **Step 2: Create an Outline**
   - Brainstorm ideas
   - Determine three sub-topics
   - Add two or three points for each sub-topic

6. ❏ **Step 3: Prepare the Presentation Slides**
   - Select an interesting template
   - Add appropriate pictures and graphic objects

7. ❏ **Step 4: Deliver Your Presentation**
   - Spark your audience's interest
     - Tell a joke or anecdote
     - Present a startling fact
   - Summarize your topic in a purpose statement
   - Inform your audience of the three main sections of your presentation

8. ❏ **Final Words**
   - Enjoy yourself!
   - Make your materials interesting and informative
   - Know what you want to say and you will have the confidence to say it

1

activity:

Modify the Slide Master

The information you wish to present in the eight slides is complete. Next, you need to enter the Slide Master view so that you can make changes that will affect every slide in the presentation. For example, you will change the font style from Tahoma to Eras Bold ITC for each slide title. You will also modify the colored boxes included with the Blends presentation template you chose when you started the presentation.

steps:

1. Press **[Ctrl][Home]** to move to the first slide in the presentation, click **View** on the menu bar, click **Master**, then click **Slide Master**

The Slide Master view appears. Any changes you make to the objects and text in this view will affect every slide in your presentation.

2. Click the **Master title style** placeholder, as shown in Figure P1-5, click the **Font list arrow**, select **Eras Bold ITC**, then click the **Decrease Font Size button** 🔼 once

To jump to a new font quickly, type just the first letter of the font you want.

3. Click anywhere in the text **Click to edit Master text styles** (first level text), click **Format** on the menu bar, click **Bullets and Numbering**, click **Character**, click the diamond symbol, as shown in Figure P1-6, then click **OK**

4. Click the **Zoom list arrow** on the Standard toolbar, then click **150%**

5. Click the Red rectangle to the left of the text Click to edit Master title style to select it, click the **Fill Color list arrow** 🎨 on the Drawing toolbar, click **Fill Effects**, click the **Texture tab**, click the **Pink tissue paper** texture, then click **OK**

6. Click the left side of the Yellow rectangle, press and hold the **[Shift]** key, then click the right side of the Yellow rectangle, as shown in Figure P1-7

You use [Shift] to select two or more objects at once.

7. Click the **Fill Color list arrow**, click **Fill Effects**, click the **Texture tab**, click the **Blue tissue paper** texture, then click **OK**

Your Blends boxes are complete.

8. Click the **Zoom list arrow**, click **Fit**, then click the **Normal View button** 🖳 at the lower-left corner of the screen to display the first slide in the presentation

9. Click **View** on the menu bar, click **Master**, click **Title Master**, click anywhere in the three colored boxes to select all three boxes and the horizontal line, press **[Delete]**, click 🖳, then save the presentation

Your screen appears as shown in Figure P1-8.

FIGURE P1-5: Master title style placeholder selected

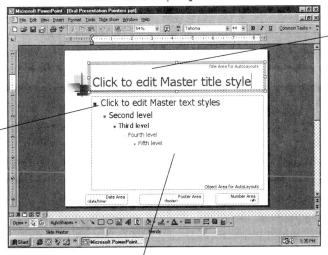

Master Title Style placeholder

First level text

Master Text Style placeholder

FIGURE P1-6: Bullet dialog box

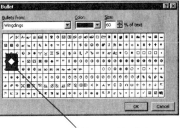

Diamond bullet selected

FIGURE P1-7: Yellow rectangle elements selected

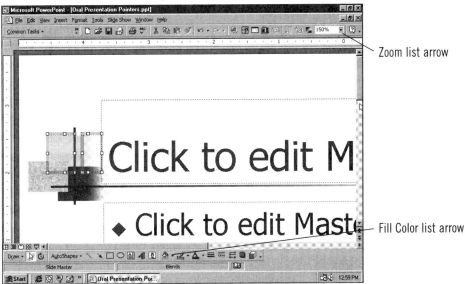

Zoom list arrow

Fill Color list arrow

FIGURE P1-8: Graphic object removed from the title slide

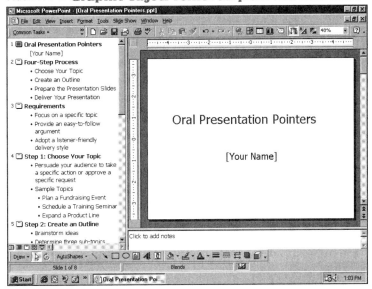

activity:

Modify Individual Slides

You need to add some clip art and geometric objects to selected slides to emphasize important points and add interest to your presentation. Start by inserting a clip art object on Slide 2. You will obtain the clip art object from Microsoft's Clip Gallery Live.

Hint

You must make Internet Explorer your default browser before you can use the Clip Gallery Live.

Trouble

If the Picture toolbar is in the way, drag it by its title bar.

steps:

1. Click the **Next Slide button** ⊻ on the scroll bar to display Slide 2, click the **Insert Clip Art button** 🖼 on the Drawing toolbar, click **Clips Online**, connect to the Internet if necessary, click **Accept** if a licensing notice appears, click in the **Search box**, type **Check marks**, then click **go**

   A selection of check mark images appears, as shown in Figure P1-9.

2. Click the **check box** below the picture of the checkbox you like best, click the **Download This Clip Now! button** 🔽, **right-click** the picture when it appears in the Insert ClipArt dialog box, click **Insert**, close the Insert ClipArt dialog box, then return to PowerPoint

3. Drag the sizing handles to resize the object and position it as shown in Figure P1-10

4. Click the **Next Slide button** ⊻ until Slide 6 appears (containing "Step 3: Prepare the Presentation Slides"), click **AutoShapes** on the Drawing toolbar, point to **Stars and Banners**, then click the **Explosion 1 shape** (first row, first column)

5. Position the mouse in the lower-left corner of the screen, then click and drag the mouse to draw the shape, as shown in Figure P1-11

   If your shape is a slightly different size, drag the sizing handles to modify it.

6. Click the **Fill Color list arrow** 🎨⊻ on the Drawing toolbar, then click the **red box**

7. Use the Basic Shapes command on the AutoShapes menu to draw a cube similar to the cube shown in Figure P1-11, click 🎨⊻, click **Fill Effects**, click the **Preset option button**, click the **Preset colors list arrow**, select **Daybreak**, then click **OK**

8. Click the **explosion shape** to select it, press and hold **[Shift]**, then click the **cube**

   You can move both objects at the same time only when they are all selected. Always use the [Shift] key to select multiple objects.

9. Click **Draw** on the Drawing toolbar, point to **Align or Distribute**, click **Align Bottom**, drag the two selected objects down so that they are positioned as shown in Figure P1-11, then save the presentation

FIGURE P1-9: **Clip Gallery Live**

go button

"Check marks" entered in the Search box

Click the Download This Clip Now! button

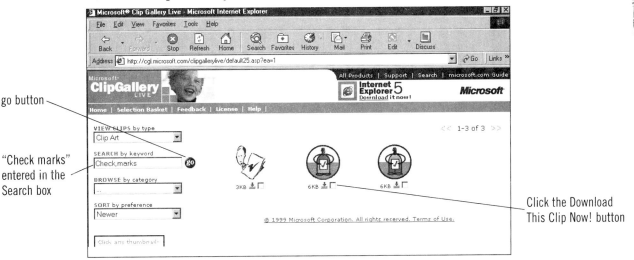

FIGURE P1-10: **Clip art sized and positioned on Slide 2**

You may have a different picture

Picture toolbar

Insert Clip Art button

Sizing handles

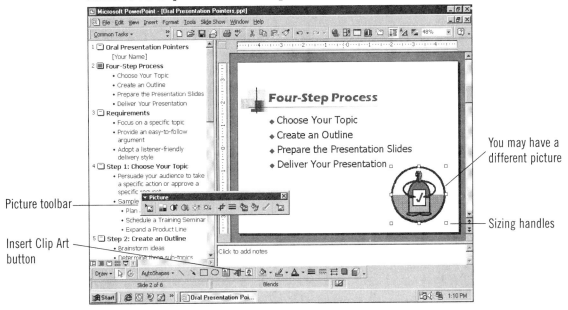

FIGURE P1-11: **Completed objects for Slide 6**

AutoShapes button

Draw button

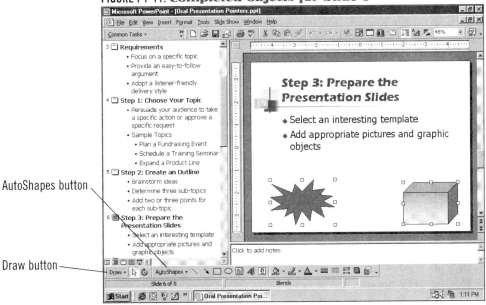

activity:

Edit and Show the Presentation

You need to add a clip art object to Slide 8, switch the order of Slides 2 and 3, add transition and build effects in Slide Sorter view, run the presentation in Slide Show view, then preview the presentation in your Web browser. Start by adding a large clip art object to Slide 9, which you will display under the text.

Trouble

If you do not have this clip art image, choose another one.

steps:

1. Click the **Next Slide button** ⬇ until you reach Slide 8, click the **Insert Clip Art button** 🖼, click in the **Search for clips** text box, type **Speaker**, press **[Enter]**, right-click the picture that appears similar to the figure shown in Figure P1-12, click **Insert**, then close the Insert ClipArt dialog box

2. Right-click the picture, click **Grouping**, click **Ungroup**, click **Yes** to convert the clip art object to a Microsoft drawing object, click **Draw** on the Drawing toolbar, then click **Group**
   If Group does not appear on the Draw menu, click the Expand arrows. You first converted the speaker picture into numerous objects and then you grouped the picture into one object so that you can now apply a gray fill. If the image becomes unselected while you are executing Step 2, click the Undo button ↺ *as many times as necessary, then try the step again.*

3. Click the **Fill Color list arrow** 🪣▾ on the Drawing toolbar, click **More Fill Colors**, click a **light gray box**, click **OK**, click the **Line Color list arrow** ✏▾, click **More Line Colors**, click a **darker gray box**, click **OK**, then drag the sizing handles to increase the size of the picture, as it appears in Figure P1-12
   At present, the speaker picture appears in front of the text.

4. Click **Draw** on the Drawing toolbar, point to **Order**, then click **Send to Back**
   Slide 8 looks quite striking!

5. Click the **Slide Sorter View button** 🔳, click **Slide 2**, then drag it to the right of Slide 3, as shown in Figure P1-13

6. Press **[Ctrl][A]** to select all the slides in the presentation, click the **Slide Transition Effects list arrow** on the Slide Sorter toolbar, then scroll down and click **Split Vertical In**

7. Click away from the slides, click **Slide 8**, then click the **Slide View button** 🔲, click **Final Words**, click the **Animation Effects button** 🌟 on the Formatting toolbar, if necessary, click the **Drive-In Effect button** 🚗, then click away from the slide title to deselect it
   If the Animation Effects button is already selected, the various animation effect buttons are visible.

8. Press **[Ctrl][Home]**, click the **Slide Show button** 🖥, then press **[Spacebar]** or click the **left mouse button** to scroll through the presentation
   The transition effect works nicely, and the animation effect on the final slide adds excitement.

9. Click **File** on the menu bar, click **Print**, click the **Print What list arrow**, click **Handouts**, click the **Slides per page list arrow**, click **9**, click **OK**, then save and close the presentation
   Your presentation is printed on one page, as shown in Figure P1-14.

Clues to Use

Grouping and Ungrouping

You can modify any clip art image or graphic on the Slide Master by first "ungrouping" it to separate it into its component elements. You can then modify individual elements or "regroup" the object and then modify all the elements at once.

FIGURE P1-12: Modified image for Slide 8

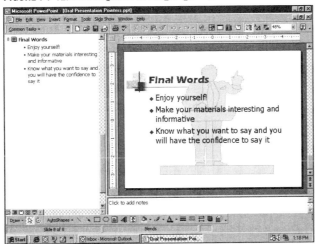

FIGURE P1-13: Slides 2 and 3 reversed in Slide Sorter view

Slide Transition
Effects list arrow

Slide view
button

Slide Sorter
view button

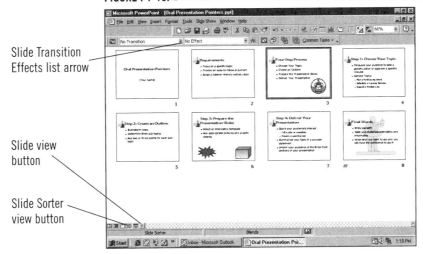

FIGURE P1-14: Slides printed as a handout

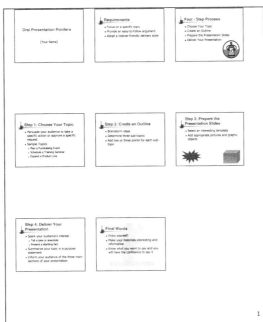

Web Page for First Night Celebration

On New Year's Eve, your community will sponsor a First Night Celebration at various venues in the town center. Family-oriented concerts and entertainment will be performed throughout the evening, culminating in a spectacular fireworks display at midnight. As a volunteer on your community's local council, you have been asked to produce an attractive Web page and poster to advertise the event. You will save time by creating both the Web page and the poster at the same time. You will Insert WordArt and Clip Art Objects, Insert Text Objects, and then Format the Poster as a Web page.

activity:

Insert WordArt and Clip Art Objects

steps:

1. From a blank PowerPoint screen, click the New button 🗅 on the Standard toolbar, click the Blank AutoLayout in the lower-right corner of the New Slide dialog box, click OK, then save the presentation as First Night 2001

2. Click the Slide View button 🖼, click the Insert WordArt button 🔷 on the Drawing toolbar, select the second WordArt style in the third row, click OK, type First Night 2001, click OK, click the WordArt Shape button 🔠 on the WordArt toolbar, then choose the Deflate Bottom shape, as shown in Figure P2-1.

3. Drag the object up to the top of the slide, resize the object so it appears as shown in Figure P2-2, then save the presentation.

Trouble
If you do not have this clip art image, choose another one, and then go on to Step 8.

4. Click the Insert Clip Art button 🖼 on the Drawing toolbar, click the Entertainment category, click in the Search for clips text box, type Success Victory Champagne Bottle, press [Enter], right-click the champagne bottle that appears as shown in Figure P2-2, click Insert, then close the Insert ClipArt dialog box

5. Click Draw on the Drawing toolbar, click Ungroup, click Yes, click away from the selected objects, click just the bubbles, click Draw, then click Ungroup
You modify the champagne bottle so that the cap and bubbles are disconnected. The champagne bottle now consists of four objects: the bottle, the bubbles, the spray, and the cap.

6. Use your mouse to drag each of the four elements so that they are positioned as shown in Figure P2-2
Take your time. Moving objects with the mouse requires practice and a steady hand! Now that the four objects in the champagne bottle image are separated, you will regroup the image and reduce its size.

7. Press and hold [Shift], click the bottle, click the bubbles, click the spray, click the cap so that all four objects are selected, click Draw, then click Group

8. Drag the lower-right sizing handle up to reduce the size of the image, position it in the center of the screen, as shown in Figure P2-3, click away from the image to deselect it, then save the presentation

FIGURE P2-1: WordArt shape dialog box

WordArt shape button

Deflate Bottom shape selected

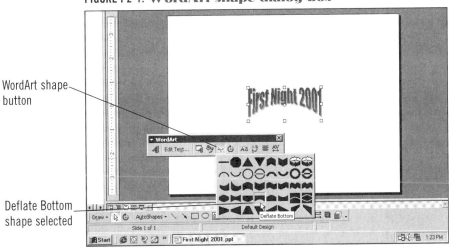

FIGURE P2-2: WordArt object and ungrouped champagne bottle

Completed WordArt object

Cap

Bubbles

Spray

Bottle

FIGURE P2-3: Champagne bottle image resized and positioned

Resized bottle image

activity:

Insert Text Objects

You need to insert four of the seven text objects required for the poster. Start by entering the text object for the subtitle: "Celebrate a Family-Style New Year's Eve."

steps:

Hint

You need to select the border so that any changes you make will be applied to all the text in the box.

1. Click the **Text Box button** 🔳 on the Drawing toolbar, position your mouse under and to the left of the WordArt object, draw a box across the screen, then type **Celebrate a Family-Style New Year's Eve**

2. Click the border surrounding the text object, click the **Increase Font Size button** 🄰 on the Formatting toolbar, click the **Bold button** 🄱 on the Formatting toolbar, click the **Center button** 🔳 on the Formatting toolbar, then drag the shaded border to position the object attractively under the WordArt object, as shown in Figure P2-4

   If the text wraps or if the box extends too far to the right, drag the corner handles to adjust the size of the text object so that all the text appears on one line and you can easily center it under the WordArt object. If necessary, move the WordArt object up a bit so that the text object does not overlap the champagne bottle.

3. Click away from the text object to deselect it, click 🔳, then draw a box starting at the left edge of the page about 1" under "Celebrate"

4. Enter the text, as shown in Figure P2-4

   The box will grow as you press [Enter] after each line. Don't worry if the box extends off the screen or if the first line wraps.

5. Click the border surrounding the text object, click the **Font Size list arrow** 🔟 ▾ on the Formatting toolbar, then click **16**

6. Click **Format** on the menu bar, click **Line Spacing**, reduce the **Before Paragraph Spacing** to **0**, click **OK**, click 🔳, then position the object as shown in Figure P2-5

Hint

Make sure you enter the name of your town in place of [Your Town].

7. Click the 🔳, draw a box about 4" wide starting at the lower-left corner of the page, type **Sponsored by: [Your Town] Community Council**, click the border, reduce the font size to **12**, then position the text object at the bottom-left corner of the screen

8. Create another text object that contains **For more information and a complete concert schedule, call 962-4491**, reduce the font size to **12**, then position the text object at the lower-right corner of the screen, as shown in Figure P2-5

   You may need to decrease the size of the second text object in order to position it at the lower-right corner.

9. Press and hold **[Shift]**, click both text objects at the bottom of the screen, click the **Draw button**, click **Align or Distribute**, click **Align Bottom**, then save the presentation

   Compare your screen with Figure P2-5.

FIGURE P2-4: **Text for description of performances**

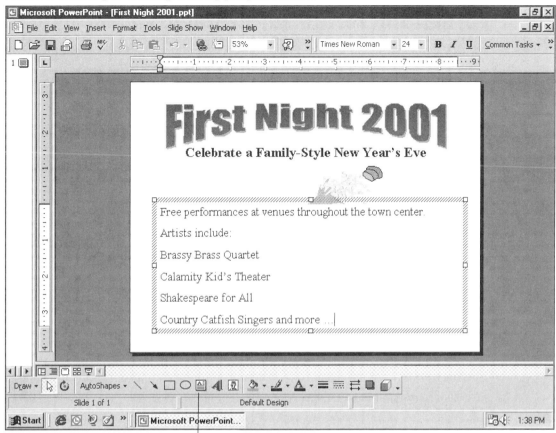

Text Box button

FIGURE P2-5: **Text objects completed**

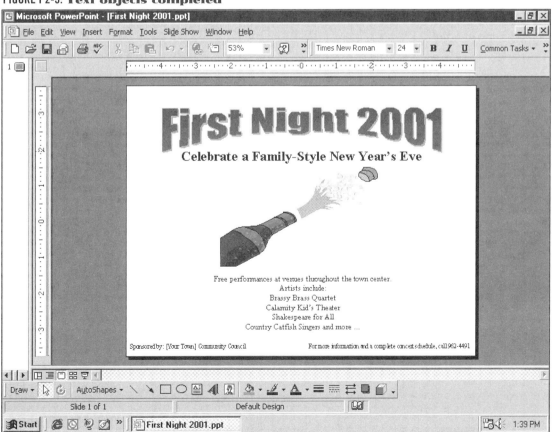

activity:

Format the Poster for Printing

You will first create the three rotated text objects, and then you will size and position all the objects on the page so that they appear as shown in Figure P2-6. If you do not like a change you make to an object, just click the Undo button and try again. Sizing and positioning a large number of objects requires time and patience. Experiment with different looks as you work so that your poster appears similar to the completed Web page shown in Figure P2-7.

steps:

1. Create a text object for **Non-alcoholic Refreshments!**

2. Select the text box (click the border), reduce the font size to **16**, resize the text object so that the text wraps to two lines, then click the **Free Rotate button** 🔃 on the Drawing toolbar
Green dots appear at the four corners of the text object.

3. Point the mouse over the lower-right green dot (the mouse pointer changes to ↻), then click and drag the dot up to rotate the object, as shown in Figure P2-6

4. Create the rotated text objects for **Outdoor Barbeque!** and **Midnight Fireworks Display!** in 16 point, as shown in Figure P2-6
You have created all the elements required for your Web page.

5. Click **File** on the menu bar, then click **Web Page Preview**
The Web page appears in your Web browser, as shown in Figure P2-7.

6. Return to PowerPoint, click **File**, click **Save As Web Page**, type **First Night**, click **Save**
PowerPoint saves the file and creates a new folder called FirstNight_files on your disk. This folder contains all the files required to display the completed page on your Web browser.

7. Click **File** on the menu bar, click **Print**, then click **OK**
Note that you can choose to print the page from PowerPoint or from your Web browser.

8. Close the Web browser, then close the presentation

Clues to Use

Publishing the Web page on the World Wide Web

The presentation you have saved as a Web page consists of several files. For example, the champagne bottle is a file and the text of the presentation is a file. PowerPoint creates these files when you save a presentation as a Web page, and then PowerPoint creates a folder to accommodate the files. If you have an Internet Service Provider and space on the Internet for Web pages, you can transfer the folder containing the files associated with the PowerPoint presentation to your web space. To find out more about how to carry a Web page live on the Internet, you will need to contact your Internet Service Provider or your technical support person.

FIGURE P2-6: Rotated text objects

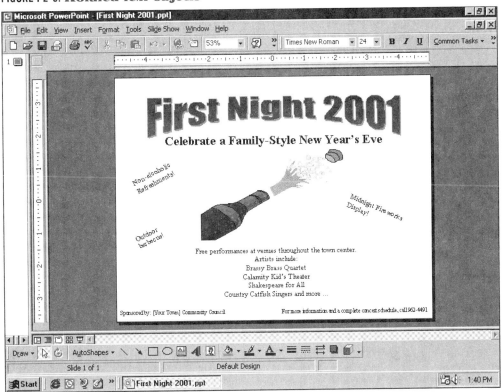

FIGURE P2-7: Web page displayed in the Web browser

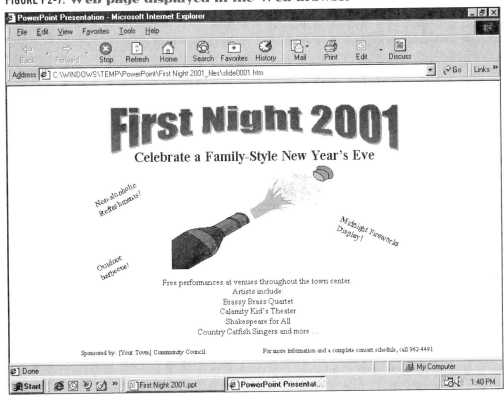

Lecture Presentation on Time Management

To give a presentation on time management to your classmates in a business course, you have decided to use PowerPoint to create black and white slides in the portrait format that you can then photocopy onto transparencies to display on an overhead projector as you progress through your presentation. You will **Create Black and White Slides**.

activity:

Create Black and White Slides

Hint

Remember to press [Tab] to indent one level and [Shift][Tab] to return to the left margin.

Trouble

If you click the Master title style placeholder by mistake, click the oval again.

steps:

1. Open a new PowerPoint presentation with the default title slide AutoLayout, click **File** on the menu bar, click **Page Setup**, click the **Portrait option button** in the Slides section, click **OK**

2. Click next to the slide icon in the Outline View pane, enter the text for the six slides in the presentation, as shown in Figure P3-1, check the spelling, then save the presentation as **Time Management Presentation**

3. Click the **Grayscale Preview button** on the Standard toolbar, click **Format** on the menu bar, click **Apply Design Template**, click **Capsules**, click **Apply**, click **View** on the menu bar, point to **Master**, then click **Slide Master**

4. Click the **Zoom list arrow** on the Standard toolbar, click **100%**, scroll up so that you can see the oval shape, then click the far-left edge of the oval to select it
   A yellow diamond appears and the oval is enclosed in a border.

5. Click **Format** on the menu bar, click **AutoShapes**, click the **Size tab**, change the width in the Size and rotate section to **6"**, then click **OK**

6. Click just below the oval shape to select the Master title style placeholder, click the **Decrease Font Size button** once, drag the placeholder up so the word **Click** appears in the oval shape, then click the **Normal view button**

7. Click the **Zoom list arrow**, click **Fit**, then add and modify clip art images as described below:

Slide #	Clip Art Object Keywords	Modification
3	Worried Confusion Risk	Size and Position
5	People Happy Joy	Size, Ungroup, fill objects with Denim texture, then flip horizontally
6	Organize Challenge Juggle	Size and position

8. Click **View**, click **Master**, click **Title Master**, click the **Master title style placeholder**, increase the font size to **36pt.**, click the **Align Left button** on the Formatting toolbar, click the **Slide view button**, display Slide 1, then press **[Enter]** after Time until the "Time Management" title appears on two lines, as shown in Figure P3-2 in Slide Sorter view

9. Click **File** on the menu bar, click **Print**, click the **Print what list arrow**, click **Handouts**, click **OK**, then save and close the presentation

FIGURE P3-1: **Outline of the Time Management presentation**

1 ❑ Time Management

[Your Name]

Business Management 101

2 ❑ Time Management Topics

- Strategies
- Time Management Techniques
- Stress Control

3 ❑ Strategies

- Use your time effectively
- Make responsible decisions
- Control your stress

4 ❑ Time Management Techniques

- Prepare daily to-do lists
- Handle paperwork as few times as possible
- Simplify repetitive work
- Perform work correctly the first time

5 ❑ Stress Control

- Control your food intake
- Exercise regularly
- Visualize non-stress situations
- Clarify work roles
- Avoid over-scheduling

6 ❑ Time Management Goal

- Control your workday rather than allowing your workday to control you!

FIGURE P3-2: **Completed presentation in Slide Sorter view**

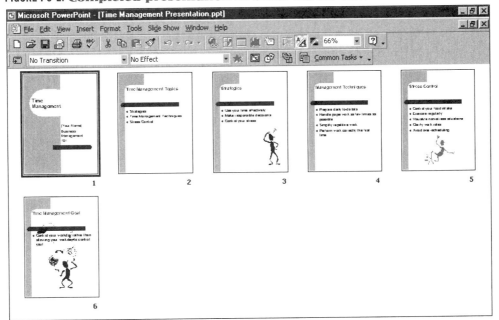

Independent Challenges

INDEPENDENT CHALLENGE 1

Create a 6- to 10-slide presentation in portrait format that you could use to help teach a specific concept or task. For example, your presentation could present guidelines for purchasing a computer system, buying a used car, taking effective vacation photographs, planning an event such as a class party or a wedding, seeing the major sites in your home town, etc. Follow the steps provided to create the presentation in PowerPoint.

1. Your first task is to determine the topic of your presentation. Think about an activity or task that you know well and that you can present in short, easy-to-understand steps. Start with the words "How to. . . ," followed by a verb and then the activity. For example, your presentation topic could be "How to Create a Balcony Garden," or "How to Plan a Backpacking Trip." In the box below, write the topic of your presentation.

   Presentation Topic: ....

2. You need to determine three main sections for your presentation. Each of these sections will cover a specific activity related to your topic. For example, the three sections for a presentation titled "How to Find a Job" could be: 1. Personal Profile, 2. Employment Sources, and 3. Interview Techniques. You will present each of these sections on one slide along with three or four bulleted points that describe it. Write the three sections of your presentation in the box below.

   Section 1: ....
   Section 2: ....
   Section 3: ....

3. Open PowerPoint and create an outline of your presentation. Save the presentation as "How to [activity]." Here's a suggested format:

SLIDE #	SLIDE TITLE	TEXT
1	Presentation Topic	Your Name
2	Overview	List the three sections in your presentation
3	Section 1 Title	List three or four bulleted points related to Section 1
4	Section 2 Title	List three or four bulleted points related to Section 2
5	Section 3 Title	List three or four bulleted points related to Section 3
6	Conclusion	Create a "motivational" slide to summarize your presentation. If you wish, you can add more slides for each of the three sections. You may discover that you have enough information in a section to require two or even three slides in order to present it effectively.

4. Switch to Slide view, change the page orientation to Portrait, then apply a Presentation Design template.
5. Switch to Slide Master view and modify the appearance of the text in the placeholders. You may wish, for example, to change the font size and style of the text in the Master Title Style placeholder. If you wish to change the bullet style, click to the right of the bullet, click Format on the menu bar, select Bullet, and then select the bullet style you prefer from the Bullet dialog box.
6. In Slide view, add clip art pictures to selected slides. Remember that you can use the drawing tools to modify a clip art image after you have ungrouped it.

7. Add one or two geometric objects to selected slides. If you wish to include a geometric object or a clip art on every slide, insert them in Slide Master view.
8. When you are satisfied with the appearance of your slides, switch to Slide Sorter view, add transition effects to all the slides, then switch to Slide Show view and run the presentation.
9. Save, print, and close the presentation.

INDEPENDENT CHALLENGE 2

Create a Web page that announces some kind of event, such as a concert series, sports tournament, or club meeting.

1. Determine the type of event your Web page will announce. Think of your own interests. In what type of event are you most likely to participate? If you are involved in sports, you could create a Web page to advertise an upcoming game or tournament. If you belong to a club, you could create a Web page to advertise a special event such as a fund-raising bake sale or craft fair.
2. Think of an interesting title for your event. For example, a Web page that announces a celebrity golf tournament could be called "Stars on Par," or a Web page that advertises running events for cash prizes could be called "Dash for Cash."
3. Determine the details that readers of your Web page will need to know in order to participate in the event advertised. You need to specify where the event will be held, when it will be held (date and time), what activities will occur at the event, and who readers should contact for more information.
4. On a blank piece of paper, create a rough draft of your Web page. Determine where you will place the various blocks of text and one or two clip art images.
5. Create the Web page on a blank PowerPoint slide. Add at least one clip art image that you have altered in some way. Remember that you need to ungroup the image before you can modify it with the Drawing tools. Experiment with the various tools available. You will soon discover numerous ways in which you can modify the available clip art images to create exciting images of your own. For ideas, refer to the Web page you created for Project 2.
6. Rotate some of the text objects and create a WordArt object for the Web page title.
7. Save your Web page frequently as you work. Creating an interesting and informative Web page takes time and patience. Experiment and remember that you can always click the Undo button if you make a change that you don't like.
8. View the Web page on your browser.
9. Save the slide as a Web page.
10. Print a copy of your Web page from either PowerPoint or your Web browser.

INDEPENDENT CHALLENGE 3

1. Create a sales flyer that advertises a special sale, promotion, or event sponsored by a company of your choice. For example, you could advertise a fall clearance sale at a local furniture store or a two-for-one deal at a local restaurant.
2. Determine the following information for your flyer:
   a. Name, address, and phone number of the company
   b. Sales information; for example, special discounts, items on sale, promotional deals, etc.
   c. Price information
3. On a blank piece of paper, create a rough draft of your sales flyer. Determine where you will place the various blocks of text and one or two clip art images.
4. Create the sales flyer on a blank PowerPoint slide. Add at least one clip art image that you have altered in some way.
5. Rotate some of the text objects, and create a WordArt object for the company name.
6. Save the sales flyer frequently as you work.
7. Print a copy of your sales flyer.

You have helped to organize a three-day convention for home-based entrepreneurs in your state or province. This convention will include seminars, booths for the entrepreneurs to promote their products or services, a keynote speech by your state governor or provincial premier, and plenty of opportunities for entrepreneurs to network. A few months prior to the convention, you will hold a meeting for local entrepreneurs to inform them about the conference and encourage them to participate. Follow the instructions provided to create and then modify the presentation that you plan to give at this meeting.

1. Start a new presentation, then enter the slide titles and text for the presentation as shown below:

SLIDE #	SLIDE TITLE	LEVEL 1 TEXT	LEVEL 2 TEXT
1	Home-Based Entrepreneurs Conventions	[Your name and the name of your town and state/province]	
2	Convention Details	Location Dates Time	[Enter an appropriate location in your hometown, e.g., "Westside Convention Center, San Diego"] May 3 to May 5, 2001 8 a.m. to 6 p.m. Banquet on May 4 at 8 p.m.
3	Convention Activities	Seminars Booth Rentals Networking Keynote Speech	
4	Seminars	Selected Seminars:	Business on the Internet Marketing Your Service Business Basic Accounting for Small Businesses Organizing Your Home Office
5	Booth Rentals	50 square feet: $1000 100 square feet: $2000	
6	Networking	Contact hundreds of local and national distributors Form new business alliances Trade success stories	
7	Keynote Speech	[Name of your governor, premier, or other leader] will present a keynote speech on:	Government Support for the Home-Based Businessperson
8	Home Is Where the Business Is!	[Create a "motivational" slide to encourage attendance at the convention]	

2. Switch to Slide view, then apply the Lock And Key Design template.

3. Switch to Slide Master view, ungroup the key image, select the shaded rectangles above and below the key image, then change the fill to use the Desert preset gradient. To apply a preset gradient, click the fill Color list arrow, click Fill Effects, click the Gradient tab, click the Preset option button, click the Preset Colors list arrow, select Desert, click OK, then click OK again.

4. Change the font style of the Master title text to Elephant.

5. Add the Desert preset gradient to the key picture on the Title Master.

6. In Slide view, add clip art pictures to selected slides. Remember that you can use the drawing tools to modify a clip art image after you have ungrouped it. Refer to the sample version of the presentation shown in Figure IC-1.

7. Select clip art images from the Online Clip Gallery or the ClipArt Gallery. The images you choose may not be the same as the images shown in Figure IC-1.

8. When you are satisfied with the appearance of your slides, print them as handouts (6 to a page).

9. Add transition animation effects to the slides in Slide Sorter view.

10. Save the presentation as Entrepreneurs Presentation.

FIGURE IC-1: **Completed presentation in Slide Sorter view**

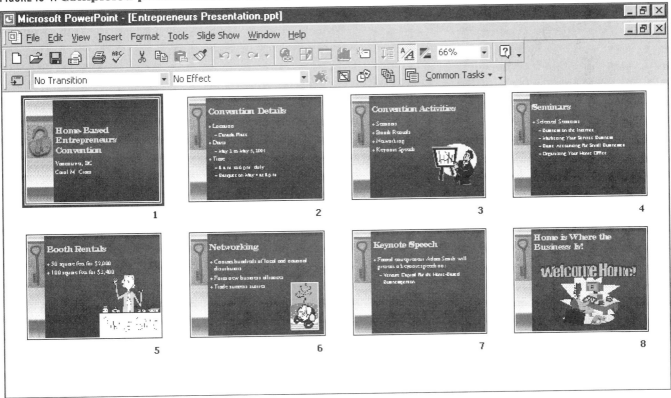

Visual Workshop

As part of a presentation on Saving Endangered Species that you are giving at a meeting of a local environmental group, you need to create the two slides shown in figures VW-1 and VW-2. Enter the slide titles, select the Nature design template, remove the "Enter text here" box from Slide 2, then add text blocks and clip art to Slide 2, as shown in Figure VW-2. Note that the clip art images you select may be different. Search for the appropriate images on the Clip Gallery Live. Save the presentation as "Saving Endangered Species", print, and close the presentation.

FIGURE VW-1: Title slide

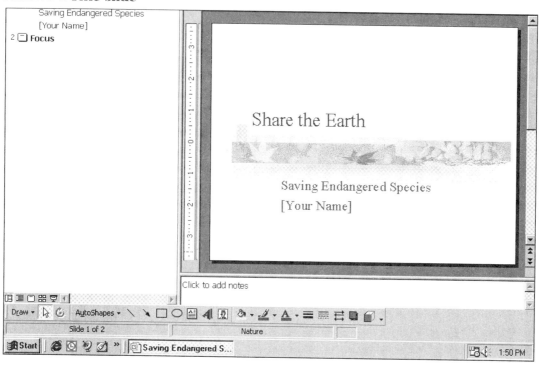

FIGURE VW-2: Slide 2

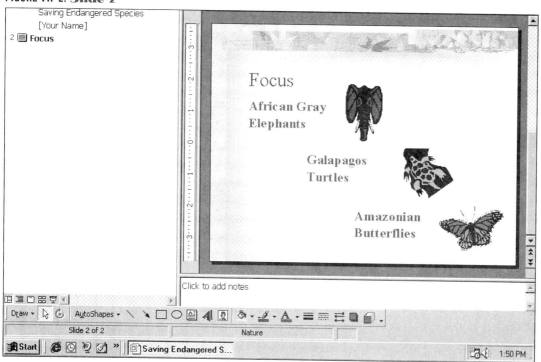

Microsoft
► PowerPoint, Word, Excel, and Access
Projects

Integrated Presentations

In This Unit You Will Create:

Sales Presentation

Career Options Presentation

Class Party Presentation

You can integrate all four Office programs to produce PowerPoint presentations that reflect a broad spectrum of company activities. For example, suppose you own a small company that sells custom-made snowboards. A group of potential investors has asked you to make a sales presentation. You already have information about your customers and products stored in an Access database, financial information stored in Excel workbooks, and sales literature stored in Word. Now you want to take elements from each of these sources and present them in a format that your investors can quickly and easily understand. The PowerPoint onscreen slide presentation provides you with a flexible medium in which to bring together information from a variety of sources. By creating links between PowerPoint and the source programs, you can also keep the presentation up-to-date and ready to go at a moment's notice. In this unit, you will integrate Access, Excel, and Word with PowerPoint to produce exciting on-screen and Web browser presentations that incorporate slide transitions and animation effects.

Sales Presentation for Fancy Free Travel

Fancy Free Travel organizes guided tours to "adventure" destinations around the world. Clients can choose adventures ranging from canoeing trips into the depths of the Amazon rain forest to survival adventures on a remote Pacific island. As a sales manager for Fancy Free Travel, you will produce an on-screen presentation for your co-workers that highlights the most popular tours and communicates your new marketing plan to further increase sales. Four activities are required to complete the sales presentation for Fancy Free Travel:

Project Activities

Create Source Materials

Much of the data you need for your sales presentation is stored in the Tours database. This database contains the Tours table that lists the sales from Fancy Free Travel's last 10 tours. The records in this table are shown in Figure P1-1. Once you have created the table in Access, you will copy it into Excel and create the two charts you plan to use in your presentation.

Create the Presentation and Add Charts

You will first work in Outline view in Word to enter the text required for each slide in your presentation, as shown in Figure P1-2. You will then send the outline to PowerPoint where all the Outline levels will be automatically transferred to slide titles and bulleted items. Once the presentation appears in PowerPoint, you will apply a PowerPoint template to the slide show.

Add a Chart and Modify the Presentation

First you will copy the chart from Excel into a selected slide, and then you will modify the chart in PowerPoint. You will then adjust the appearance of the slide show in Slide Master view.

Update the Presentation

A few weeks after you give your presentation, new sales figures are entered into the Access database. You decide to once again give the presentation to a different group of co-workers, but you want the new presentation to contain the new data entered in the Access database. Fortunately, you linked the table in Access with the charts in Excel, which you then linked to the slides in PowerPoint. You will change some of the figures in the Access table, then apply some transition effects and animation effects to produce a whole new slide show. Figures P1-3 and P1-4 show the original and revised versions of one of the slides in the presentation.

FIGURE P1-1: First ten records in the Tours table

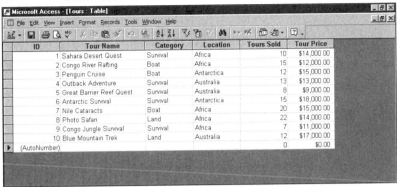

FIGURE P1-2: Presentation outline entered in Outline view in Word

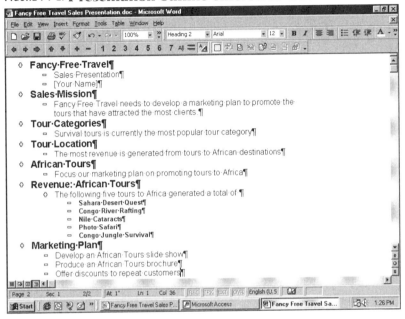

FIGURE P1-3: Version 1 of Slide 4

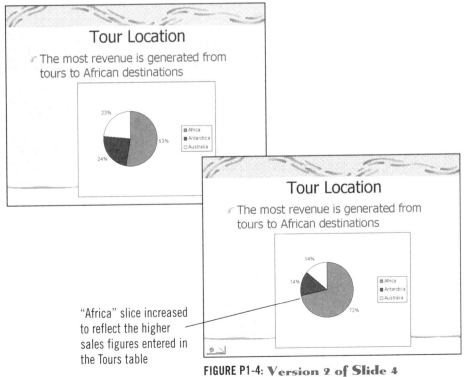

"Africa" slice increased
to reflect the higher
sales figures entered in
the Tours table

FIGURE P1-4: Version 2 of Slide 4

SALES PRESENTATION FOR FANCY FREE TRAVEL

activity:

Create Source Materials

You need to create the Tours table in Access, then copy the table to Excel and create two charts required for your presentation.

steps:

1. Start **Access**, create a blank database, access the drive where you plan to store all your files for this book, type **Fancy Free Travel Database** in the File name box, then click **Create**

2. Double-click **Create table in Design view**, then enter the five field names and select the appropriate data types as shown in Figure P1-5

3. Click the **Datasheet View** list arrow ▦▾, click **Yes**, name the table **Tours**, click **OK**, click **Yes** to create a primary key, then enter the records for the Tours table as shown in Figure P1-6
   Your Access table is complete.

4. Close and save the Tours table, click **Tours**, then click the **Copy button** ▣ on the Database toolbar

5. Start **Excel**, click **Edit** on the menu bar, click **Paste Special**, click the **Paste link option button** (the Biff5 format is the default), click **OK**, then save the worksheet as **Fancy Free Travel Sales Presentation**
   The Tours table appears in Excel.

6. Click cell **G2**, enter the formula to multiply the Tours Sold by the Tour Price (=E2*F2), copy the formula down the column to cell **G11**, click the **Currency Style button** 🔘 on the Formatting toolbar, click cell **G12**, double-click the **AutoSum button** Σ on the Standard toolbar, then adjust the width of column B so that all the row names are visible
   You should see $1,900,000.00 in cell G12.

7. Click cell **B14**, type **Survival**, press [Tab], type **Boat** in cell **C14**, press [Tab], type **Land** in cell **D14**, then click cell **B15**, and enter the formula that adds the total tour sales for each Survival tour, as shown in Figure P1-7

8. Enter the formulas required to calculate the total tour sales for the Boat tours and the Land tours, then use the Chart Wizard to create a column chart from cells **B14** to **D15**, as shown in Figure P1-7
   Make sure you position and size the chart as shown in Figure P1-7. Note that you must enter formulas to calculate the values in cells B15 to D15 so that the chart will automatically be updated when you change selected values in the Tours table.

9. Enter the tour locations and formulas in cells F14 to H15 as shown in Figure P1-7, create a pie chart from the data, then save the workbook
   Your pie chart should appear as shown in Figure P1-7. Note that the values in cells F15 to H15 must be formulas that calculate the total sales for each location. For example, the formula in cell F15 is =G2+G3+G8+G9+G10, which calculates the total sales of tours to Africa.

FIGURE P1-5: Design view of the Tours table

Number type selected for the Tours Sold field

Currency type selected for the Tour Price field

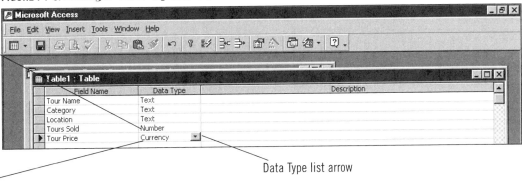

Data Type list arrow

FIGURE P1-6: Records for the Tours table

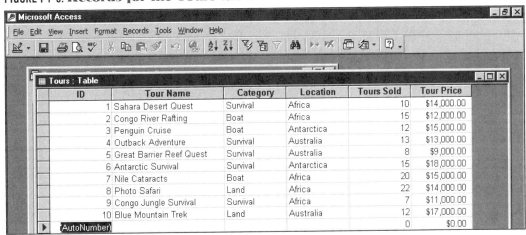

FIGURE P1-7: Completed column and pie charts

Formula for cell D15: =G9+G11

Enter formulas for cells F15, G15, and H15

Formula for cell B15: =G2+G5+G6+G7+G10

Select the Show percent option button in the Chart Wizard and do not display a chart title

Formula for cell C15: =G3+G4+G8

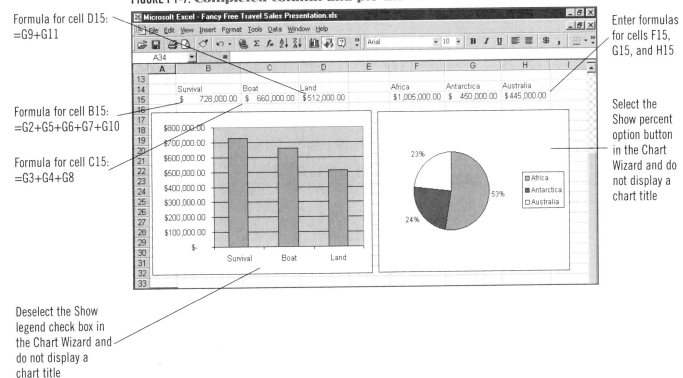

Deselect the Show legend check box in the Chart Wizard and do not display a chart title

activity:

Create the Presentation

You've created the source materials required for your presentation. Now you need to use Word to create an outline of your presentation. You will then send the presentation to PowerPoint where you will apply a PowerPoint template.

steps:

1. Start **Word**, then click the **Outline View button** 📄

2. Type **Fancy Free Travel**, press **[Enter]**, press **[Tab]**, type **Sales Presentation**, press **[Enter]**, type your name, press **[Enter]**, then save the document as **Fancy Free Travel Sales Presentation**

3. Press **[Shift][Tab]**, type **Sales Mission**, press **[Enter]**, press **[Tab]**, type the text for the remaining slides, as shown in Figure P1-8, then check the spelling
Remember to press [Tab] to move the cursor to the right and [Shift][Tab] to move the cursor to the left. Don't worry if your text formatting is different from Figure P1-8. You will modify the correct heading styles in the next step.

4. Save the document, click **File** on the menu bar, click **Send To**, then click **Microsoft PowerPoint**
In a few seconds, the outline appears in PowerPoint.

5. Click **Format** on the menu bar, click **Apply Design Template**, select **Sumi Painting**, then click **Apply**

6. Click **View** on the menu bar, click to **Master**, click **Slide Master**, click the Master title style placeholder and drag it up so that the text (not the border of the box) appears just below the blue border

7. Click the Master text styles placeholder and drag it up so it appears just below the Master title styles placeholder

8. Save the presentation as **Fancy Free Travel Sales Presentation**, click the **Slide View button** 🔲 then click the Slide 6 icon in the Outline pane to move directly to Slide 6
The slide title and text should appear similar to Figure P1-9.

FIGURE P1-8: **Outline of the Fancy Free Travel Sales Presentation**

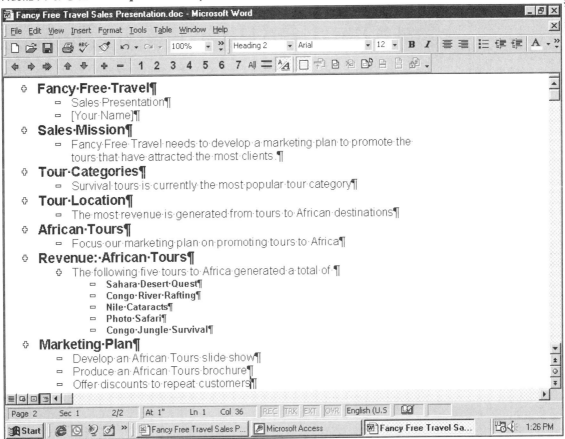

FIGURE P1-9: **Slide 6 text**

Slide 6 selected

Slide title and slide text moved up

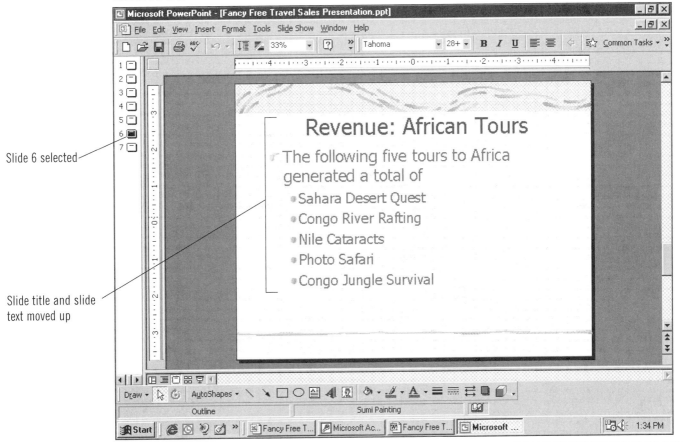

activity:

Add a Chart and Modify the Presentation

You first need to copy the column and pie charts from Excel and then paste them as links on selected slides. You will then obtain a motion clip and a sound clip from Microsoft's Clip Gallery Live and insert them on Slide 5.

steps:

Hint

You may need to click a hyperlink to jump to the Clip Art Gallery.

1. Show **Slide 3**, click the **Microsoft Excel program button** on the taskbar, click the **Column chart**, click the **Copy button** on the standard toolbar, click the **PowerPoint program button** on the taskbar, click **Edit** on the menu bar, click **Paste Special** (you may need to expand the menu to see Paste Special), click the **Paste link option button**, then click **OK**

2. Drag the sizing handles and reposition the chart so that it appears as shown in Figure P1-10

3. Copy the pie chart from Excel, paste it as a link into Slide 4, resize and position the pie chart so that it fills the slide attractively, as shown in Figure P1-11, then save the presentation

4. Click **Slide 5** in the Outline pane, click the **Insert Clip Art button** on the Drawing toolbar, click **Clips Online**, then click **OK** and **Accept**, if necessary

5. Click the **View Clips list arrow**, click **Motion**, click in the **Search box**, type **elephant**, click **Go**, click the **check box** next to the elephant motion you chose, then click to download the motion clip

6. **Right-click** the elephant image in the Insert ClipArt dialog box, then click **Insert**
   While you are still in the Insert ClipArt dialog box, you can go back to the Clip Gallery Live and download a sound clip.

7. Click the **Internet Explorer program button** on the taskbar, click the **View Clips list arrow**, click **Sounds**, type **Africa** in the Search box, click **Go**, click to download the sound of your choice (e.g. African Drums), **right-click** the clip, click **Insert**, then close the Insert ClipArt dialog box and close Internet Explorer

8. Click **Yes** to have the sound play automatically in the slide show, click the **Slide Show button**, hear the sound and watch the elephant move, press **[Esc]** twice, then size and position the elephant and move the sound icon to the lower-left corner, as shown in Figure P1-12

9. Save the presentation

FIGURE P1-10: **Sized and positioned column chart on Slide 3**

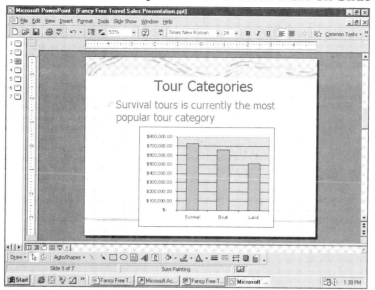

FIGURE P1-11: **Completed pie chart on Slide 4**

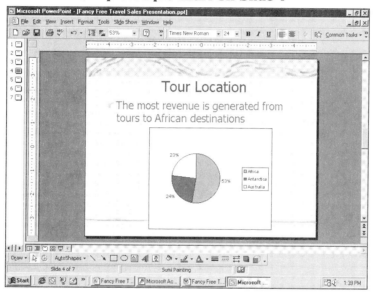

FIGURE P1-12: **Motion and Sound clips sized and positioned**

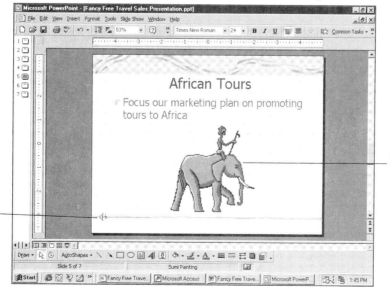

Increase the size of the motion clip

Move the sound icon here

activity:

Update the Presentation

After you give the sales presentation, the number of tours sold increases. You need to open the Tours table in Access, change the number of tours sold, then update the links to the charts in PowerPoint. Change the AutoLayout for Slide 1, and then you will enter the total number of African tours sold on Slide 6 as an object linked to the Excel workbook and Access database.

steps:

1. View **Slide 1**, click **Format**, click **Slide Layout**, select the **Title Slide** layout, then click **Apply**

2. Switch to Excel, click cell **F15** (contains the total revenue from African tours), click the **Copy button** 📋 on the Standard toolbar, switch to PowerPoint, view Slide 6, click after **of**, click **Edit** on the menu bar, click **Paste Special**, click **Paste link**, then click **OK**

3. Size and position the Excel object as shown in Figure P1-13, then save the presentation

4. Click the **Microsoft Access program button**, open the **Tours table**, then enter new values for the Tours Sold column, as shown in Table P1-1

5. Close the Tours table, switch to PowerPoint, click **Edit** on the menu bar, click **Links**, press and hold the **[Shift]** key, click the three links entered, click **Update Now**, then click **Close**

6. Verify that the new amount ($2,209,000.00) appears
   Word automatically updates the links, but using Update Now is faster.

7. View Slide 3, note how the Boat column has increased, double-click **Survival** in the bulleted text, type **Boat**, then view Slide 4 to see how the Pie chart has changed to reflect the new data you entered in the Tours table
   You may need to wait a few minutes to see Africa's slice increase from 53% to 72%. If you've waited more than five minutes and the slice still hasn't changed, right-click the Pie chart in Excel, then click Update Link.

8. Click the **Slide Sorter View button** 🔳, press **[Ctrl][A]** to select all the slides in the presentation, click **Slide Show** on the menu bar, click **Slide Transition**, click the **Effect list arrow**, click **Random Transition** (bottom selection), then click **Apply to All**
   When you select Random Transition effects, PowerPoint applies a different effect to each slide.

9. Click the **Preset Animation list arrow** on the Slide Sorter toolbar, click **Random Effects** (bottom selection), as shown in Figure P1-14, click the **Slide Show button** 🖥, then click the mouse button to move from slide to slide
   You can select different slide transitions and build effects for each slide in Slide Sorter view.

10. Save your presentation, print a copy of the handouts (9 to a sheet), close the presentation, then save and close the files in Access, Excel, and Word

FIGURE P1-13: Excel object sized and positioned on Slide 6

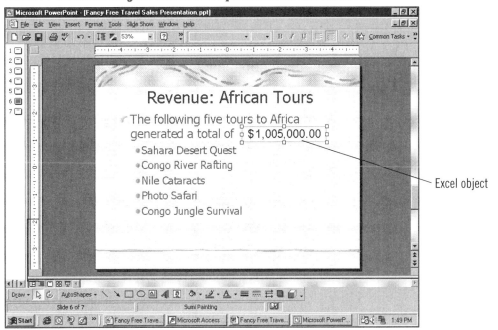

Excel object

TABLE P1-1: New information for the Tours table

TOUR NAME	TOURS SOLD
Sahara Desert Quest	20
Nile Cataracts	80
Congo Jungle Survival	30

FIGURE P1-14: Animation effect selected

Animation Effect list arrow

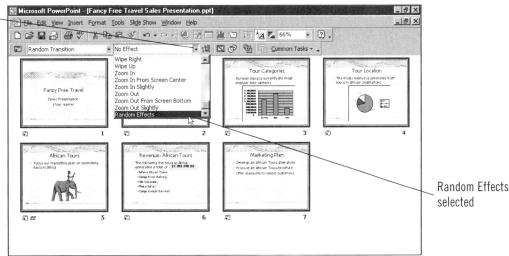

Random Effects selected

Clues to Use

Re-establishing Links

To re-establish links, you should start with the application that does not contain links and then open the remaining files in the order in which they are linked. For this presentation, the order of files is Access, Excel, and PowerPoint.

Career Options Presentation

As the marketing coordinator at Amherst Business College, you will prepare a presentation to inform potential students of the courses offered and the career options they can expect after graduating from the college. For this project you will **Create the Source Materials and the Presentation, Add Charts,** and **Add Hyperlinks and Preview the Presentation on the Web Browser.**

activity:

Create the Source Materials and the Presentation

You plan to include two charts to demonstrate the employment success of former students. The statistics you need for your charts are entered in an Access table. First create the Access table, then create the charts, and finally enter the slide titles and text required for the presentation.

steps:

Hint

Remember to select Paste Special from the Edit menu.

1. Create an Access database called **Amherst Business College**, create a new table called **Employment Table** with a primary key, then enter the fields and records in Datasheet view, as shown in Figure P2-1

2. Close the table, click **Employment Table**, click the **Copy button**, switch to Excel, paste the table as a link in a blank worksheet, then save the workbook as **Career Options Presentation**

3. Select cells **B1** to **E5**, click the **Chart Wizard button** on the Standard toolbar, click **Next** to accept the Column chart type, click **Next** again, click the **Legend tab**, click the **Bottom option button**, then complete the Chart Wizard steps

4. Select cells **C2** to **F6**, then click the **AutoSum button** Σ on the Standard toolbar

5. Click the **Chart Wizard button** on the Standard toolbar, click **Pie**, then click **Next**

6. Click the **Collapse Dialog Box button**, select cells **C1** to **E1**, type a **comma (,)**, select cells **C6** to **E6**, click the **Restore Dialog Box button** [restore.tif], click the **Rows option button**, if necessary, then click **Finish**

7. Position the two charts side-by-side, increase the chart sizes so that the data is easy to read, as shown in Figure P2-2, **right-click** the legend in the column chart, click **Format Legend**, click the **Font tab**, select the **10 pt.** font size, click **OK**, use the same procedure to modify the size of other text elements in the charts, if necessary, then save the workbook

8. Open a blank presentation in PowerPoint, enter the slide titles and text required for the presentation, as shown in Figure P2-3, check the spelling, then save the presentation as **Career Options Presentation**

FIGURE P2-1: Employment table

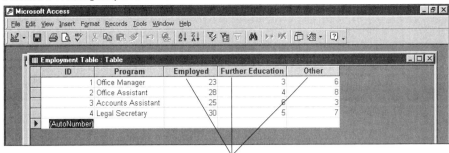

Change the Data Type to Number for the
Employed, Further Education, and Other fields

FIGURE P2-2: Completed charts in Excel

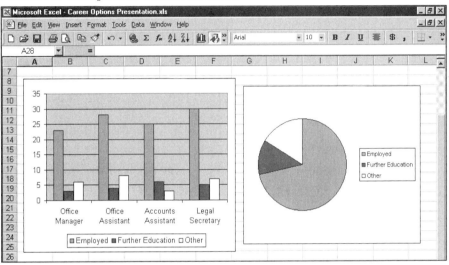

FIGURE P2-3: Career Options Presentation outline

1 ☐ Career Choices
   Amherst Business College
   [Your Name]

2 ☐ Program Objectives
   • Develop marketable skills
   • Achieve computer expertise
   • Qualify for employment
   • Build a solid foundation for further education

3 ☐ Marketable Skills
   • Document and Word Processing
   • Accounting Procedures and Spreadsheet Analysis
   • Office Management
   • Small Business Development
   • Business Writing
   • Desktop Publishing
   • Internet Communications

4 ☐ Employment Opportunities
   • Administrative and Executive Assistants
   • Accounting Assistants
   • Office Managers
   • Legal Secretaries

5 ☐ Special Features
   • Intensive hands-on training
   • Three-week employment practicum
   • Career counseling

6 ☐ Employment Statistics

7 ☐ Graduate Profile

8 ☐ Program Overview

9 ☐ Core Courses

10 ☐ Amherst Business College

activity:

Add Charts

You need to apply a presentation template, copy and modify the two Excel charts, then create an organizational chart for Slide 8.

steps:

1. Click Format on the menu bar, click Apply Design Template, select Notebook, then click Apply

2. Switch to Excel, click the Column chart, click the Copy button 🗐, switch to PowerPoint, view Slide 6: Employment Statistics, delete the "Click to add text" box, click Edit on the menu bar, click Paste Special, click the Paste link option button, then click OK

3. Size and position the chart attractively on the slide, click Format on the menu bar, click Object, click the Picture tab, click Recolor, click the Fills option button, click the list arrow next to the blue color, click the Follow Accent Scheme Color (turquoise) box, as shown in Figure P2-4, click OK, then click OK

4. View Slide7: Graduate Profile, delete the "Click to add text" box, paste the pie chart as a link, then modify the colors, size, and position of the pie chart so it appears attractively on the slide
Use your own judgment to determine the best colors to use. You will need to experiment!

Trouble

If a message appears asking you to install the Organization Chart feature, check with your instructor or technical support person.

Trouble

If four boxes already appear on your screen, just type **Legal Secretary** in the far right box, and do not click the Right Co-worker button.

5. View Slide 8: Program Overview, delete the "Click to add text" box, click Format on the menu bar, click Slide Layout, click the Organization Chart layout, click Apply, then double-click the org chart icon

6. Type Core Program in the top box, click the far left box, type Office Manager, click the middle box, type Office Assistant, click the far right box, then type Accounts Assistant

7. Click the Right Co-worker button Co-worker: , click the Accounts Assistant box, type Legal Secretary, click away from the boxes, then delete the "Type title here" text in each box, if shown

8. Click and drag your mouse across Chart Title to select it, press [Delete], press [Ctrl][A] to select all the boxes in the chart, click Styles on the menu bar, then click the middle selection in the top row, as shown in Figure P2-5

9. Click File on the menu bar, click Exit and Return to Career Options Presentation, click Yes, resize the table to match Figure P2-6, then save the presentation
Slide 8 appears as shown in Figure P2-6.

FIGURE P2-4: **Recolor dialog box**

Click here to change the color of the blue bar

Turquoise color box

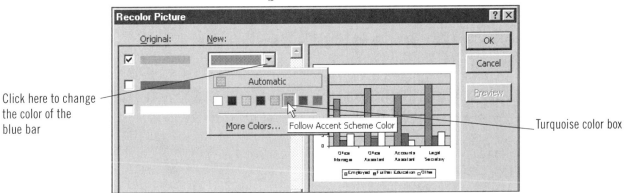

FIGURE P2-5: **Groups dialog box**

Vertical style selected

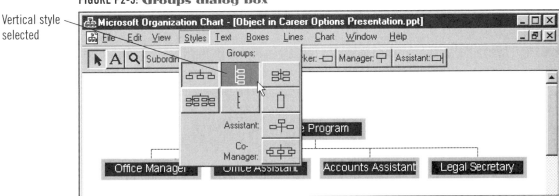

FIGURE P2-6: **Completed organizational chart on Slide 8**

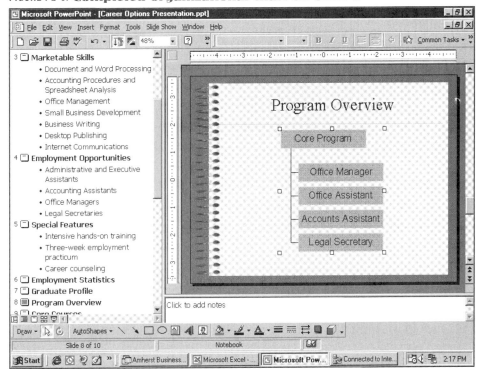

activity:

Add Hyperlinks and Preview the Presentation on the Web Browser

You will add a table to Slide 9 and a WordArt object to Slide 10, create hyperlinks that jump from selected text in one slide to another slide, then preview the presentation in your Web browser.

steps:

1. View Slide 9: Core Courses, delete the "Click to add text" box, click the Insert Table button ▦ on the Standard toolbar, then drag the mouse across the table grid to create a table of four rows and two columns
   In a few seconds a blank table form will appear on the slide.

2. Enter the text for the table, as shown in Figure P2-7

3. Click and drag the column divider to the left to decrease the size of column 1 so that "Accounting Procedures" fits on one line, click the border of the table, click the Fill Color list arrow ▢▾ on the Tables and Borders toolbar, then click the Follow Background Scheme Color box (it is cream)

4. Click away from the table, position it attractively on the slide, then save the presentation

5. Click the Next Slide button ⬇ to move to Slide 10, delete the "Click to add text" box, click the Insert WordArt button ◀ on the Drawing toolbar, click the second style in the fourth row, click OK, type Make Career Choices, press [Enter], type That Make Sense, select the Comic Sans MS font, then click OK

6. Click the 3-D button ▣ on the Drawing toolbar, click No 3-D, click the Fill Color list arrow ▢▾, click the Follow Accent Scheme Color (turquoise) box, then size and position the object as shown in Figure P2-8

7. Scroll to Slide 2, select the text Qualify for Employment in the Outline pane, click the Insert Hyperlinks button 🔗 on the Standard toolbar, click Place in This Document, click 7 Graduate Profile, then click OK

8. Click File on the menu bar, click Web Page Preview, then maximize the Web browser if necessary
   The presentation appears in the Web browser as shown in Figure P2-9.

9. Click the slide titles to the left of the slides to move from slide to slide, test the hyperlink in Slide 2, close the browser, print a sheet of handouts (9 slides to the page), then save and close the files in PowerPoint, Access, and Excel.

Trouble

If the Tables and Borders toolbar is not visible, click **View** on the the menu bar, point to **Toolbars**, then Click **Tables and Borders**.

Integration

FIGURE P2-7: **Text for the Word table**

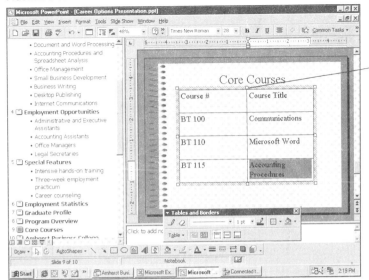

Drag the column divider to the left to increase the width of column 2

FIGURE P2-8: **Slide 10 completed**

Insert WordArt button

Fill Color button

3-D button

FIGURE P2-9: **Presentation viewed in the Web browser**

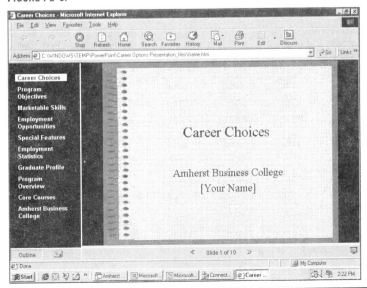

Class Party Presentation

You are on a committee formed to organize a class party to celebrate the end of a year-long business administration course at Mariposa Community College in Louisville, Kentucky. Your job is to create a slide show presentation that will inform your classmates about the party and encourage them to attend. As you create the presentation in PowerPoint, you will enter some of the data in Word and Excel and then copy it into PowerPoint. Often you will find that you need to retrieve data from other applications for inclusion in a PowerPoint presentation.

steps:

1. Create a new presentation in PowerPoint, enter the outline as shown in Figure P3-1, check the spelling, then save the presentation as **Class Party Presentation**

   Instead of selecting one of the PowerPoint templates, you will add a custom background to your presentation.

2. Switch to Slide view, click **Format** on the menu bar, click **Background** , click the **Background fill list arrow**, then click **Fill Effects**

3. Click the **Preset option button**, click the **Preset colors list arrow**, select **Late Sunset**, click **OK**, then click **Apply to all**

   As you can see, most of the text on the slide is not visible.

4. Click Format on the menu bar, click **Slide Color Scheme**, click the left scheme in the top row, then click **Apply to All**

5. Switch to a blank Word document, type **Date:**, press **[Tab]**, type **June 10**, press **[Enter]**, type **Time:**, press **[Tab]**, type **6 pm to ?**, press **[Enter]**, type **Place:**, press **[Tab]**, then type **Le Figaro Restaurant**

6. Press **[Ctrl][A]** to select all the text, click the **Copy button** 📋 on the Standard toolbar, switch to PowerPoint, view **Slide 3: Party Details**, delete the "Click to add text" box, click **Edit** on the menu bar, click **Paste Special**, click **Unformatted Text**, click **OK**, increase the font size to **40**, then position and size the text attractively on the slide

   Select Unformatted Text in the Paste Special dialog box to copy text from Word into PowerPoint.

7. Switch to a blank Excel worksheet, enter the data shown in Figure P3-2 in cells A1 to D2, select cells **A1** to **D2**, click the **Copy button** 📋 on the Standard toolbar, switch to PowerPoint, view **Slide 4: Cost Breakdown**, delete the "Click to add text" box, click the **Chart Wizard button** 📊 on the Standard toolbar, click **Chart**, click **Chart Type**, click **Pie**, click **OK**, select columns **A** to **D** in the datasheet, click the **Paste button** 📋, then delete rows 2 and 3 in the datasheet

8. Click away from the datasheet to place the pie chart on the slide, position the pie chart attractively on the slide, double-click the pie chart, move the legend to the lower corner, click the white line around the pie chart, press **[Delete]**, then click away from the pie chart to deselect it

9. Add a WordArt object and a clip art image from the Clip Gallery Live to Slide 5, similar to Figure P3-3, add animation effects to selected slide elements in Slide view, add slide transitions and builds in Slide Sorter view, compare your screen with Figure P3-3, run your slide show in Slide Show view, print it, close the Word and Excel documents without saving them, then save and close the presentation

   Ideas for Slide 5 include "We Deserve a Break!" or "Let's Celebrate!" as a WordArt object, accompanied by an appropriate clip art picture. Use your imagination to create an interesting and motivating slide.

FIGURE P3-1: **Outline for the Class Party presentation**

1 ☐ Class Party

   Business Administration Class

   Mariposa Community College

2 ☐ Purpose

   • Celebrate the end of a long, hard year

   • Share employment search tips

   • Show appreciation to our great instructors

3 ☐ Party Details

4 ☒ Cost Breakdown

5 ☒ _____

   You will create a
   WordArt object on
   this slide

FIGURE P3-2: **Data for the Slide 4 pie chart**

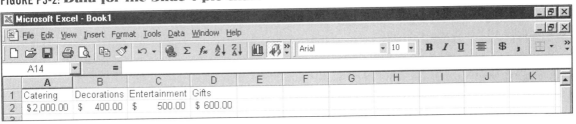

FIGURE P3-3: **Class Party Presentation in Slide Sorter view**

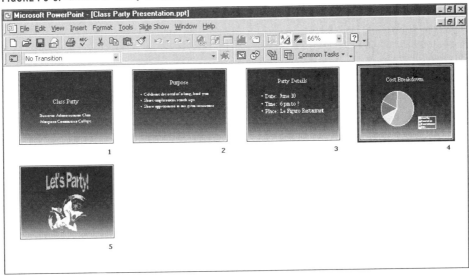

Clues to Use

Enhancing the Look of a Slide Presentation

You can achieve an almost limitless variety of looks by working with the options available in the Custom Background and Slide Color Schemes dialog boxes. You can format a textured or patterned background, select your own colors for each element on a slide, and modify any of the preset shading patterns.

In Iependent Chillen jes

INDEPENDENT CHALLENGE 1

Create an onscreen presentation of 8 to 10 slides that highlights sales information and recommends marketing strategies for a company of your choice. You could create a presentation for a movie production company that presents the revenues from the last 10 movies produced and recommends producing movies in the most popular category. Alternatively, you could create a presentation for a theme park that shows the revenues from 10 rides and then offers marketing suggestions for attracting more customers to the two most popular rides. For ideas, check the business section of your local newspaper, surf the World Wide Web, or browse through the clip art categories. For example, the roller coaster clip art image in the Entertainment category may inspire you to create a presentation involving a theme park. Follow the steps provided to create a table in Access, charts in Excel, the presentation in PowerPoint, and a presentation booklet in Word.

1. You need to know the name of your company and the type of products or services that it sells. For example, you could call your company Vitamin Vigor and describe it as a retail operation that sells vitamins, herbal teas, and other health products. Write the name and a brief description of your company in the box below:

Company Name: ....
Description: ....

2. Start Access, create a database called [Company Name] Sales Presentation, and create a table consisting of at least 10 records. Call the table [Product] table (e.g., Rides table). Include fields in the table that you will be able to use in charts. For example, a table for the theme park presentation could include the following fields: Ride Name, Category (e.g., Kiddie, Moderate, and Hair-raising), Number of Riders, and Ride Price.

3. Copy the table and paste it as a link into Excel. Create two charts that illustrate sales information about your company. For example, you could create a pie chart that shows the breakdown of ride sales by category and a column or bar chart that demonstrates the revenue from each of the 10 rides listed in the Access table.

4. Switch to PowerPoint, create an outline of your presentation, then save it as [Company Name] Sales Presentation. Following are some ideas to help you get started.

Slide #	Slide Title	Text
1	[Company Name]	Sales Presentation [Your Name]
2	Mission	Write a one- or two-sentence description of your company's goals. For ideas, refer to Slide 2 of the Fancy Free Travel sales presentation you created for Project 1.
3	[Product] Categories	Write one sentence describing a chart that illustrates the breakdown of sales by category.
4	[Product] Sales or Location	Write one sentence describing a chart that is the breakdown of sales by location or overall sales, depending on the type of chart you have created.
5	[Most Popular Product/Category]	Write a sentence describing your marketing plan, e.g., to focus on a specific product category.
6	Revenue: [Most Popular Product/Category]	List the products that generated the most income in the category you've chosen to focus on, then copy the total revenue from the category from Excel into PowerPoint.
7	Marketing Plan	Write two or three points describing your marketing plan.
8	Conclusion	Create an interesting "motivational" slide to conclude your presentation.

Add additional slides to your presentation, if you wish.

5. Switch to Slide view and apply a presentation template or a custom background. Spend some time experimenting with the wide variety of looks you can achieve by working with the options available in the Custom Background dialog boxes. Don't forget to check out the preset backgrounds!

6. Switch to Slide Master view and modify the appearance of the text in the placeholders. You may wish, for example, to change the font size and style of the text in the Master Title Style placeholder. Add a clip art image to the Slide Master, if you wish.

7. In Slide view, copy the charts to the appropriate slides (paste them as links) and add clip art pictures to selected slides. Remember that you can use the Drawing tools to modify a clip art image after you have ungrouped it. You may need to recolor the charts so that they are clear and easy to read on the slide background or template you have chosen.

8. Add motion and sound clips that you have downloaded from the Clip Gallery Live to selected slides.

9. When you are satisfied with the appearance of your slides, switch to Slide Sorter view and add some slide transitions and build effects. You can also add animation effects to selected slides in Slide view.

10. Preview your slide show and make any formatting adjustments required.

11. Change some of the values in the Access table, then update the charts in PowerPoint.

12. Print the presentation slides as handouts (9 slides to the page), then save and close all files.

INDEPENDENT CHALLENGE 2

Create a presentation that informs an audience about a specific college program or organization. Imagine that your audience will be people interested in attending the program or joining the organization. Your presentation needs to inform them about the program or organization and encourage them to enroll or join. If you wish, adapt the presentation you created for Project 2 to suit the needs of a program or organization of your choice.

1. Determine the program or organization about which you will present information. For example, you could present information about a charity organization, such as M.A.D.D. (Mothers Against Drunk Driving), the Cancer Foundation, or a Community Arts Group. Create meaningful names for each of your files.

2. Think of an interesting slant regarding the program or organization. The presentation you created for Project 2 was called "Career Choices" because it focused on how the business program at Amherst Business College helps students obtain employment in office management and administrative positions. A presentation to encourage people to join a Children's Hospital Association could be called "Caring for Kids".

3. Create a table in Access that lists certain statistics regarding the program or organization. For example, you could list three or four of the activities funded by the Children's Hospital Association and then three categories of funding (for example, Corporate, Private, and Government). For ideas, refer to the Access table you created for Project 2.

4. Copy the Access table to Excel and create one or two charts from the data.

5. Create the presentation outline in PowerPoint. Include at least eight slides in your presentation. The information you present should inform your audience about your program or organization and encourage their participation. Allow at least one slide for a Word table and one slide for an organization chart.

6. Copy the charts from Excel into PowerPoint.

7. Create an organizational chart on one of the slides. For example, you could create a chart that shows the various activities funded by your organization or the electives students can take after completing the required courses.

8. Switch to Slide view and apply a presentation template or a custom background.

9. Switch to Slide Master view and modify the appearance of the text in the placeholders.

10. Add clip art images to selected slides. Modify the clip art images to suit the message you are trying to communicate.

11. Create a hyperlink from text on one slide to another slide.

12. Preview the presentation in your Web browser.

13. Change some of the values in the Access table, update the charts in PowerPoint, print a copy of your presentation as a handout with nine slides to a page, then save and close all files.

INDEPENDENT CHALLENGE 3

Create a presentation that proposes a special event, entertainment, or party to a group of your choice. For example, you can create your own class party presentation similar to the presentation you created for Project 3. Alternatively, you can create a presentation that proposes a class reunion, a company picnic, or a weekend seminar. Create meaningful names for each of your files.

1. Create an outline in PowerPoint that includes slide titles with the following information:
    a. Type of party or event
    b. Purpose of the party or event
    c. Location, time, and cost
    d. Chart showing the cost breakdown
    e. "Motivational" slide
2. Use as many slides as you wish. For ideas, refer to the presentation you created for Project 3.
3. Enter the party details in Word, then copy, and paste them as unformatted text into PowerPoint.
4. Create a worksheet in Excel that shows the cost breakdown for the party, copy the data into a datasheet that you create in PowerPoint, then create a pie chart.
5. Modify the presentation, use custom backgrounds, templates, slide transitions, slide builds, and animation effects, then print a copy. Save and close all files.

INDEPENDENT CHALLENGE 4

Your supervisor has asked you to create a presentation that will convince the executives of your company to launch a Web site on the World Wide Web. The company is called Balloon Magic and sells all kinds of balloons and novelties for parties, conventions, and special events. You and your supervisor feel that a presence on the World Wide Web would greatly assist the company's recent decision to expand its mail order department. Follow the instructions provided to create and then modify the presentation that you plan to give to the executives. Save all the files you create as Balloon Magic.

1. Open a blank presentation in Outline view, then enter the slide titles and text for the presentation as shown below:

Slide #	Slide Title	Level 1 Text
1	Balloon Magic	Publishing on the World Wide Web
2	Purpose	Publish a Web site on the World Wide Web to promote Balloon Magic's products Provide online ordering to Web customers Connect with other balloon and novelty businesses
3	Web Overview	The World Wide Web has grown at an incredible pace over the past three years, nearly doubling its users every year
4	Web Users Profile	65% of Web users are in their mid-thirties and make over $65,000 per year
5	Business on the Web	40% of businesses advertising on the Web over the past year report a 30% increase in revenues 20% report more than a 50% increase in revenues
6	Web Launch Strategy	Create a Web site Establish links with related businesses Launch the Web site on the Internet Access server
7	First-Year Costs	Web site costs for the first year break down as shown in the table following
8	Goals	Increase mail order revenues by 30% in year 1 Increase mail order revenues by 40% in year 2 Hire an in-house "Web master" to service the Web site at the end of year 1

2. Apply the Daybreak preset background in the Gradient tab of the Fill Effects database to all the slides.

3. Switch to Slide Master view, change the font in the Master Title Style placeholder to Gill Sans Ultra Bold, reduce the font size to 40 pt., insert a motion clip of a balloon from Clip Gallery Live, then size and position the image in the lower-right corner of the slide master. Refer to Figure IC-1 as you work.

4. Switch to Slide view, view Slide 3, open a blank worksheet in Excel, enter the data shown below:

1998	1999	2000	2001
20	45	80	150

5. Select the data in the Excel worksheet, click the Chart Wizard button, click Next, click the Series tab, click in the Category (X) axis labels text box, collapse the dialog box if necessary, then select the cells containing the years (e.g. cells A1 to D1).

6. Expand the dialog box, click Series 1, click Remove, click Next, type Millions as the Y-axis title, then click Finish.

7. Click the legend, click Delete, right-click the gray grid area, click Format-Plot Area, click the None option button in the Area section, click OK, right-click the chart area, click Format Chart Area, then remove the white background from the chart area.

8. Copy the chart and paste it as a link in Slide 3.

9. View Slide 7, create a table consisting of two columns and three rows, then enter the text as shown below.

Web Page Design $300
Server Space for One Year $1,200
Web Page Maintenance $300

10. Modify the font size and column width as shown in Figure IC-1.

11. Add clip art pictures, sound clips, and motion clips to selected slides. Remember that you can download clips from the Clip Gallery Live and modify a clip art image after you have ungrouped it.

12. In Slide view, add preset animation effects as listed below to the bulleted text in the slides specified.
Slide 2: Drive-in Effect
Slide 4: Camera Effect
Slide 5: Typewriter Text Effect

13. In Slide Sorter view, add slide transition and build effects to selected slides, preview the slide show, make different choices as required, then print the slides in your presentation as a handout of nine slides to one page.

FIGURE IC-1: **Completed presentation in Slide Sorter view**

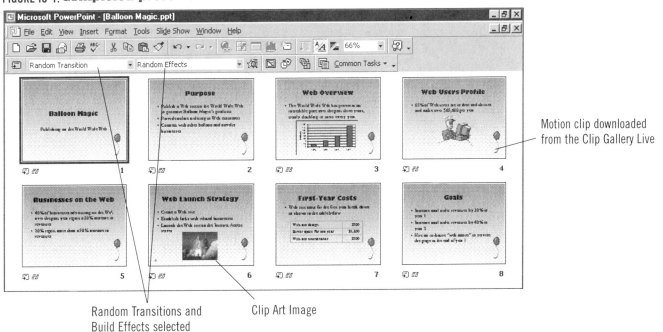

Motion clip downloaded from the Clip Gallery Live

Random Transitions and Build Effects selected

Clip Art Image

Visual Workshop

For a course on tourism in the Caribbean, you have decided to create a presentation that focuses on popular hotels on the various Caribbean islands. One of the slides in the presentation will be a pie chart that shows the breakdown of hotel guests by location. Create the Hotels table in an Access database called Caribbean Hotels, as shown in Figure VW-1, answer Yes to create a Primary Key, copy the table and paste it as a link into Excel, then create a pie chart that shows the number of guests at each location (e.g. Jamaica, Cuba, etc.). Open PowerPoint, select the Title Only AutoLayout, then copy the pie chart and paste it as a link into the slide. Add a title to the slide, apply the Water droplets texture as the background, then insert an appropriate clip art image. Switch to Access, change the number of guests who stayed at the Montego Bay Resort on Jamaica to 600, switch back to PowerPoint, update the link so that the Jamaica slice increases to 53%, as shown in Figure VW-2, then print a copy of the slide. Save all documents as "Caribbean Tourism".

FIGURE VW-1: **Hotels table**

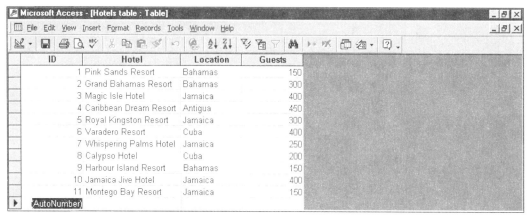

FIGURE VW-2: **Completed slide**

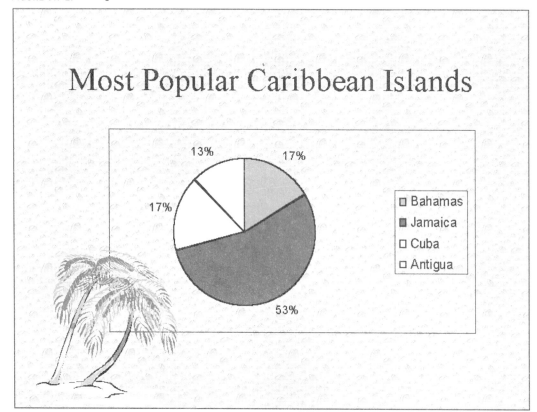

Microsoft
► World Wide Web Projects
with Internet Explorer 5.0

College and Job Search

In This Unit You Will Explore:

PROJECT 1 ► **College Programs for Studying Abroad**

PROJECT 2 ► **Summer Job Opportunities**

PROJECT 3 ► **Resume Posting**

You can use the World Wide Web to find information about colleges and universities all over the world. Many college sites consist of hundreds of pages containing information about courses, prerequisites, professors, student groups, and even dormitory accommodations. Many sites also allow you to register and even take courses online. Another fast-growing area of the World Wide Web concerns job opportunities. Companies and organizations around the world post job vacancies, and individuals post their resumes. For specialized jobs, in particular, the World Wide Web's employment resources provide valuable opportunities for job seekers. ► In this unit, you will explore some college sites that offer overseas study programs, look for a summer job, and post your own resume on the World Wide Web.

PROJECT 1

College Programs for Studying Abroad

You've decided that you would like to investigate the possibility of studying in a foreign country for an academic term or even a full year. From the hundreds of programs offered, you need to select one that suits your academic interests and is located in a country to which you want to travel. To help you choose the best program, you will search the World Wide Web for information about programs for studying abroad and then create a table in your word processing program that compares five of the programs that most interest you. Four activities are required to complete this project.

Project Activities

Search for Study Abroad Programs

Several sites exist that contain databases of Study Abroad programs. A **database** contains information related to a specific subject, project, enterprise, or business. For example, a database can contain all the names and addresses of a company's clients or a list of all the universities that sponsor Study Abroad programs. Often, databases are organized both by subject and by location. You can search a database for a program on a specific subject, such as Physics, or for a program in a specific country, such as Mexico. Some of the sites that list Study Abroad programs are maintained by a particular university and provide information only on programs sponsored by that university. Other sites provide information on programs sponsored by universities all over the world. You will start your search for one of these databases by first going to the Infoseek search page and then entering the keywords "study abroad" as your search terms. Table P1-1 describes five of the major search tools. As you develop your Web-surfing skills, you will learn to identify the search tool best suited to finding the type of information you require.

Identify a Program

You will go to the studyabroad.com Web site and explore its links to Art History programs in Italy.

Set up a Comparison Table

Next, you will set up a comparison table in Microsoft Word that includes headings for the types of information you need to gather about four Study Abroad programs.

Gather Information and Print the Comparison Table

Finally, you need to choose the types of programs and locations that interest you, gather information about each program, and copy this information into the table. You will find the required information at a variety of college sites. Figure P1-1 lists information about four Study Abroad programs related to studying art history in Italy. The document you produce will include information about four of the programs organized into a table.

TABLE P1-1: Description of major search sites

SEARCH TOOL	DESCRIPTION	TIPS AND COMMENTS
MSN	• Default search engine on Internet Explorer • Features directory listings and search engine capabilities • Provides a short description of each site found	• Click the results/page list arrow to select how many results to show per page (from 10 to 100)
Excite	• Features both directory listings and search engine capabilities • Offers a good news search service (NewsTracker) • Provides a review of each site found	• Searches every word on every page of the Web. • Click Show Titles to remove reviews and see more sites on the screen at one time
Infoseek	• Includes a "human-compiled" directory of Web sites • Provides lists of pages in related categories	• Use to find pages in the categories provided • Good for finding related categories; useful reviews
AltaVista	• One of the largest search engines on the Web, in terms of pages indexed • Popular with both researchers and basic users	• The "Ask AltaVista" feature allows you to enter questions as search terms (for example, the question "What is the capital of Bulgaria?" would return the correct answer
Yahoo!	• Organizes sites by category • Provides both a summary and a link to the related category • Largest human-compiled guide to the Web	• Use for finding sites in specific categories • Great source for sites related to geographical location (e.g., Regional)

FIGURE P1-1: Comparison table of study abroad

Studying Abroad Programs

Institution	LEXIA PROGRAM PROFILE: *Venice, Italy*
Field of Study	ITALIAN CIVILIZATION SEMINAR
Field Trips	Each program typically includes several one- or two-day trips in the site city and surrounding areas or neighboring countries. In addition, short excursions within the city are also an important part of the program. These excursions help introduce students to the host country and region, enabling them to extend their learning outside of the classroom.
Requirements	Primarily open to individuals who are in good academic standing at any college or university, have completed at least one year of college, and who have a minimum grade point average of at least 2.5.
Cost	$17,450 (academic year)
Program URL	http://www.lexiaintl.org/venice.html
Institution	**Academic Programs International, Granada Spain**
Field of Study	**SPANISH LANGUAGE & CULTURE PROGRAM**
Field Trips	Numerous excursions all around Spain including Madrid, Salamanca, Toledo, El Escorial, Cadiz, and Osuna.
Requirements	Students must have a 2.75 GPA and be in good academic standing at their U.S. university.
Cost	$5,100 (one term)
Program URL	http://www.academicintl.com/index/
Institution	**Eastern Michigan University's Asian Cultural History Tour**
Field of Study	Social, economic, and political problems of key Asian countries.
Field Trips	Non-stationary program—ongoing trav... ...ing Beijing, A...

activity:

Search for Study Abroad Programs

You will use Infoseek to search for a site that includes a large Study Abroad database. In Infoseek, you can choose to follow links to various categories or you can enter your own search terms. You will enter the search terms "studying abroad" in the Infoseek search box.

steps:

1. Connect to the Internet, start Internet Explorer 5.0, then, if the MSN (Microsoft Network) home page does not appear on your screen, click in the **Address box**, type **www.msn.com**, then press **[Enter]**
The MSN home page appears. On this page, you can select the search engine you want to use to conduct your search and then enter the search terms.

2. Click the **using list arrow**, then select **Infoseek**, as shown in Figure P1-2

3. Click in the **Search the Web for** text box

4. Type **study abroad**, then press **[Enter]**

5. When the list of Web sites appears, scroll down the list to find the hyperlink called **studyabroad.com**, as shown in Figure P1-3
Note that a different list of results may appear on your screen or the hyperlink to the studyabroad.com site may be different. Check for the studyabroad.com address as shown in Figure P1-3.

6. Click the **studyabroad.com** hyperlink or, if you cannot see the studyabroad.com site in your list of results, click in the **Address box** at the top of the screen, type **www.studyabroad.com**, then press **[Enter]**
The studyabroad.com home page appears similar to Figure P1-4. Note that some of the links to educational institutions may be different on the page that appears for you. Large sites such as studyabroad.com are updated frequently.

7. Click the **Favorites button** 🔲 on the toolbar, then click **Add**

8. Click **OK** to add the address of the studyabroad.com Web site to the list of favorites on the computer you are using
Once you have added a Web site to your list of favorites, you can use Windows Explorer to copy the studyabroad.com address to a disk

9. Click 🔲 again to close the Favorites panel

Saving a favorite to a disk

If you are working on a computer at your school or office, you may not be able to save favorites. However, you can choose to save your favorites to a disk so that you can view them on a different computer. To save a favorite to your Project Disk:
Click Favorites on the menu bar, then click Organize Favorites. Right-click the favorite you wish to save to a disk. Click Send To, click 3½" Floppy, then click Close.

FIGURE P1-2: Selecting the Infoseek search engine from the MSN search page

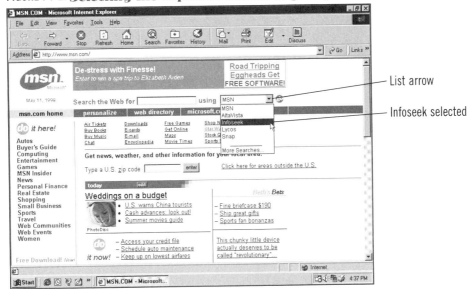

List arrow

Infoseek selected

FIGURE P1-3: Hyperlink to the studyabroad.com Web site

Address box

www.studyabroad.com link

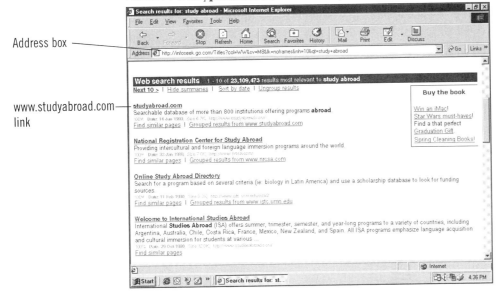

FIGURE P1-4: studyabroad.com Web site

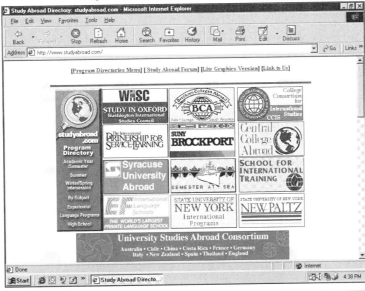

activity:

Identify a Program

From the studyabroad.com Web site, you can choose various ways to search for a study abroad program that interests you. For example, you can search for programs by country or by subject, or you can search for specific types of programs such as internship programs or summer law programs. You will start off by searching for programs in Italy, and then narrow your search by specifying programs related to art history.

steps:

1. Scroll down the studyabroad.com page to find a section related to searching for a study abroad program that appears similar to Figure P1-5

The links and text on the page that appears on your browser may be different, depending on whether the studyabroad.com Web site has been re-designed or updated.

2. Click a link such as <u>**Academic Year and Semester programs by Country**</u> as shown in Figure P1-5

3. Scroll to **Italy** in the list of destinations, then click **Italy**

4. Click **Select**, then scroll down the page that appears

On the map of Italy that appears, you can click the area that interests you to see a list of the programs offered.

5. Click the **Back button** ⇐ on the toolbar **twice** to return to the list of search options

Rather than select an institution at random, you can narrow your search by focusing only on the institutions that offer art history programs in Italy.

6. Click <u>**Academic Programs by Subject**</u>, select **Art History** from the list of choices, click <u>**Art History — Europe**</u>, then select **Italy** from the list of countries

Note that you may need to use a different method to access the required information, depending on how the studyabroad.com Web site has been updated.

7. Click **Find**, then scroll through the list of results

A page similar to Figure P1-6 appears. The results on your page may be different. As you can see, each entry (listed alphabetically) consists of the location of the study abroad program, a brief description, and contact information—usually in the form of a link to an e-mail address.

8. Click the link to **Lexia International** or, if the link to Lexia International does not appear in your list of programs, click the **Address box**, type **www.lexiaintl.org**, press **[Enter]**, then follow the links to find the Lexia Web site for Venice that appears similar to Figure P1-7

The Lexia Web site describing its program in Venice, Italy, appears similar to Figure P1-7.

FIGURE P1-5: Country search link selected

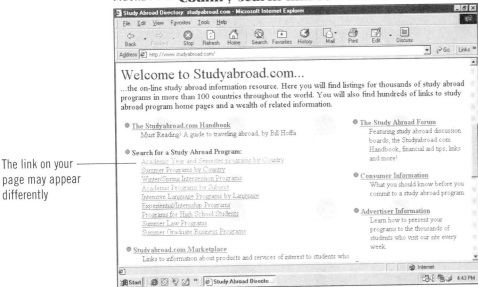

The link on your page may appear differently

FIGURE P1-6: List of art history programs in Italy

Link to the sponsoring institution's Web site

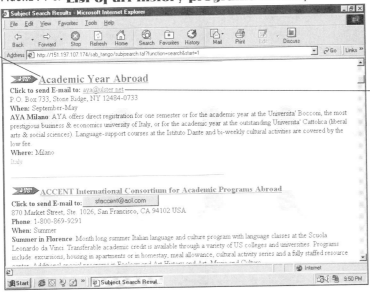

Link to an e-mail address

FIGURE P1-7: Lexia's Venice program Web site

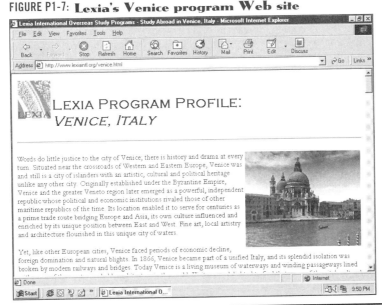

activity:

Set Up a Comparison Table

You need to develop a system to gather information and enter it in a table you create in Microsoft Word. First, you will set up the table in Word, and then you will copy information about Lexia's cultural program in Venice into the table. Once you have completed these steps, you can go on to gather information about other programs and locations of your choice.

steps:

1. Start Word, click **Table** on the menu bar, click **Insert** click **Table**, type **2** for the number of columns, type **25** for the number of rows, then click **OK**

2. Move the mouse over the dividing line between columns 1 and 2 until you see ◄║►, click ◄║►, then drag the column divider to the left to reduce the width of column 1 to approximately 1.5"
   Type the labels in rows 1 to 6 as shown in Figure P1-8, then save the document as "Studying Abroad Programs" to the disk where you plan to store all the files for this book

3. In Internet Explorer, scroll down the Lexia Venice page to view the information provided

4. Select **LEXIA PROGRAM PROFILE: Venice, Italy** at the top of the page or similar text that includes "Lexia"

5. Press **[Ctrl][C]** switch to Word, **right-click** the cell next to Institution, then click **Paste**

6. Switch to Internet Explorer, then use the Copy and Paste commands to transfer the information required for your table, as shown in Figure P1-9, using links provided at the bottom of the page
   After you follow links to find some of the information, use the Back button to return to the Lexia Venice site. Some of the text you paste into the Word table will not be formatted with the same font as the other text in the document. You will fix this problem in the next activity. Take your time gathering the information. Concentrate on finding information that you feel would be relevant to a student interested in attending the Lexia program in Venice. The information you find may not match exactly the information shown in Figure P1-9.

7. Make sure you are at the page containing the Lexia Program Profile for Venice, Italy, click the **Address box** in Internet Explorer, press **[Ctrl][C]** switch to Word, click the table cell next to Program URL, then press **[Ctrl][V]**

8. Save the document

Hint

You can use the [Ctrl][C] and [Ctrl][V] keystroke commands to speed up the copy/paste process.

FIGURE P1-8: **Table setup**

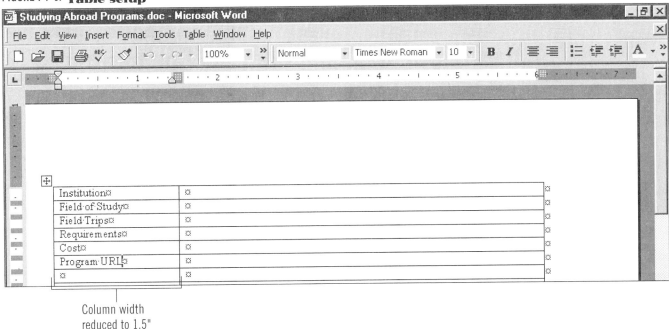

Column width
reduced to 1.5"

FIGURE P1-9: **Information about the Lexia program in Venice**

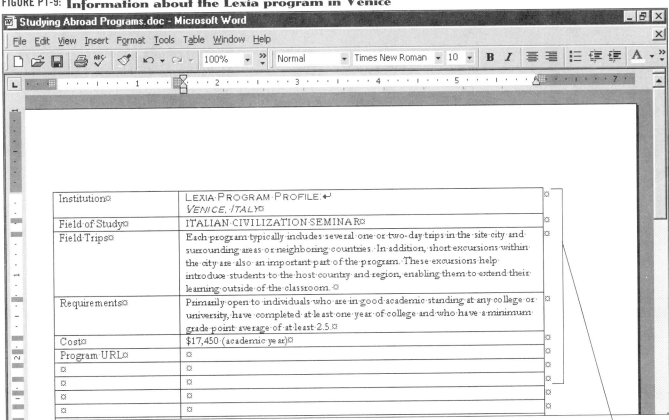

The information you
copy may be slightly
different

activity:

Gather Information and Print the Comparison Table

You need to gather the information required for your table from a variety of sites, and then format the table attractively for printing. The formatted table is shown in Figure P1-10 with information about Lexia's program in Venice along with information about three additional programs in a variety of fields. Your table will contain information about the Venice program and three different programs related to your own interests.

Hint

Use Copy and Paste to copy the row headings down the table.

steps:

1. Decide what field of study and location you prefer, apply the techniques you have learned to identify three programs from the studyabroad.com Web site that interest you, then gather the information required for your table

   Remember to add to your list of favorites the Web sites that you will need to show again. To find programs, use the search tools provided on the studyabroad.com Web site. If you cannot find information required for a specific cell in your table, just enter "Not Available". If necessary, summarize information in your own words instead of using the Copy and Paste functions.

2. In Word, press **[Ctrl][A]** to select the entire document, click the **Font list arrow**, select **Times New Roman** (or another font of your choice), click the **Font Size list arrow**, then select **12**

3. Press **[Ctrl][Home]** to move to the top of the table, press **[Enter]** twice to move down the table, type and center **Studying Abroad Programs** at the top of the page, press **[Enter]** then enhance the text with **20 pt.** and **Bold** as shown in Figure P1-10

4. Select the first row of your table, then enhance the text with **14 pt.** and **Bold** as shown in Figure P1-10

5. Double-click the **Format Painter button** ◇ on the Standard toolbar, then click to the left of each of the remaining three program names to enhance them with 14-pt. and Bold
   You may need to click the More Buttons button to find the Format Painter button. When you have finished formattting the program names, click the Format Painter button to turn it off.

6. Enhance the table form attractively
   You can choose to add border lines, shading, and additional text formatting. In the sample table in Figure P1-10, the row labels were right-aligned and bolded, border lines were added, the rows containing the university names were shaded, the cost information was bolded, and the URLs were italicized. You decide how best to format the information you have gathered.

7. View your document in Whole Page view, make any spacing adjustments required so that the table appears attractively spaced over one or two pages, print a copy of your table, then save and close the document

Studying Abroad Programs

Institution	**LEXIA PROGRAM PROFILE:** *Venice, Italy*
Field of Study	ITALIAN CIVILIZATION SEMINAR
Field Trips	Each program typically includes several one- or two-day trips in the site city and surrounding areas or neighboring countries. In addition, short excursions within the city are also an important part of the program. These excursions help introduce students to the host country and region, enabling them to extend their learning outside of the classroom.
Requirements	Primarily open to individuals who are in good academic standing at any college or university, have completed at least one year of college, and who have a minimum grade point average of at least 2.5.
Cost	$17,450 (academic year)
Program URL	http://www.lexiaintl.org/venice.html
Institution	**Academic Programs International, Granada Spain**
Field of Study	**SPANISH LANGUAGE & CULTURE PROGRAM**
Field Trips	Numerous excursions all around Spain including Madrid, Salamanca, Toledo, El Escorial, Cadiz, and Osuna.
Requirements	Students must have a 2.75 GPA and be in good academic standing at their U.S. university.
Cost	$5,100 (one term)
Program URL	http://www.academicintl.com/index/
Institution	**Eastern Michigan University's Asian Cultural History Tour**
Field of Study	Social, economic, and political problems of key Asian countries.
Field Trips	Non-stationary program—ongoing travel through several Asian countries including Beijing, Agra, Hanoi, Jaipur, and Shanghai.
Requirements	College sophomores, juniors, and seniors of any major are eligible. Applicants must have completed at least 30 hours of college credit with a 2.5 GPA before the tour begins.
Cost	$7,595
Program URL	http://www.emich.edu/abroad/ACHT/asindx.html
Institution	**Boston University: The Belize Archeological Field School**
Field of Study	Archeology
Field Trips	Scheduled travel to Tikal; field trips to Lamanai, Cerros.
Requirements	Not available.
Cost	$11,885 per semester tuition
Program URL	http://web.bu.edu/abroad/belize.html

Summer Job Opportunities

You could spend days—weeks even—surfing the hundreds of job search databases on the World Wide Web. To make your search as efficient as possible, you need to focus on a specific job category and location. In this way, you make sure that you look only for jobs that meet specific criteria. For example, you could decide to search only for jobs as a Web page designer in San Francisco that require a background in both journalism and graphic arts. For Project 2, you will compile listings for summer job opportunities. To complete this project, you will **Explore National Park Jobs** and then **Compile Four Additional Postings**.

activity:

Explore National Park Jobs

To begin your search for summer job opportunities, you will find a site that lists jobs available in various national parks throughout the United States.

steps:

1. In Internet Explorer, click in the **Address box**, type www.altavista.com, then press [Enter]

2. Click in the search box, type **Where can you find summer job postings?**, click **Search**, then add the list of search results that appears to your list of favorites
   You will return to this list to explore sites related to job opportunities that interest you. Note that asking questions in AltaVista can sometimes produce good results.

3. Scroll down the list of search results, click **Summer Employment Opportunities**, then click **Cool Works** or, if this link does not appear, click in the Address box, type www.coolworks.com, then press [Enter]
   The Cool Works site appears similar to Figure P2-1.

4. Click **National Parks**, click **Grand Canyon National Park**, click **Grand Canyon National Park Lodges**, scroll down the page, then click **The Jobs**
   Note that you may need to follow different links to find a list of jobs offered at the Grand Canyon National Park Lodges.

5. Scroll down the page to read the various positions available

6. Select one of the positions in the Food and Beverage Department, copy it, open a blank document in Word, paste the description as shown in Figure P2-2, then save the document as **Summer Job Opportunities**

7. In Internet Explorer, scroll to the top of the page, select the text **Grand Canyon National Park Lodges**, then copy it above the job description in Word

8. In Internet Explorer, scroll to the bottom of the page, click **To Apply**, then click **Application Form**
   If Adobe Acrobat Reader is installed on the computer you are using, the application form will appear in Acrobat Reader as shown in Figure P2-3. You could print this form, complete it, and then mail it to the Grand Canyon Lodge. If Acrobat Reader is not installed on your system, go on to the next step.

9. Click the **Back button** ⇦, close Acrobat Reader, if necessary, select the address of the Grand Canyon Lodge, copy and paste it to your Word document, then save the document

FIGURE P2-1: Cool Works site

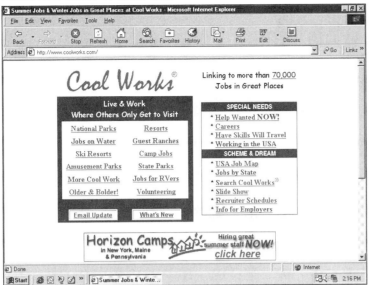

FIGURE P2-2: Position copied to Word

The position you select will be different

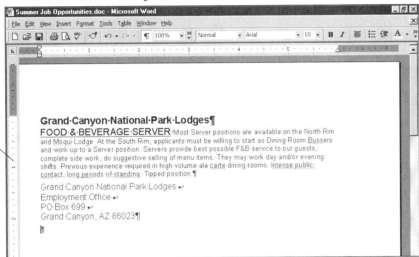

FIGURE P2-3: Application form viewed in Acrobat Reader

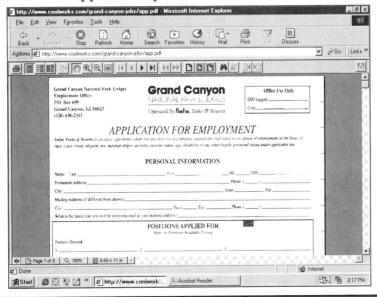

activity:

Compile Additional Postings

You need to find information about three additional positions for a summer job that interests you, and then copy the information to your word processing document.

steps:

1. In Internet Explorer click the URL in the Address box, then copy it below the contact address in Word

2. Move to the top of Word, then type and format **Summer Job Opportunities** as shown in Figure P2-4

3. Format the National Park job posting so that it appears similar to Figure P2-4

Note that you will need to remove extra spaces and hard returns, add Bold to selected headings, remove bold from body text, and increase the font size of the company/organization name.

4. Determine the type of summer job you might enjoy

5. In Internet Explorer, check out the Cool Works site and other sites listed in the Excite search results

6. Identify three summer jobs that interest you, then copy and paste the information into Word so that the completed document lists four summer job postings (including the posting for Grand Canyon National Park)

Try to gather information from at least three different sites. Once you have identified a job that interests you, you need to copy the name of the company or organization, the job description, the contact information, and the URL to your word processing program. Note that the contact information may be an e-mail address.

7. Format the document attractively over one or two pages, print a copy, then save and close the document

Use the Format Painter to apply consistent formatting to each of the four descriptions. A sample Summer Job Opportunities document appears in Figure P2-5. This sample document includes jobs from a variety of fields. Your Summer Job Opportunities document should list postings that interest you and for which you are qualified.

FIGURE P2-4: National Park job position formatted

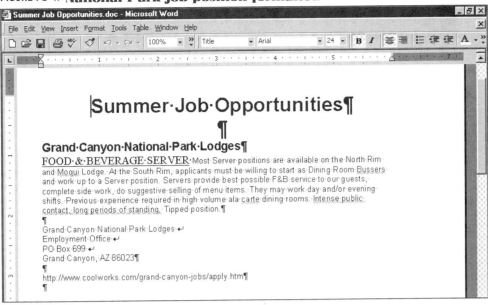

FIGURE P2-5: Sample list of summer job opportunities

Summer Job Opportunities

Grand Canyon National Park Lodges
<u>FOOD & BEVERAGE SERVER</u> Most Server positions are available on the North Rim and Moqui Lodge. At the South Rim, applicants must be willing to start as Dining Room Bussers and work up to a Server position. Servers provide best possible F&B service to our guests, complete side work, do suggestive selling of menu items. They may work day and/or evening shifts. Previous experience required in high volume ala carte dining rooms. Intense public contact, long periods of standing. Tipped position.

Grand Canyon National Park Lodges
Employment Office
PO Box 699
Grand Canyon, AZ 86023

http://www.coolworks.com/grand-canyon-jobs/apply.htm

Denali Windsong Lodge
<u>FRONT DESK CLERK: $8.00/HOUR</u>
Denali Windsong Lodge is a seventy-two room lodge located one mile north of the entrance to Denali National Park. Denali National Park is known for its wildlife viewing, photography, hiking, and mountain biking opportunities. There is a low cost shuttle running into the Park, and most activities are within easy walking distance.

Alaska Tour & Travel
A service of Alaska Windsong Lodges
P.O. Box 22-1011
Anchorage, AK 99522

http://www.alaska-tour.com/Jobs.html

Crestwood Valley Day Camp
<u>DAY CAMP COUNSELLORS</u>
Crestwood Valley Day Camp is centrally located in the Bayview and Lawerence area in Toronto. Crestwood is in search of enthusiastic and fun day camp counsellors for July and August camp this summer. If you are pursuing a career with children, Crestwood would be an excellent addition to a resume as Crestwood Valley Day Camp is affiliated with Crestwood School - and is therefore highly respected.

Crestwood Valley Day Camp
Toronto, ON, Canada
(416) 444 – 9595

http://www.summerjobs.com/do/where/jobtree/Canada

Moon Beach Camp
<u>WATERFRONT DIRECTOR</u>

Certified lifeguard responsible for coordinating the swimming and watercraft programs. Moon Beach Camp is located on the shores of Moon Lake and Little St Germain Lake in the heart of Wisconsin's Northwoods approximately 30 miles North of Rhinelander and 8 miles West of Eagle River.

Contact: (715) 479-8255

http://www.ucci.org/mb-jobs.html

Resume Posting

New resume-posting services are appearing on the World Wide Web almost daily. Although many of these services charge a fee for posting your resume, you can still find some services that will post your resume for free. Employers seeking job candidates can search for key words to access resumes of candidates who may suit the offered position. Once you have posted your resume, you can update it and check whether any employers have accessed it. In Project 3, you will **Create Your Resume**, and then **Post Your Resume**.

activity:

Create Your Resume

To post your resume on one of the free services, copy it from your word processing program and paste it into the space allocated on the Web site. Any formatting included in your resume, such as bolding and font sizes, will be lost. Your first step, therefore, is to create an unformatted text version of your resume. If you already have a resume on file, you can save it as a new file, then remove all the formatting.

steps:

1. If you have your resume on file, open it in Word, or create a one-page resume similar to the sample resume shown in Figure P3-1

   If you need to create your resume, make sure you include an objective along with information about your education and work experience. The objective states the type of position you are looking for and usually the location that interests you. For example, if you are seeking employment as an accountant, you could enter "To obtain employment as a Cost Accountant for a service-oriented business in the Little Rock area" as your objective. Use the resume shown in Figure P3-1 as your guide. If you have already created your resume, make sure you include an objective.

2. Save your formatted resume as **My Resume**, then save the resume again as **Resume for Posting on the Web**

   You now have two copies of your resume. Next, remove the formatting from the "Resume for Posting on the Web" version.

3. Press **[Ctrl][A]** to select all the text, click **Format** on the menu bar, click **Style**, select **Normal** from the list of styles, then click **Apply**

4. Press **[Ctrl][A]**, click all the formatting buttons on the formatting toolbar twice to remove all the bold, italics, and underlining, then remove other enhancements such as border lines

5. If your resume includes a table, select the table, click **Table** on the menu bar, click **Convert**, click **Table to Text**, click the **Paragraph Marks option button**, then click **OK**

6. Add hard returns where required to separate the various sections of the resume

7. Select the first heading, click **Format** on the menu bar, click **Font**, click **All caps**, click **OK**, then format the remaining headings in All caps, as shown in Figure P3-2

8. Use semicolons to separate information originally included over several lines

9. Save the unformatted resume

FIGURE P3-1: Sample resume formatted

JOYCE ALLAN
2131 Dollarton Hwy.
North Vancouver, BC V7H 1A8
Phone/Fax: (604) 929-4431
e-mail: joyce@commerce.ca

Objective

To apply my organizational and computer skills as an Administrative Assistant in a service-based company or organization

Education

1999-2000:	**Capilano College**, North Vancouver, BC
	Administrative Assistant Certificate

- Computer Skills: Microsoft Office 2000: Word, Excel, Access, PowerPoint, FrontPage, Publisher, and Adobe PageMaker 6.5
- Business Communications and Organizational Behavior
- Basic Accounting and Bookkeeping
- Administrative Procedures
- Internet Communications

1993-1997:	**Point Gray Senior Secondary School**
	Grade 12 Graduation

Work Experience

1998-1999:	**Best Bookkeeping**, 3095 West George Street, Vancouver
	Office Assistant (part-time)
	Responsibilities included:

- Maintaining company records
- Formatting documents in Word 97
- Organizing company database with Access 97

1996-1997:	**Camp Haida**, Gambier Island, British Columbia
	Camp Counselor (summers)
	Responsibilities included:

- Supervising groups of 10 campers aged 9 to 11
- Organizing crafts and sports activities
- Assisting with general office duties

Volunteer Experience

1995-1998:	**Mother's March**, North Vancouver Chapter
1999-2000:	**Capilano College Applied Business Technology Department**
	Student Activities Coordinator

References

Available on request

FIGURE P3-2: Sample resume: formatting removed

JOYCE ALLAN
2131 Dollarton Hwy.
North Vancouver, BC V7H 1A8
Phone/Fax: (604) 929-4431
e-mail: joyce@commerce.ca

OBJECTIVE
To apply my organizational and computer skills as an Administrative Assistant in a service-based company or organization

EDUCATION
1999-2000: Capilano College, North Vancouver, BC; Administrative Assistant Certificate; Computer Skills: Microsoft Office 2000: Word, Excel, Access, PowerPoint, FrontPage, Publisher, and Adobe PageMaker 6.5; Business Communications and Organizational Behavior; Basic Accounting and Bookkeeping; Administrative Procedures Internet Communications
1993-1997: Point Gray Senior Secondary School; Grade 12 Graduation

WORK EXPERIENCE
1998-1999: Best Bookkeeping, 3095 West George Street, Vancouver; *Office Assistant (part-time)'* Responsibilities included: Maintaining company records; Formatting documents in Word 97; Organizing company database with Access 97
1996-1997: Camp Haida, Gambier Island, British Columbia; *Camp Counselor (summers)* Responsibilities included: Supervising groups of 10 campers aged 9 to 11; Organizing crafts and sports activities; Assisting with general office duties

VOLUNTEER EXPERIENCE
1995-1998: Mother's March, North Vancouver Chapter
1999-2000: Capilano College Applied Business Technology Department; *Student Activities Coordinator*

REFERENCES: Available on request

activity:

Post Your Resume

First you will search for sites on Yahoo! that allow you to post your resume for free. You will then post your resume on the CareerShop site. On this site you will need to logon. If you do not wish to logon to the site, just read the directions, then try searching for and logging on to a different site.

steps:

1. In Internet Explorer, click in the Address box, type **www.yahoo.com**, click **Go**, click **Jobs** under the Business & Economy hyperlink, then click **Resumes**

2. Add the Web page to your Favorites folder

As you can see, hundreds of sites offer resume-posting services. You can return to this list to find additional Web sites that will accept resume postings. The CareerShop site is one of the sites listed. You can reach it quickly by entering its address in the Address box.

3. Click in the Address box, type **www.careershop.com**, then press **[Enter]**

The Career Shop site appears similar to Figure P3-3.

4. Scroll down the page that appears, then follow links to find the resume-posting form that appears similar to Figure P3-4

You may be able to click Resume, as shown in Figure P3-3, and then click the Post Resume tab.

5. Complete the form with the required information

Note that you will be required to enter your e-mail address and to make up a login name. Choose a simple name that you will remember (such as your own name!). As you complete the form, you do not need to enter personal information such as your home address or telephone number if you do not wish. Make sure you do enter information in the text boxes that are marked with an asterisk.

6. When you have completed the form and are ready to copy your resume into the text box provided, return to Word, press **[Ctrl][A]** to select the text of your unformatted resume, press **[Ctrl][C]**, return to the resume posting page, click in the text box in the Career Shop site, then press **[Ctrl][V]**

7. Click **Submit** at the bottom of the page

8. Return to the Yahoo! list of search results, explore some of the other sites listed, then post your resume to at least two more sites

Some of the sites charge a fee to post resumes, so you will need to spend some time finding sites that do not charge fees. The process required to post your resume will differ from site to site. Follow the directions provided on each site.

9. After you have posted your resume to a site, copy the site's URL to a blank document in Word, enter a brief description of each site to which you successfully posted your resume, save the document as **List of Resume Posting Sites**, then print a copy

A sample list of resume posting sites appears in Figure P3-5. Note that you may wish to include the posting date and the date on which you received a reply. Over the next few weeks, check the sites to which you posted your resume. You may even receive an e-mail from a potential employer!

FIGURE P3-3: **Career Shop Web site**

You can click Resumes to go to a page to post your resume

FIGURE P3-4: **Form for posting a resume**

You must enter information in the boxes marked with an asterisk

You can omit private information if you wish

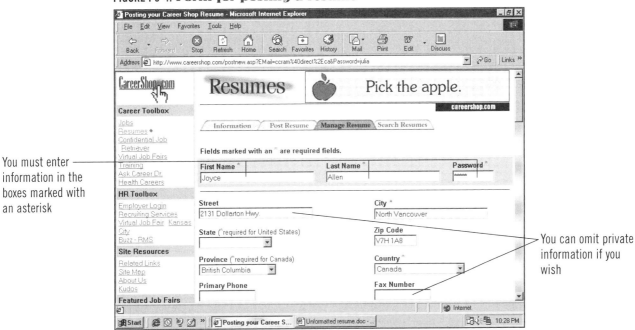

FIGURE P3-5: **Sample list of resume posting sites**

Resume Postings	
March 10 to March 16, 2001	
Web site	**Career Web**
URL	http://www.cweb.com/
Posting date	March 10, 2001
Comments	Needed to log on with a user name and password and then to complete an extensive form. Also provided space to enter the text of a cover letter and an unformatted resume. Main focus was on registering for jobs in the United States, although an option appeared to also register with a Belgian employment service. I received confirmation e-mail after I posted my unformatted resume and a cover letter.
Web site	**Monster Board**
URL	http://my.monster.ca/
Posting date	March 15, 2001
Comments	Needed to log on with a user name and password. The site then sent a new username and password. After logging on with the new username and password, I posted an unformatted resume. Monster Board sites are available for the United States, Australia, Canada, and the United Kingdom.
Web site	**Career City**
URL	http://www.careercity.com/
Posting date	March 16, 2001
Comments	After logging in, I was asked to complete a detailed form and then to post my unformatted resume. This site also allowed me to view the posted resume and then make changes to it. The resume and description that employers would see was very attractively presented.

Independent Challenges

1. Search for three colleges in a location of your choice that offer a two- or four-year program that interests you, and then create a table in Word to present the results of your search. Follow the steps provided to organize your search, and then present your search results.

   Determine where you would like to attend college and the type of program that interests you. For example, you could decide that you'd like to obtain a four-year degree in Business Administration from a college in Hawaii or a two-year degree in Computer Programming from a college in Ontario. If you wish, you can choose to search for colleges outside your home country. In the box below, write your preferred location and program:

   Location ....

   Program ....

2. Set up a table in your word processing program that lists the information categories shown below. Once you begin to search for colleges, you will fill in the table with the information required.

   College Name ....

   Location ....

   Department ....

   Program Description ....

   Degree/Certificate ....

   Yearly Tuition ....

   Special Features ....

   Contact Addresses/e-mail ....

   College URL ....

3. Save the document in your word processing program as "My Search for a College".

4. Connect to the Internet, then use Excite or Yahoo! to search for colleges in the location of your choice (for example, enter "Colleges in Ohio" or "College Accounting Programs in New York"). You will need to spend some time narrowing your search.

5. Add to your Favorites the college sites that interest you.

6. Once you have found three colleges that meet your needs, use the Copy and Paste functions to copy the required information to the table in your word processing program. You will need to follow numerous links in the college sites you select in order to find the required information. For the Special Feature section, enter information that you feel makes the colleges interesting to you. For example, a special feature may be that one of the colleges offers reasonable student accommodations or interesting extracurricular programs or is located near an area that you particularly wish to explore.

7. Make sure you include the URL of each of the three college sites you choose.

8. Format the completed table attractively, then print a copy.

INDEPENDENT CHALLENGE 2

Search a variety of employment databases to find five job postings in your area of expertise and preferred location.

1. Determine the type of job for which you are qualified and the location in which you prefer to work.
2. Identify possible titles for the job. For example, you could look for jobs as an Administrative Assistant, an Office Manager, an Elementary School Teacher, an Accounts Manager, and so on. Try to identify at least four or five job title variations so that you have several possibilities for keyword searches.
3. Create a document in your word processing program titled "Job Postings for [Job Title] in [Location]", then save the document as "My Job Postings".
4. Connect to the Internet, then initiate searches for job postings in your area of expertise. You may wish to start with some of the job search databases. The Web site at www.monsterboard.com is particularly good.
5. As you find job postings appropriate to your area of expertise and preferred location, copy the postings to your word processing document. Note that your document should include the name of the company, the job title, the job posting, the contact information (address or e-mail), and the URL of the site on which the posting appeared.
6. Gather information related to five postings.
7. Format the word processing document attractively, then print a copy.

INDEPENDENT CHALLENGE 3

Search a variety of employment databases to find the qualifications for ten jobs that you feel you could apply for once you have received the required training.

1. Identify the job area in which you would like to work. For example, you may decide that you would like to work in the Film industry.
2. Identify the specific job type for which you would like to obtain qualifications. For example, if you are seeking work in the Film industry, you can decide that you want employment as a Key Grip or a Location Manager or a Production Assistant. You may need to check some job databases related to your preferred area to determine the position types that interest you.
3. Search a variety of employment databases to find ten postings for the job you have selected. To increase your chances of success, do not limit your search to a specific geographic location. Your goal is to find out what qualifications you need to apply for the jobs of your choice.
4. Create a document in your word processing program titled "Qualifications for [Job Title]", then save the document as "Qualifications for [Job Title]". Set up a table in the document that appears as shown below:

Job Title	
Academic Qualifications	
Skills	
Years of Experience	
Other Qualifications	
Posting URL	

5. Copy the required information from the postings you have selected to the table in your word processing document. Note that you need to gather information about qualifications from ten job postings in the area of your choice. Each of the postings should relate to the same type of job.
6. Format the table attractively in your word processing document, then print a copy.

INDEPENDENT CHALLENGE 4

You need to find information about jobs available in countries other than your own. Follow the instructions provided to perform the searches required.

1. Open the AltaVista Web site at www.altavista.com, then enter search terms that include the type of job you'd like to find and the country you'd like to work in. For example, you could enter "Japan teaching English" if you wanted to find job teaching English in Japan.
2. Add the list of search results to your Favorites.
3. Explore some of the results to find postings for jobs that interest you in the country of your choice.
4. When you find a listing that interests you, copy it to a new document in Word, then save the document as "Jobs in [name of country or location]."
5. Conduct further searches in AltaVista to find jobs in other countries. Try a variety of search terms. If you were looking for jobs teaching English, for example, you could enter the terms "Teaching English in China, " Teaching Jobs in Europe, Mexico: Teaching English, English Teaching: India, and so on. Note that you can try the Web site at www.jobs.edunet.com. This site includes a database that you can search by country.
6. Find at least ten postings for jobs in various countries worldwide. Make sure you copy the postings to Word.
7. Apply consistent formatting to the postings in Word.
8. Sort the postings in alphabetical order by country.
9. Add a title to the document, format it attractively on one page, then print a copy. Figure IC-1 is a sample list of postings for jobs teaching English in European countries.

FIGURE IC-1: **Sample list of job postings**

Technical Writing Jobs in European Countries

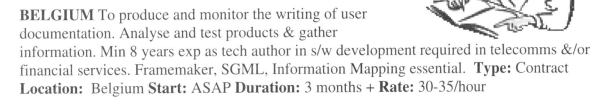

BELGIUM To produce and monitor the writing of user documentation. Analyse and test products & gather information. Min 8 years exp as tech author in s/w development required in telecomms &/or financial services. Framemaker, SGML, Information Mapping essential. **Type:** Contract **Location:** Belgium **Start:** ASAP **Duration:** 3 months + **Rate:** 30-35/hour

GERMANY Must have investment banking experience, will be analysing requirements and writing relevant documentation. **Type:** Contract **Location:** Frankfurt, Germany **Start:** ASAP **Duration:** 6 months **Rate:** Good

UNITED KINGDOM Design & writing of User Guides, Reference Manuals, Presentations, technical documentation, MS Office, SGML,HTML, Corel Draw, Quarkexpress, MS Frontpage. **Type:** Contract **Location:** Portsmouth, Hampshire **Start:** Beginning/Mid June **Duration:** 6-12 months **Rate:** Up to 20/hr

LONDON English degree, must be flexible, mobile; ability to document clearly, minimising ambiguity; ability to evaluate the situation & discuss at all levels; ability to drive the processes & obtain sponsors by persuasion & influence, 2 years experience. **Type:** Permanent **Location:** London **Start:** ASAP **Salary:** 25k - 35k

SWITZERLAND English mother tongue technical author with excellent German language skills needed for a variety of documentation & translation tasks. **Type:** Permanent **Location:** Switzerland **Start:** ASAP **Salary:** CHF60k

SWITZERLAND You must have solid experience in Technical Writing with strong liaison skills. A degree is a must. **Type:** Contract **Location:** Basel, Switzerland **Start:** ASAP

WEST MIDLANDS 1-2 years minimum technical writing. Knowledge of Word, Homesite & HTML HMP Workshop. Experience of producing online help. **Type:** Permanent **Location:** Birmingham, West Midlands **Start:** ASAP **Salary:** Dependent on experience

Hot Spots

You need to find one Web site related to jobs in your state or province and one Web site related to a college or university that you may wish to attend. To find these sites, you will explore the listings from the Excite and Infoseek Web sites. First, go to Excite at www.excite.com, then follow the Careers category link to find a site related to employment opportunities in your state or province. You decide the specific job category that interests you. When you find appropriate listings, print the page by clicking File, Print, and OK. Figure HS-1 illustrates four classified advertisements that appeared on a search for jobs related to personnel and human resources in British Columbia. Next, go to Yahoo! at www.yahoo.com, then follow the Education category link to find the Web site of a college or university in a location of your choice. Print a copy of the first page in the Web site. Figure HS-2 illustrates the Web site for the University of Durham in England.

FIGURE HS-1: **Sample job listings**

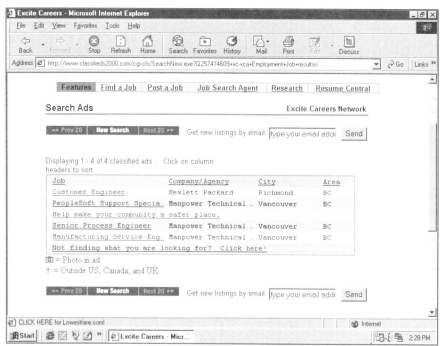

FIGURE HS-2: **University Web site**

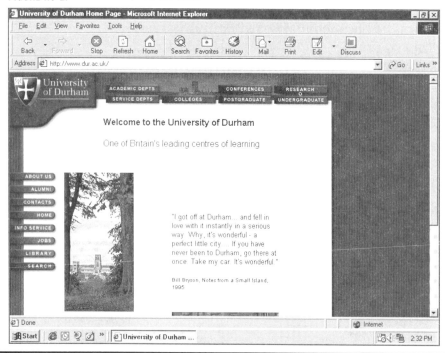

Index